What others are saying about
Progress Not Perfection: Your Journey Matters

"Kate's focus has always been progress, not perfection. She first became my coach a dozen years ago. At the time I didn't want to admit that I needed one, but I did. And she took me on. She encouraged—never criticized. She asked questions—never judged. She was always supporting progress—never expecting perfection. She modeled for me what her book is all about. She has lived the principles she outlines—and her book shares what she has learned in a delightful way. If you can't get Kate—at least get her book—you owe it to yourself."

Bob Pike CSP, CPAE—Speakers Hall of Fame
Chairman/CEO, The Bob Pike Group
Founder Editor, the Creative Training Techniques newsletter

Reading *Progress Not Perfection* is like having a private coaching session with Kate Larsen but without her bright smile and warm hugs. Kate is someone who lives what she teaches and is one of the most authentic people we have ever come across. This book is a rare insight into Kate's past and has all the tools and ideas to take your life to a more peaceful and happy place. You will enjoy the journey and all the learning along the way.

Peter and Kathie Davis
Co-founders of IDEA Health & Fitness Association

"Kate Larsen shares the wisdom, insights, tools, and strategies for living on purpose, and by design. She is the ultimate encourager, and your life will never be the same after you read the final pages."

Mark LeBlanc
Owner, Small Business Success, Author of *Growing Your Business!*

"What an AMAZING book this is—a simple, yet challenging manual one can use for the rest of one's life to understand the choice one has to make to live intentionally and fully. I especially loved the "workouts" and "workins" at the end of each chapter. Kate has shared her own personal progress openly and honestly, and the result is a book I will keep close for years to come as I continually strive to live more purposefully. Thank you, Kate, for giving us new clarity and hope."

Barbara A. Glanz
Author of Balancing Acts—More Than 250 Guilt-free, Creative Ideas to Blend your Work and your Life

"Kate Larsen teaches you in this book what I learned from her about the qualitative balance of life. Until I met Kate I was lacking this component. I was driven by the 'at all costs' concept. In fact, one of my heroes was Machiavelli! Now one of my heroines is Kate Larsen. *Progress Not Perfection: Your Journey Matters* is a must-read, must-understand and must-practice experience."

Bob Esquerre, MA, MES, NSCA-CPT, NASM-CPT, ACE-CES
International Consulting Director
Esquerre Fitness Group International

"*Progress Not Perfection* is a whole life, holistic approach to health and well-being. Kate helps you create a present, and a future, overflowing with possibilities. It is compelling, thought-provoking, inspiring, and uplifting all at once. It's like having a heart-felt talk with a perceptive and caring friend. This book is a keeper."

Beth Rothenberg
PCC UCLA faculty, certified professional coach

PROGRESS
not
Perfection

Your Journey Matters

Kate Larsen

Andover,
Minnesota

Author photography by Treleven Photography

ISBN 13: 978-1-931945-51-6
ISBN 10: 1-931945-51-9

Library of Congress Catalog Number: 2006934414

Printed in the United States of America

First Printing: October 2006

10 09 08 07 06   5 4 3 2 1

Expert Publishing, Inc.
14314 Thrush Street NW,
Andover, MN 55304-3330
Andover,   1-877-755-4966
Minnesota   www.expertpublishinginc.com

Irene Weeks
My mom, friend, confidante, cheerleader, and
role model.

Jack Larsen
My precious husband, soul mate, love, inspiration, and God's perfect partner for me.

To the Memory of Aunt Bobbie
My aunt, godmother, and faith-filled woman.
At forty-five years young, she left us too early.
She would love to have lived the truths shared
in this book, especially for her five beautiful
children—all to be done for the glory of God.

Contents

"It is good to have an end to journey toward; but it is the journey that matters in the end."

—*Ursula K. LeGuin*

Acknowledgments

The dream of this book was birthed more than a dozen years ago. The first outline was drafted more than six years ago. Had anyone told me the arduous journey that lay ahead of me, I may have given up before I got started. A burning desire kept me moving along. I believe God put that desire in my heart. Then He provided me with the travel companions I needed to make it happen—in His time, not mine.

Many authors share in their acknowledgments an appreciation for the sacrifices made by family members who "patiently endured fast food meals and an absent parent" during the writing of their book. While I totally understand the need for that dedication and attention, I was not willing to miss that time or those meals with my family. Nor was I willing to forgo exercise and many of the other things that add richness to my life. Ah, competing values. I suppose they will always exist. Because I chose to write this way, at times I made myself crazy not completing the book sooner. However, time marches on and here it is.

I could not begin to adequately thank all of those who read and reread the chapters and stories in this book. I must however, try to do so.

Elaine Duffy, you were a wonderful lifeline to sanity in my office. I am eternally grateful for your dedication, patience, and willingness to work alongside me. Your family has also been an inspiration to me. To Sharron, my editor, who never would have guessed it would take me so long to get this project completed, your patience and expertise were amazing. I believe I have finally stopped ending every sentence with an exclamation point. Kathy Heil, you are a gem for reading the entire manuscript and making recommendations that I know improved this work in such a short amount of time. April Durrett, the wonderful editor of my many articles over the years, you always make me sound better. Becky Pluth, you came into my life at the perfect time to reenergize me, offering to partner with me on the workbook that will enable this material to come to life for my clients, friends, and family. And, Pat Shauer, the angel and copy editor extraordinaire who helped me finally cross the finish line with the manuscript. You took my hand the last mile of this marathon and pulled me safely to the finish.

I have been blessed with many cheerleaders who have helped keep me to the task and made it fun in doing so. In addition to my mother, Irene, I have had my sisters and their husbands, Peggy and Danny Suerth, Tara and Chris Stauber, and Bridget and Gary Keating. My brother, Mike and his wife, Amy Gormaly. My special soul-mate sisters Amy and Laura. Between the three of us mothers, we have raised nine boys. I think that qualifies us for special places in heaven with our husbands right next to us. David Grady and Bill Middleton—thank you for sharing your wives and kids with me. You each have special hearts.

I share a great deal about the wealth of friends in this book. My life has been made richer by the support, love, and encouragement received from my special friends Janet and Dan Dryer, Kelli and Greg Hueler, and Karen and Michael Vannurden.

I know that my efforts were perpetually lifted up in prayer by my prayer warrior friends: Jean Detroi, Joy Hall, Linda McCormick, Jan Wyder, Kathy Heil, Mary Lee Jennings, Alicia Hauer, Jana Lavell, Amy Macgowan, my dad, and Carol Travilla (thank you for your encouragement to write many years ago). Carol Clark and Rachel Soffer, you are both strong, powerful, women who live with integrity. You have been a joy to work with.

What would I have ever done all those years ago in 1989, when I began speaking, without my National Speakers Association peers? You probably don't realize your ongoing impact in my life. Elizabeth Jeffries, Sue Rusch, Mark LeBlanc, Bob Pike, Barbara Glanz, Tim Richardson, Alan and Christine Zimmerman, and Glenna Salsbury.

Beth Rothenberg has been one of my most vocal and enthusiastic advocates. Thank you for your confidence in me and never-ending enthusiasm and encouragement. Bob Esquerre, a peer and collaborator in the personal training industry, you are a blast to work with. You recognized the impact of coaching in the fitness field ahead of the wave.

Margaret Moore, visionary extraordinaire, invited me to play and grow in the wellness coaching industry in amazing ways. Thank you for helping me think bigger.

My peers at Blanchard Coaching, you have inspired me to a higher level of coaching and for that, I am grateful. With special thanks to Linda Miller, Madeleine Homan, and Joni Wickline who have challenged and encouraged me to try new things.

How fun it is for me to be able to thank Sallie Dede for introducing me to the joy of exercise and the impact of teaching fitness as a vocation. You drilled into me the belief and conviction that alignment and core strength were critical to the health of my body. I have expanded that into every area of my life. Alignment is essence of powerful movement and expression.

I must add a special acknowledgment to a crew who have supported, challenged, and encouraged me both in health and recovery—the Thursday Night Exercise Crew. You know who you are. You're the best!

This book is far more engaging and empowering because of the stories that bring the message to life. I have to thank my clients and workshop participants who graciously allowed me to share their stories and their names. (I did not use your names because it made my life far easier in the end. You will likely recognize yourself on these pages though.)

Jack, my husband of more than twenty-four years, is a dream. He has encouraged me to grow, live fully, and share my energy and enthusiasm for life with others. He is the Prince Charming I dreamed of marrying.

How do I capture in mere words the love, affection, and joy I find in my sons, Kiel, Jamie, and Christopher. They light up my world and make all that I do more meaningful. It is for their legacy that I strive to live wisely with integrity and character.

Ultimately, this is all about glorifying God and serving others with a love and compassion I hope is evident to all. I am so grateful for my many blessings and for you who decided to read this book. God bless you.

Preface

Do you want to experience the joy of living a purpose-filled, healthy, and connected life? If you're frazzled, fried, frustrated, and fatigued, you are not alone. The message contained within this book is that you *can* live a fuller, healthier, joy-filled life. Despite the busyness of your current schedule and demands—it *is* possible. If you have not had the energy and contentment you've wanted, consider this new refrain "up till now." Up till now it's been impossible to be healthy in every area of your life. And, now you will have a way. You can be healthier in more areas of your life than you've ever been before. That health will provide you with the energy, joy, and hope you passionately want to share with the world.

Most working professionals want to fill their lives with positive, healthy influences and choices. My goal is to direct you toward balancing your work and life to help you manage stress and align yourself with your highest personal values.

> *"He who has health has hope, and he who has hope has everything."*
> *Arabian Proverb*

In this book, I will guide you on a journey of reflection and action. If you want more energy, fun, and joy in your world, you will find a strategic framework and step-by-step game plan to walk you through the process of decision-making skills needed to achieve your desires. You will find that your plan will require a shift in both your attitudes and behaviors. But, don't worry, I'll break it down so the steps are easy to follow. You'll discover the best place to start is by *giving yourself permission* to take better care of yourself. Unless you truly commit to giving yourself permission to take care of your *self*, your life will never change. You will continue to experience fatigue, frustration, and a nagging sense of discontent years beyond this reading.

I've heard it said a person's mission is not to **discover** his or her purpose and mission, but to **uncover** it. And then, to pursue fulfilling that mission. To do that requires you have the energy, creativity, and focus to do so. This growing, evolving, and becoming takes a lot of effort and stamina. My hope for you is that you become proficient at self-coaching. Your decisions will connect to your values and personal life mission.

This book addresses three areas: (1) lifestyle choices, (2) self-talk habits, and (3) empowering action ideas that enable you to be proactive. By focusing on these areas, you can truly lead the life you want—not the life you're living by default.

Make Lifestyle (Health) Choices

The first goal deals with reflection, assessment, and commitment to lifestyle choices and behaviors. Each can give you more energy for living a joy-filled, healthy life. Positive choices help you take charge of your life. It's time to make the choices you need to nurture you from the inside out.

Adopt Positive Self-Talk Habits

The second goal reveals to you the power and impact of self-talk on your moods, choices, and overall health. When you monitor your self-talk, you unleash your greatest potential and shut down your most severe critic—yourself. This book will help you turn up the volume on your inner head chatter so you can choose the tone and positive direction of your self-talk. By learning the questioning and reflective skills used by professional life coaches, you can incorporate self-coaching techniques to skillfully shift your life, your health, and your sense of fulfillment in life.

Empower Yourself and Stop Being Bullied

The third goal encourages you to stop being bullied by the media, the culture, and other people in your life. Are you maintaining a daily lifestyle pace that leaves you physically, emotionally, spiritually, intellectually, and financially drained? If you answer yes, then you are being bullied. Our culture subtly advocates looking good on the outside, regardless of the cost on the inside (in our hearts and spirits).

This book blends my experiences with clients, conversations with other coaches, and insights gained through corporate and association interviews about the issues that impact the energy, productivity, and satisfaction of working professionals everywhere.

In the introduction, I expand upon my eight "I Choose To" commitments to give you a sense of *where* you can go, *what* you can achieve through this book, and *how* to use the support of the exercises contained within it. The goal is not for you to adopt my commitments, but to create your own based upon what you learn about yourself and your life as you read. You will have the opportunity to create your own agreements at the end of this book. However, feel free to write down your ideas as you read, reflect, and reevaluate your daily choices. I offer a multitude of fun, creative, intellectually, and spiritually challenging exercises for you to do alone or with friends. I hope you read with a highlighter and pen in hand. Write in the margins, fill in the blanks, and mark the passages you want to revisit. If you can't bring yourself to mark in the book, keep a notebook handy and use that instead.

To live a life filled with energy, joy, and contentment is a challenge. Up till now you haven't found the direction you've needed to choose differently, to choose consistently. Choose to take charge of your life by taking care of your health inside and out. I'm so glad you've joined me on this journey!

Before you go any further, you might want to get a sense of me, the author. Why? Because if you and I share similar heart desires, then you'll love the rest of this book.

One month after I sent my manuscript for this book to my editor, I found a painful lump in my right breast. One week later I was diagnosed with breast cancer. After surgery the doctor determined that I had a Stage II cancer and recommended eight rounds of chemotherapy. This crisis in my life enabled me to reflect upon what I had written in this book—from a new perspective. Had I done something wrong? Had I been living the message authentically? Would I do anything differently knowing what I knew now? No, I had not done anything wrong. I had done everything right as it related to what I had control over in my life. I discovered my level of health allowed me to bounce back stronger, sooner than I would otherwise have. Living authentically? Absolutely. Regrets? None. I wouldn't change any words in this book—either for my clients and/or future readers.

The journey through cancer did change me though. I can't deny that. I am so grateful for the depth of insights I experienced. I now know firsthand unrelenting pain, frustration, discouragement, and the uncertainty of not knowing when, once again, I could live the way I had in the past. I also discovered a world of joy and love rarely experienced. I chose to focus on the care, gracious giving, and abundant nurturing I experienced from others.

Shortly after my first round of chemo, we celebrated Thanksgiving. I was filled with joy to be able to say, "I felt as though I have been tested and found true." I trusted God in the midst of a very frightening and uncertain time. I considered it a gift.

Why did I get cancer? And, why at that particular time of my life? Who knows? When I shared the results of the biopsy with my then twelve-year-old son, he said, "Mom, if you can get cancer—anyone can!" Maybe that's the message. Anyone can get cancer. We cannot control all things in life. However, by taking charge of what you can control, you can let go of the outcomes knowing you're doing the best you can and enjoy peace, contentment, and joy. The message will be abundantly clear in the book: small choices make a BIG difference. Take charge of your small choices and you will take charge of your life.

Introduction

The summer I turned fifteen started in the strangest, yet ultimately, most wonderful way. I'll never forget the frustration, fear, and anxiety I felt that first week after the end of my freshman year. Not out of school for more than two weeks and I had already gotten myself into big trouble. I sat one morning in the office of a social psychologist named Esther Robinson. My parents had brought me in to see her; they said I had a problem. She escorted my parents into the waiting area after introductions were made, returned to her office, turned to me, and said, "So, Katie, tell me about you. What keeps you busy each day?" I went on to tell her—in depth—what kept me busy each day. Had you been there, you would have heard a story that went something like this:

"Gosh, where do I start? I was born one month before my mother turned twenty-one. Fifteen months later Molly was born. Mom never saw Molly though. Molly was born with birth defects and suffered from anencephaly. She died three months later in the hospital. Peggy was born when I was two and a half. Michael came along when I was five; Tara when I was six. I remember caring for and treating Tara like she was my baby. She was like a doll to me; I loved watching her. When I was nine and a half, Bridget was born, and I had a baby to care for again.

"When I was ten, Mom had to go back to work. I'm in charge after school on Mondays and Wednesdays and most Saturdays while she's gone. I have to get home right after school because by six o'clock sharp, I have to have dinner on the table, the house cleaned up, the laundry done, and take care of the four younger kids.

"Also, from when I was ten until twelve, I cleaned the apartment for an elderly couple, Fred and Clara Warvel, in the building behind our house. Clara was an invalid and Fred a pleasant man who sat out on his porch for hours a day visiting with the neighborhood kids, giving out candy. That was my first paying job.

"At twelve, my mom was able to get me a job at the retail store she worked at—Winsberg's. I work there on Thursdays and Sundays.

Sometimes on Saturdays. Initially, I worked in the backroom of the uniform department until I could get a workers' permit to work out on the floor of the boy's department. I love selling Converse gym shoes and matching up fun outfits for customers.

"I'm a pretty good student. I've been on the honor roll since fourth grade. I try really hard to maintain my grades. I made the Honor Society this year. I play on the basketball team. I really want to make first string next year, so I have to work extra hard to prove myself. During the season, we practice every day, sometimes before school, sometimes after school. And, of course, on some days we have games.

"I have lots of friends. They say I'm kinda like an Ann Landers because I always know what to say to make them feel better. My boyfriend just broke up with me." I remembered pausing for a long time here because I started to cry and was embarrassed and trying to pull myself together.

"I'm really devastated, but my friends think I'm so together that I can't tell them. You know the reason my parents brought me in here is because I got caught drinking. I mean, it was eighty degrees outside, I didn't eat, my boyfriend broke up with me and I was—over served. There's really nothing wrong with me. Did they tell you my dad went in for alcoholism treatment? They probably think I have it or something. Well, I don't. I'm just fine."

Esther did a lot of nodding of her head. She smiled, sighed, looked wide-eyed, and finally said, "Katie, you're a busy young lady! How do you feel about everything you're doing?"

I don't think anyone had ever asked me that question in a way that I felt truly safe to answer. Something in her demeanor enabled me to feel safe. I became transparent. I felt my "I'm happy and fine mask" slide right off my face.

"Feel?" I said. "Not that good actually. My mom brought me into the doctor last month. He says I have the beginnings of an ulcer and if I don't start to do things differently, I'll have even *more* pain. But, I don't even know where to start. I have to keep my grades up, I want to make first string on varsity next fall, I have to work, we don't have any money,

I have to baby-sit, and it's not like I can tell my parents no. I'm so embarrassed and sad my boyfriend broke up with me." With despair in my voice I asked, "What's wrong with me?"

Esther called my parents back in and said, "You're right, Katie has a problem. It's you." I sat dumbfounded as she clearly expressed her concern for me. She called a spade a spade and laid everything on the line for my parents. *They* needed to change, and she would work with me to change.

Esther helped release me, both from my parents' tight control and my unhealthy need to perform perfectly. I'd love to tell you I was transformed overnight. However, I've discovered becoming oneself takes a lifetime. Getting comfortable in your own skin takes more patience and time than I'd ever like to admit. However, it helps immensely when you become focused and intentional and strive to stay on the right path. The "right" path for me was revealed as I worked with Esther.

Following a few more sessions, Esther taught me two very important truths that I continue to speak about and teach thirty-some years later. I genuinely believe Esther saved my life and gave me my sanity. I believe her counsel changed the course of my life.

Those two truths were that I could, and should, trust my own instincts, and that I am responsible for my choices. If I'm not happy with my life, it's my own doing. I can trust my instincts. My "gut" told me something was wrong in our home. The adults in my life wouldn't, or maybe couldn't, acknowledge it. My gut began to eat itself out literally—I had developed an ulcer.

> *"Most worthwhile achievements are the result of many little things done in a single direction."*
> *Nido Quebin*

Esther also showed me that the power to be joy-filled, satisfied, or loved comes from within my heart and mind, not outside circumstances and people. She emphasized that although I could not control all of my circumstances (especially at fourteen years old), I could control my response to my circumstances. Alter my attitude and my reality would change; my perspective creates my reality.

The bottom line, regardless of my age, circumstances, and financial state, is that I am responsible for my choices. I am not a victim, unless I allow it.

I cannot claim to have mastered these truths; however, they impact and inspire my choices to this day. I became increasingly aware of the self-talk I developed, which sabotaged my confidence, self-esteem, and courage. I continue to tune into (and silence) that small, nasty voice that still wants to criticize me, make me feel small and inadequate, and diminish my spirit. I am grateful this voice has become more of an encourager that supports me and challenges me to live in truth and challenges the lies when my negative voice attacks.

Meeting and working with Esther was the first significant event that changed the trajectory of my life. The other was directed by my mother. While my father was in treatment, Mom started attending Al-Anon, the group meeting established for the family members and friends of alcoholics. The influence of that program on my mom and ultimately all five of us kids was pivotal and powerful. My mom heard, believed, and acted on the premise that, "all it takes is one emotionally healthy parent to raise emotionally healthy, responsible kids." Yes, two healthy parents would have been better, but that was not her option. She did what she could with what she had—it was more than enough.

My formative teenage years were spent hanging around my mother and her friends from Al-Anon. I watched the results of decisions made by women before they had found their voice or discovered themselves. I wanted to learn from them and choose differently. I hungered to learn from their mistakes so I would not have to endure the same pain of broken relationships, poor health, and an inability to engage in positive self-care. My passion for sharing the message to take charge of your choices so you take charge of your life, I believe, blossomed then. The honesty, reflection, and action called for in the Al-Anon twelve-step program showed me I could make better decisions day-to-day. Those better decisions made moment-to-moment, created and continue to create the life I experience today. The good and the bad!

I want to help others stomp out the bully voice that pushes, pulls, and strains them. The bully voice causes you to compare yourself to others—guaranteeing you will always come up short. I love encouraging people, and I thrive on being a part of that process. I recognize today that it's not about me. It's about God using me as a tool, and I continue to be humbled by His patience and grace with me.

Since I will ask you to consider what you want in your life and what you will intentionally choose to do with your life and health, it may be helpful to share with you what I want, what I strive for and what I hope for others. You may have a sense of where you want to go in life and what you want to achieve, but do you have a plan—a strategic plan to make it happen? Do you know what you want for yourself? Have you considered what you want for others?

May you be encouraged, inspired, and entertained by what you read here.

In Changing My Life, I Hope to Change Your Life
I want to:

❑ continue to develop my character—becoming more loving, authentic, and generous.

❑ be humble, loving, patient, selfless, honest, generous, joy-filled, contented, and healthy in every area so I have wonderful energy and capacity to love and give of myself.

❑ only strive for God's approval (not everyone else's) and be used as a tool for Him.

❑ be an encourager to the timid, discouraged, and overwhelmed.

❑ be patient—with myself and others trusting God's timing and refining.

What I want for you:

- ❏ to know and experience the feeling of being loved for exactly who you are.
- ❏ to take responsibility for your decisions and yourself.
- ❏ to know you have the power to change.
- ❏ to be able to see how uniquely and wonderfully designed you are.
- ❏ to be able to let go of the definition of success created by others and create your own.
- ❏ to slow down and enjoy your life—your children, families, friends, work, hobbies, and nature.
- ❏ to take great care of your body and health through smart lifestyle choices.
- ❏ to be kind to yourself.
- ❏ to balance your personal desires with your responsibilities to others.
- ❏ to take control of your life—one choice at a time.

I will never forget the sense of shock and sadness when over the course of twenty-four hours, both Kirby Puckett's and Dana Reeve's deaths occurred. They were forty-five and forty-four years old. Both left children, family, and friends mourning. The stark reality is that we do not know how much time we have here on earth. That perspective propels me to live my life, however brief or long, with purpose and intention. Knowing my mission and striving to live according to how I believe I am called to requires my immediate and ongoing attention. How about you?

To live out my mission statement requires me to make commitments to being a certain way with others and myself. To remind me of my intention and responsibilities, I live according to the following eight "I Choose To" statements. Notice that six of the eight describe how I want to "be." See if any of these have meaning for you. (You will find your own copy in appendix A of this book for you to use or fine tune.) Each statement is followed by an application thought for you to consider.

Kate's Eight "I Choose To" Statements for Living Life with Joy and Energy

I will consider myself blessed (some might say "successful") in life if I can live with joy and energy, while having a positive impact on the people, community, and world around me. I'll successfully accomplish this as long as I do it without sacrificing my health and primary relationships at home. And above all else, I want to do it to glorify God, not me.

1. I choose to be **intentional** about my choices.

2. I choose to assess the **cost/investment** that my choices involve.

3. I choose to **live congruently** according to my deepest values that glorify God.

4. I choose to be **persistent and patient** with the process, while always reaching beyond my current comfort zone.

5. I choose to be **present** in the moment.

6. I choose to be **authentic** with others and myself.

7. I choose to create **reserves/margin** in my life.

8. I choose to be **flexible** because it allows for spontaneity in my life.

1. I choose to be intentional about my choices.

Being intentional simply means I employ behaviors and thinking habits that are thoughtful and directed toward a certain outcome. If I want to be healthy and whole as a woman, wife, mother, daughter, friend, coach, or peer, then I need to make decisions that naturally improve the probability of that occurring. I realize there is a great deal over which I have no control in this world, so I choose to take charge of the things I can control or influence.

I am going to guess you have areas of your life you would like to improve. Start by focusing on the choices you make each day that impact your energy. Every meal you eat, conversation you have, item you purchase, movie you watch, book you read, or seminar you attend needs to support or encourage better health—physically, emotionally, spiritually, financially, and interpersonally. Take responsibility for your choices and changes—simple to say, and challenging to do.

2. I choose to assess the cost/investment my choices involve.

We each have limited resources of time, energy, and money. When I say yes to one activity, I say no to another. When I make commitments to one person, I, by default, say no to another person. I use up my resources of time, energy, or money throughout the day. Days add up to weeks, weeks to months and years. Some or all of my resources (time, energy, money, etc.) will become depleted without my being able to take time for rejuvenation, renewal, or refreshment. That is why I believe so strongly in great self-care.

What are your choices costing you today, and, more importantly, what could they be costing your future? For instance, if you recognize that distance has grown between you and your husband or wife, what is/will be the cost of not being proactive about spending more time together? Understandably, you're busy and it would be really challenging to carve out the time.

One of the most prevalent times divorce occurs is at twenty years, just as the kids leave home and your time together is free again. Will your partner be someone you want to spend time with and enjoy?

3. I choose to live congruently according to my deepest values that glorify God.

My greatest desire is to glorify God with my life. For me, the way to live life has been established in the Bible—God's instruction manual and love letter. This book acts as my compass and springboard for living according to my deepest values. It helps me sort through what is appropriate, expedient, fruitful, excellent, and true for me. That helps me make decisions on a day-to-day basis. The Bible may or may not be *your* true compass for living. What *is* important is that you know what you live for and *how* you want to live. What motivates and inspires you as you struggle to make best decisions in the moment? Until you can clearly identify and articulate your guiding values, principles, and motives, you will make inconsistent choices that may or may not serve you well.

Years ago, I read a quote by Chuck Colson that said, "If you were dragged into a court of law this day, is there enough evidence to convict you of being a Christian?" What a simple, clear, and telling way to look at my life choices. For instance, if I say my family members are the most important people in the world to me, would there be enough evidence to convince a jury?

I could share more of my deeply held values here, but who cares? This is about *you* and *your* values. What is important to you? If you value something deeply, is there enough evidence in your life to convict you of living out that value?

Most adults I work with come to identify their values only while in the midst of difficult times. Few have been intentional or proactive about making consistent choices tied deeply to their values throughout their lives and clearly expressed to their children. Have you clearly articulated your values, goals, and character qualities you want to see develop in your children on a *consistent* basis?

There will always be interesting and worthwhile opportunities to participate in. You will always have a multitude of engaging activities to choose from. Some days the only way to choose, the only way to say, "No, thank you," is to select what to do based upon your highest, clearly identified, and articulated values.

4. **I choose to be persistent and patient with the process, while always reaching beyond my current comfort zone.**

Each year when I run Grandma's half marathon in Duluth, Minnesota, I feel I stretch myself. Actually, each time I get up to speak in front of an audience, I stretch myself. Writing and placing my opinions and ideas out there takes persistence and courage. Raising kids requires oodles of patience and persistence. Taking care of myself is essential to having the patience and persistence I need on a number of levels—intellectual, spiritual, or relational. What risks have you taken in the last year that made you feel alive, proactive, or proud?

Most highly regarded people are lifelong learners. Remaining open-minded and willing to learn allows you to reach beyond your comfort zone. As you learn and strive to put into practice new insights, you take the risk of failing. Trying new things can feel uncomfortable or threatening. Some of your personal goals are probably tied to being willing to take a chance and try something new. *Risk falling down.* The best way to prepare yourself to risk is to develop strong supportive relationships with those who will encourage you, stand by you, and hold you up—if necessary. If you have not built a good strong support network of people in your life, do that first. Then if you fall down, you'll have others to pick you up and dust you off.

As you remind yourself to be patient and persistent with your journey, keep in mind, ***the goal is progress—not perfection.*** Pursuing perfection sets you up for disappointment. As you do the best you can day in and day out, one choice at a time, you can be proud of your effort. Pursue excellence and you can have peace of mind. Pursue perfection and nothing will ever be good enough. Contentment is the natural result of doing things to the best of your ability and letting the outcome go.

5. I choose to be present in the moment.

It is truly amazing how much time I spend somewhere other than here—in the now. I now recognize quickly that when I am anxious, I am in the future rather than the present. When I am angry, I'm in the past. Yes, the past may be ten minutes ago. The future could be two hours from now. Either way, worrying or being angry is not going to improve my disposition or health, so why would I want to remain there? If, in the moment, I am able to consciously choose how I want to think (positively) and react (proactively), then I can make a positive difference or better handle situations and people.

Think of a recent situation that caused you to be anxious. Maybe you're anxious now. Consider for a moment what you could do right now to relieve some of your anxiety. If you can do something—do it! Even if that means you put this book down now and take care of the task, pray, or take action—do it!

If you can't do anything about the situation, circumstance, or person you're anxious about, you can intentionally let it go until you can act, reflect, or change your situation. Forget your knee jerk (habitual) response of getting worried. Yes, your anxious or angry response is habit. Consider breaking the habit to reduce or get rid of your negative emotions. A great place to start to change these habits is to pay attention to the conversations you have in your head. Listen to the chatter that others can't hear going on in your mind, but you can. Think about the last time you got anxious. I'll bet if you tuned in to the running dialogue in your head, you would have heard fear-based comments. Those comments start flying around in my head whenever I begin to get overwhelmed with work. If I let you listen in, you'd hear comments like, "Kate, you'll never get this all done. There's no way. You're going to end up disappointing your clients, participants, and meeting planner. Of course, then you'll probably be so caught up in all this, you'll be cranky with the kids." You get the idea. I've learned I have to stop that negative rambling or I end up in a nervous twit in thirty seconds. Working on your self-talk is something we'll do a lot throughout our work in this book. Here's a family example from not long ago.

One morning I had the opportunity to work with one of my sons who was anxious about a test. I asked if he had studied. Yes. Was he rested and clear headed? Yes. Would this test make or break his academic career? No. Would he prefer to perform well? Yes. Okay then, he's done everything he can; the rest is out of his hands. Don't worry. Worrying will only suck the life and energy out of you. You can ask yourself the same type of questions the next time you feel anxious. Just before his test he said he thought about our conversation and actually found himself relaxing. He did beautifully on the exam.

It's almost a guarantee that if you're worried, your mind is in the future and that what you're saying to yourself is not supportive, positive, or proactive. If you're angry, you're rehashing a situation, conversation, or comment and feeling victimized or helpless about it. Maybe you're wanting to replay it or redo it—either way, you're in the past. Come back to the present and decide what you can do and what you want to say to yourself so you do not feel like a victim or someone who is out of control. It is important to *learn* from the past and *plan* for the future. However, it's unproductive to stay out of the present for too long.

6. I choose to be authentic with others and myself.

One of the commitments I made to myself after working with Esther was to become the girl on the inside whom people saw on the outside. Most adults would have described me as positive, enthusiastic, and engaged. In truth, I was fearful, insecure, and angry. Faking it wasn't working. As a grown woman, I can honestly say that what you see is what you get with me. Do your insides (genuine feelings and thoughts) match what others see on the outside? To be healthy physically, emotionally, financially, or spiritually, you have to be authentic about who you really are. Express yourself without apology, but with appreciation.

In the Disney movie *The Lion King*, the young cub Simba runs away from his pride after the death of his father, the King of the Lions. He decides he would rather be a fun-loving, relaxed, somewhat irresponsible party animal (pun intended) as his young friends were. Along the way, he realizes that he must be who he was called to be. He knows it in his core. He sees it when he reflects on his choices and direction for life. While fun initially, trying to be someone he wasn't and ignoring who he was, took more from him than he realized. Ultimately, to the joy of his pack and family, he returns to rule as he was meant to from birth. His pride and joy at the conclusion of the movie caused tears for me—yes, I am a mush—but also reminded me that we each need to take heed of who we are and what we are called to do in life.

I am not necessarily talking about your career, while that can be part of the equation. I'm referring to recognizing your temperament and natural giftedness, tuning into what gives you energy, joy, and pleasure.

Is there some activity, career responsibility, volunteer activity, or commitment you've made that you recognize is a bigger drain on you than it's worth? Be aware that you can contribute in other ways. Honestly consider whose expectations you are trying to live up to. Listen to your heart, soul, and body; be true to your wiring. God has designed you for special things. Look for a way to commit to those activities and people who enable you to shine, excel, and serve without being drained and depleted.

Being authentic doesn't mean you toss out everything that's not a fit for you in your life. What it does mean is that you honestly step back and review what has fueled you, encouraged you, and fit in your life. Being authentic releases you from hiding your weaknesses and fears; it allows you to drop the mask that hides the real you. I strive to keep my mask off each day. I invite you to join me in being authentic and real.

7. I choose to create reserves/margin in my life.

The concept of margin was best described by Dr. Richard Swenson in his book *The Overload Syndrome: Learning to Live Within Your Limits*. "Margin is the space between vitality and exhaustion. It is our breathing room, our reserves, our leeway. Margin is the opposite of overload, and therefore the antidote for that vexatious condition."[1]

Swenson goes on to say, "Without margin, we are chronically exhausted, chronically late, chronically rushed. Without margin, we

> *"Every day you mismanage your eating, exercise, sleep, relaxing, and connecting time, you pay a price. It may be the price of anxiety, low energy, fatigue, loneliness, or an ongoing sense of dissatisfaction."*
> *Kate Larsen*

are overloaded. Margin, on the other hand, tells us to guard our reserves. Create buffers and fortify them."

Most days, creating margin for myself means leaving fifteen minutes between coaching calls, it means allowing for traffic when going to appointments, it includes exercise time four days a week and quiet time every day—sometimes both in the morning and at night. I simply do the best I can while remaining flexible due to life's unexpected complications. Creating margin in your life will be done differently during each decade of your life. The activities that relaxed me years ago do not hold any interest for me today. The things I do for fun now did not even occur to me ten or fifteen years ago. When we were first married, Jack and I had fun entertaining a lot. We shopped, cooked, enjoyed many dinner parties. Today, I find it much

"We rarely change until the pain of remaining the same becomes greater than the pain of going through the change."
Kate Larsen

more fun to go out to dinner and not have to cook and clean. During my kids' toddler years, finding time for exercise required a different kind of juggling than it does today. It's easy to schedule the day from sunrise until midnight. Doing so is not smart though. In the long run, you can pay a high price for keeping an unrelenting pace. Margin is a gift I give myself, and it's one you can give yourself.

8. I choose to be flexible because it allows for spontaneity in my life.

Do you like change or do you prefer to have circumstances and people remain fairly steady? Personality assessments identify both types of people. With the world and events changing so rapidly, being able to be flexible with your schedule and expectations is important—if not essential—even if you prefer status quo.

To be fully physically healthy, it is important to remain flexible throughout your life. Being limber prevents injuries, reduces tension, and improves your postural and structural alignment (which basically means that you stand straight and tall, with minimal limitations in your joints, ligaments, and muscles).

It's also important to be mentally flexible. Some people are spontaneous by nature and resist structure. Others require so much structure in their lives that being spontaneous creates more stress than it's worth. As with most things in life, being somewhat structured, yet flexible, is the healthiest place to be physically and emotionally.

Consider what structures need to be in place for you to be more flexible. What do you need to know, complete, or arrange for you to be flexible and spontaneous? Once you know, take the steps to take care of those things and tell others.

Give Yourself Time to Evolve

Keep in mind that becoming healthier, more balanced, and more positive takes time. The habits required to achieve these goals require practice. Be patient with yourself. At the same time, it's your responsibility and your opportunity to take care of your life one choice at a time. Up till now it's been tough. However, now you can choose differently.

It's time to listen to yourself. Tune in to what your body is asking of you. Turn up the volume on your self-talk. The conversations you have with yourself (that no one else hears) set the tone for your attitude and perspective each day. Tuning into your body and turning up the volume on your self-talk will impact each and every small choice you make. Keep the idea of small choices making big differences in mind as you read this book. Decide what small choices you can incorporate into your life. Don't try to change everything. It will overwhelm you. Instead, take small steps, make small choices, and reap large rewards in the long run. Now get going. The rest of your life awaits you!

Create A New Foundation

Where do you begin to create the energy and the life you want to have? A great place to start is by fortifying your personal foundation. For our purposes, a foundation is, "That upon which anything is founded; that on which anything stands and by which it is supported; the lowest and supporting layer of a superstructure; groundwork; basis." Think of your foundation as the inside stuff making who you are that no one else sees. Your foundation is made up of your values, internal motivators, perspectives, and aspirations. What the world sees is the building built upon your foundation. The world gets its view of your values from your externals—your physical self and behaviors that are observed. Building a strong foundation for your life means you know and understand yourself. You make decisions that are in alignment with what you value and desire. A foundation remains strong with good maintenance and attention. The same is true of the body, spirit, and mind. Create a good foundation, and your body, spirit and mind will remain strong if you pay attention to them and maintain them.

A building's foundation is made up of cement, water, and/or steel. Your foundation is made up of your values, hopes, dreams, motivations, calling, goals, and beliefs. Your choices result from the health and well-being of your foundation. Failure to maintain your personal foundation will result in a weakened life, both personally and professionally. Your health, relationships, financial decisions, eating choices, and other matters will show the fissures and cracks that come from neglect. If you don't lead yourself well, you will not be healthy—physically, emotionally, financially, interpersonally, or spiritually. Sometimes when we come into adulthood our foundation is cracked. Sometimes our foundation was built in such a way that it causes us to stand off-center. Cracks can be created in childhood by family or life circumstances beyond a child's control. Alcoholism, dysfunctional adults, depression, mental illness, financial strain, and any number of other causes impact a child's perspective. A child may grow up with cracks in his foundation that may manifest themselves in unhealthy adult behavior. These behaviors include, but are not limited to, an inability to handle feedback, resistance to authority, insecurity about self-worth, etc. In other words, as much as we want to stand upright and true, we're standing on a foundation that, up till now, won't support a completely healthy life.

My husband and I put our house on the market in 1991 so we could move from Illinois to Minnesota. Our realtor mentioned we might seriously want to consider having the crack in our foundation fixed before going to market. We investigated what repairing this five-foot long crack in the unfinished basement would cost. (Note that this was a crack we hadn't seen change at all in two and a half years.) When we found it would cost more than a thousand dollars, we said forget it. Let the new owners fix it if they want. We didn't hide it, nor did we fix it. Well, it proved to be a problem for experienced homebuyers. They recognized the dangers of having cracks in the foundation of a home. After a number of months of fighting the desire to save some money, we had the crack fixed. Shortly thereafter, the house sold. I can't claim fixing the crack sold the house, though I do know fixing it didn't hinder the sale. Fix what cracks you can. It will save you far more to work on the problem now rather than later. Usually later means after the crisis. Let's begin in the basement of your foundation.

Think Prevention Versus Treatment

When asked whether you are healthy, do you automatically think about your physical health? Most people do. Women and men who are intentional about living by their values think of health on multiple planes. They approach their health and life from a preventative versus a treatment perspective. They do what they can to *avoid* illness, stress disorders, and pain. Pursuing and creating personal health and well-being allows you to lead an authentic, abundant life—the kind of lives my clients describe wanting. Those who live according to their values find success, health, and personal leadership are natural outcomes of their choices.

"Things which matter most must never be at the mercy of things which matter least." Johann Wolfgang Von Goethe

The secret to successfully living by your values is two-fold. The first is to be able to know and clearly articulate your values. The second is to intentionally cultivate *healthy relationships in every area of your life*, including a healthy relationship with yourself. When you have a healthy relationship with yourself, you genuinely appreciate your beauty, strength, contributions, worth, and uniqueness as a human being. You recognize your strengths and acknowledge your areas of potential growth (weaknesses) without fixating on them. You also then possess the courage and conviction to live according to your highest calling or your truest values.

In our fast-paced, impatient culture, many people neglect to take the time to sort through personal values and often end up adopting others' values to get to the next achievement in life. I appreciate the definition of authenticity provided by Ruderman and Ohlott of The Center for Creative Leadership. "Authenticity is the desire to have a healthy alignment between inner values and beliefs and outer behaviors," they say. "An authentic person understands her priorities and emotions. She is in touch with what matters to her and has fashioned her life in accordance to those priorities."

Where do your priorities align with *your* values? Values that we believe are our own but may not be, usually start with "I should" or "I must." For instance, a value statement you may make consciously or unconsciously of, "I value cleanliness. I should keep my home spotlessly cleaned or it will appear I am neglecting my duties at home." If you find yourself agreeing with this statement to any degree, I encourage you to

4

ask if it's cleanliness you actually value. Is cleanliness a message left over from childhood or one you have decided upon intentionally as an adult? I intend no judgment about it either way. The point is that unless you (and your family) clarify what cleanliness means and looks like, you may have unrealistic expectations, or false ones, undermining your peace of mind.

Your behavior is the most accurate indicator of your true character. Ultimately our behavior is simply the acting out of our deeply held values. We can value something, for instance health, yet find another value appears to have more control over our choices. An example would be junk food. While you value health, your choice of eating nutritionally deficient snacks may indicate expediency or pleasure is more important than your health. You may recognize exercise is critical to your health, yet sleep thirty minutes longer rather than getting up to walk. It's a fairly well-known truth that humans will go to great lengths to avoid pain. It may be that up till now, eating healthier and exercising brought more visions of pain than joy or satisfaction. As you learn to choose differently after reading this book, you will understand that the potential future pain of losing your vitality and health is not worth the immediate gratification of fast food or a skipped workout.

Self-leadership is the conscious determination to make choices that reflect values that are congruent with your deeply held convictions—even when it's difficult or challenging to do so. Self-leadership requires personal discipline, vigilance, awareness, and honesty. Self-leaders also engage the help and resources of others to help them live congruently with their personal values despite the culture's influence and lure.

It is difficult to make consistent lifestyle choices that the media and culture strive to sabotage at every turn. If an alien dropped out of the sky and, determined to learn more about us as humans by observing our media in print, radio, TV, and the Internet, it is certain he would agree that it's the stuff we consume and the physical beauty we aspire to that is most important to us. However, in talking individually with clients, family, and friends, those are rarely the things they place first in their lives. The real telling choices are where we spend our time, energy, and money. By using our resources to support the things and people we value most, we succeed in life because we live life according to our values and not others' expectations and standards.

Identify Your Personal Values

The best and most troubling place to begin when it comes to identifying your values is to explore your present behavior. At the end of this chapter you will have the opportunity to take the congruence test for yourself. (You can even stop here to take it before you continue.) If you take the time to do this, you'll make some interesting discoveries. For instance, if financial security is important to you, you'll see wise, thoughtful purchases versus impulse items. Or not. Assuming you value your spouse or your relationship with your kids, you ought to be able to see *unhurried*, non-chauffeuring time spent together. Consider whether what you *say* is important to you is the same as what you *do* with your time, energy, and money.

If you recognize a need for more time, money, or energy for your personal renewal and self-care, consider what that would look like in your life. Would you hire cleaning help, a pick-up laundry, or food delivery service? Would you delegate more tasks at home or work? Would you benefit from a personal trainer or nutritionist? How about an art or photography class? I wonder right now if that small voice in your head is saying, "Oh yes, yes, yes, I'd love that! How can I do this?" Or is that voice resisting these ideas suggesting, "You can't afford such luxuries or indulgences."

Giving yourself permission to nurture and healthfully care for yourself doesn't have to prompt feelings of guilt. Once you alter your perception of self-care as being a "guilt stimulator" to becoming a "life enhancer," you will more willingly strive to make time for your own care.

Put Your Values to Work

After so many years of doing workshops, reading books, and reviewing assessment tools, I can tell you that everyone seems to list different values. It would be helpful for you to pause now to take the Values Clarification exercise included in appendix B to sort through your most important areas of concern, growth, and opportunity.

Once you have clearly identified and can articulate your values, you can then begin the powerful process of intentionally cultivating *healthy relationships in every area of your life* according to those values. For many, the most important of all relationships is with yourself. I actually put my relationship with God even before myself because what I believe about who God is and how I am called to live and love myself is an extension of that intimate relationship.

> "The time you enjoy wasting is not wasted time."
>
> Bertrand Russell

That relationship creates the strong foundation from which I operate.

Before focusing on your outside relationships, go within and cultivate a healthy positive relationship with yourself. Get to know and love *you*!

Cultivating Healthy Relationships

Measuring the health and vitality of different facets of your life is an important step for enjoying an abundant life. Like pieces of a puzzle that fit together to form a picture, your life consists of pieces representing your finances, health, interpersonal relationships, faith, career, etc. Pulling out one piece at a time and examining your vitality, strength, and contentment in that area is important. For instance, without a healthy relationship with yourself, you won't allow yourself time to have fun, relax, set boundaries, or succeed. You need a healthy relationship with money, or financial pressures will sabotage your efforts to control your life. You need healthy relationships with your family and friends to provide you support, emotional energy, and joy as you juggle your busy life.

Some women are so busy, so engaged, and active in their lives, they never slow down. Except when they crash or burn out. At the other extreme are those who are stuck in a rut or are paralyzed due to insecurities and limited thinking. They are inactive or disengaged from life. Somewhere in the middle are women who balance the many facets of their lives to remain healthy in every way: physically, financially, emotionally, relationally, intellectually, and spiritually.

If you want to make a difference in your corner of the world *without* forfeiting your health and relationships in the process, you must live intentionally and purposefully.

"To light a candle is to cast a shadow."
Ursula K. LeGuin

Many people are concerned that if they slow down, they'll fall down and never get their motivation back again. The opposite applies to those who are stuck. Some are living mediocre lives and they know it. They're ready to be unstuck. Others are living mediocre lives and don't realize it. They haven't identified their dis-ease or acknowledged their lack of contentment or energy comes from being stuck. When they take the time to reflect and evaluate what they need and *want* to improve their energy, joy, or contentment, they become ready to get unstuck. High achievers can be stuck too— their busyness prevents their acting on the things they *really* need to do.

"Busyness is the germ that destroys the health of your relationships."
Kate Larsen

After speaking on the topic of balancing work and life since 1989, I admit that "balance" has become a meaningless, overused word. I knowingly resort to using the word balance because it implies something most people aspire to achieve. Balance for those I work with is really about living a life that takes into account the many facets of who they are. It does not imply something akin to balanced scales. That level of equilibrium, if it exists, doesn't last long. A balanced life leaves time for the pursuit of health, connectedness to others, and the creative use of one's skills, talents, and passions.

To live a balanced or integrated life does not mean you need to operate at an optimum level in every area of your life all the time. It's important to recognize and accept the ebb and flow brought with each season of life.

When my boys were in their toddler and early school years, I taught aerobics classes during the morning times. Arriving around 9:00 a.m., I worked out or taught class until 11:30 a.m. That gave me a chance to exercise, socialize, and shower, and gave the boys a chance to have some fun too. Today, with a business to run and other responsibilities, I don't take extended hours to exercise, and I generally teach during other non-prime work hours. As my season of life has changed, so have my workout hours, my social times, and the amount of time I put into my work. Is there an activity or commitment you have today that doesn't fit into your life as well as it used to? It's easy to transition into a new season of life dragging along activities that no longer enhance your life and that of your family.

The Importance of a Solid Foundation

Fluctuating life circumstances impact the rhythm of life, and the resulting impact is directly measured by the foundation you lay for yourself. A balanced life enables you to withstand storms and natural crises without destroying your health and relationships. Having a strong personal foundation is key to successfully juggling the demands of life. Most people aren't spending enough time on their foundation. Overemphasizing any one area of your life while ignoring other important areas can lead to disaster when troubles in life hit. And it's guaranteed that troubles will hit. It's a fact of life too many people ignore.

Here's the good news: A well-balanced person who has healthy relationships in most areas of life will weather the storms with less damage and cost to their life.

Sallie had been a highly successful real estate agent for fifteen years when she called me. She said she was beginning to recognize that her lack of attention to her health and lifestyle habits had begun to eat away at her energy and her body was beginning to retaliate. She had some generally good habits, yet recognized if she didn't begin to make some changes, her busy life would be permanently impacted, one small unhealthy choice at a time.

We started by evaluating what she wanted to see changed. What exactly did she mean by, "I want to increase my energy?" (Many agents who knew her would have said, "She's got plenty of energy!" For her, it wasn't her ideal, and it was *her* ideal that mattered.) She said a key indicator that her energy was increasing for the better would be if she didn't slump exhausted in her car at 3:00 p.m., and she wanted energy at night when she got home to engage more in conversation or activities with her husband. She also wanted to take care of more things at home from writing cards to friends to organizing rooms and reading casual books.

With some fine-tuning to her diet, experimenting with exercise routines, and adjusting some of her expectations for her day, Sallie saw a vast improvement in her energy in a matter of weeks.

You, too, can have more energy if you make some small changes in your daily routine.

Choose to Burn Up, Not Out

Life is short. My sons think it's absolutely morbid that I read the obituaries. I simply turn the page of the paper and there they are. When I see someone who was in their thirties, forties, fifties, or sixties, I think, *Oh, how sad; they were so young.* What is eye opening for me is how often I see those ages in the write-ups. We don't know how short our stay on earth is. I want to go out of this world burned up, not burned out. If that's the case for you, then you need to get active immediately.

To live a life that enables you to burn up instead of out requires you live differently from most people around you. It requires you live with intention, purpose, passion, self-discipline, and patience.

A great life, a successful life, isn't a matter of chance. It's a matter of choice. It's the result of thoughtful assessment, reflection, and assimilation that leads to intentional planning and action. It is also a matter of making conscious commitments— challenging commitments.

Many achieve success for *short* periods of time in specific areas of their lives. Most people want to lead lives with meaning, impact, and depth. They want to possess the energy to pursue hobbies, careers, relationships, and activities that last throughout their lives. They don't want to pay with their health and relationships for their short-term success. Yet, that seems to be exactly what many are doing.

Follow Your Desire With Action

You've probably picked up on this already, but my goal with this book is to help you develop healthier thinking habits so you will develop healthier behavioral habits. Until you are clear about what you value, what you are willing to do (or not do) to live by your values, and how to best pursue them, you will not experience lasting change. Change occurs due to action, not just thinking. Creating a lifestyle that is sustainable for a lifetime will be the greatest gift you give to yourself, your family, and your work.

> *"Goals determine what you're going to be."*
> *Julius Erving*

Throughout this book, I will suggest positive attitudes or self-talk that will enhance your efforts, encourage you, and lift your spirits.

Exercises to Help You Change Your Life Through Action

In an effort to create a way for you to make wise choices, you will find what I termed "workouts and workins" at the end of each chapter. Yes, workins is a new word. Yes, workins work!

Workouts make you sweat, push yourself, challenge your current level of physical fitness. Workouts require action. Workout exercises in this book are action oriented so you can proactively apply the ideas and concepts of the chapter to your life.

Of course, before your behaviors become habit, your attitudes and self-talk must change to support your effort and commitment to new action. Therefore, you will get to also do workins for your mind. These exercises are designed to shift your thinking, perceptions, and attitudes by stretching and strengthening your mindset, thereby making them work within. Practiced regularly, workins will stretch, strengthen, and develop your positive attitude and determination muscles. Keeping a journal as you write your insights, commitments, observations, and plans for the choices and changes you will be incorporating into your life can be tremendously helpful. But if writing a journal doesn't appeal to you, that's okay. Do the workins and workouts anyway.

Self-management implies an active pursuit of healthy relationships—beginning with your relationship with yourself. When you have a healthy positive relationship with yourself, you will be able to do so with others. Self-management suggests the choices you make will be preventative versus rehabilitative.

If you want to make a difference in your corner of the world, *without* forfeiting your health and relationships in the process, you must live intentionally and purposefully. A fulfilling life is built one choice at a time. It is not built by chance. It is built by choice. You can do it!

TRAINING TIPS

- Once you alter your perception from self-care being a guilt stimulator to a "life enhancer," you will more willingly strive to make time for your own care.

- Without a healthy relationship with yourself, you won't allow yourself time to have fun, relax, set boundaries, or succeed.

- If you want to make a difference in your corner of the world without forfeiting your health and relationships in the process, you must live intentionally and purposefully.

- A well-balanced person who has healthy relationships in most areas of life will weather the storms with less damage and cost to their life.

- A great, successful, fulfilling life isn't a matter of chance. It's a matter of choice.
- Self-management suggests that the choices you make will be preventative versus rehabilitative.
- Your behavior is the most accurate indicator of your true character.
- Pursue life based upon your strengths, not focused on your weaknesses.

WORKINS ➤

1. Complete the Values Clarification exercise in appendix B. What five things do you value most?

1. _____

2. _____

3. _____

4. _____

5. _____

After you have completed the extended Values Clarification exercise, take your list of five top values and finish the following sentences for each.

A. Because I value _____ (fill in a value), I will _____ _____ (state the benefit/reward you expect to see in your life for living according to your values).

B. The thought(s) I will hold in my head and heart is/are _____, _____, (list the attitudes, mantras, verses, or principles that will encourage you to delay gratification, persevere, or hold firm when the going gets tough and you want to quit or cheat).

C. The strength(s) I have that will work to my advantage is/are _____,
_____, and _____.

2. Would others describe you as:
- well-rounded, congruent in your behaviors and stated values?
- healthy?
- connected deeply with others?

3. If not, would it be important to you for others to describe you this way? Why?

4. What do your answers suggest you need to do?

5. Are you ready and willing to do so?

6. Are there cracks in your foundation? If so, where are they?

7. What will it take to fix them?

8. Are you willing to do what it takes to make sure you have the energy and capacity to be successful without forfeiting your health or close relationships?

WORKOUTS

1. Take the congruence test below for yourself; take out your checkbook, credit card receipts, and PDA or calendar. Examine what your

choices reveal in the manner in which you spent your time, energy, and money for the past two weeks. You will examine each of the two weeks separately.

A. My favorite thing to do alone is _____
_____. I did that for
___ minutes, ___ hours *this* week.

My favorite thing to do alone is _____
_____. I did that for
___ minutes, ___ hours *last* week.

B. I enjoyed ___ minutes, ___ hours with my spouse *this* week.

I enjoyed ___ minutes, ___ hours with my spouse *last* week.

C. I relaxed and thoroughly enjoyed my kid(s) for ___ minutes, ___ hours *this* week.

I relaxed and thoroughly enjoyed my kid(s) for ___ minutes, ___ hours *last* week.

D. I spent ___ minutes, ___ hours having fun with a friend *this* week.

I spent ___ minutes, ___ hours having fun with a friend *last* week.

E. I spent ___ dollars eating out, buying coffee/soft drinks/tea, snack foods *this* week.

I spent ___ dollars eating out, buying coffee/soft drinks/tea, snack foods *last* week.

F. The largest purchase I have made in the *last month* has been? _____.

I shopped around to get the best price with the most quality for ___ days or ___ months.

G. I averaged ___ hours of sleep *this* week.

I averaged ___ hours of sleep *last* week.

H. I engaged in an activity that stimulated my thinking (intellect) ___ minutes, ___ hours *this* week.

I engaged in an activity that stimulated my thinking (intellect) ___ minutes, ___ hours *last* week.

2. What patterns emerge from your answers?

3. What is the biggest surprise from your examination of how you spend your time, energy, and money?

4. What, if anything, are you ready and willing to adjust? What small changes would move you in the direction you would like to go?

5. By when will you do this?

6. Whom can you tell to help you remain accountable?

Build On Your New Foundation

Mary Beth called one morning while I was sitting at my desk working and shared with me her concerns about her rising anxiety, constant frustration with never feeling like she was getting anything done, despite always being busy. She said, "I honestly don't have time for myself right now but realize if I don't do something differently, I'll regret it later." Too many working professionals are frazzled, fried, and frustrated with their lack of energy, their heightened sense of anxiety, and relentless pace. Does this ring true for you? If yes, I know you want to make different choices in your life. You recognize that you need to make adjustments to your lifestyle to increase your energy, reduce your stress, and find time to enjoy the special people in your life. You also know you need to take better care of yourself. If you're tired of being tired, you are not alone.

Good Intentions Into Action

Lifestyle factors can be modified to improve health, improve the quality of life, reduce medical care costs, and enhance workplace productivity. Researchers, clinicians, and health care professionals are striving to get this message into the workplace. You don't need to wait to make lifestyle changes that will impact your productivity and effectiveness at work or home. You can begin immediately.

What do you need more of in your life? What do you want less of? Take a deep breath and prepare for some reflection. Reflection requires a slowing down that's unknown to most people today. Reflection allows you to integrate learning and make new ideas a part of yourself. Reflection is a synthesis of old and new that encourages insight and understanding. Without reflection, learning escapes. It is only through the exploration of your inner self that you change your outer self. Reflection helps you distinguish shades of meaning and builds conscious action based on clarity and purpose. Reflection enables you to wisely determine the new habits you need to adopt and old habits you need stop. As with any skill, new habits require time for consistent practice. You have the opportunity to practice every day with each choice you make.

Looking Better or Living Better
—Choose Your Focus

Newspapers, magazines, radio, and TV are filled with information on diets and weight-loss programs, fitness memberships, gadgets, and gizmos to get into shape. The messages emphasize losing weight and exercising to look better and feel better.

20

For decades, our culture has focused on *looking* better instead of *living* better. The message is if you lose weight, you'll look better. If you look better, you'll feel better. If you feel better, you'll be more productive, effective, and energetic. You'll have more patience and creativity and handle conflict better. You will attract other people to yourself.

In theory, this is terrific. The problem is, it doesn't work. Looking better does not guarantee feeling better or thinking better. I'll never forget Kayla, an absolutely beautiful woman with whom I taught exercise classes. She was fit, sculpted—beautiful. The problem was, she didn't know it. She was always focused on her physical flaws that were—to my eyes—non-existent. I don't think she ever enjoyed or appreciated her looking great because she didn't think great. She needed to *think better* to live better and enjoy life better.

Thinking better results in choosing better. If you make better choices, you'll naturally lose weight, exercise more often and more consistently, which generally translates into *being* a more pleasant, effective, authentic person. Did I mention healthier too?

Another beautiful woman I taught with acknowledged that in years past she had struggled with an eating disorder. She said her focus, which wasn't healthy, realistic, or positive, just about killed her. She reached out for help to learn how to think better. Thinking better meant challenging the truth of her negative self-talk. Thinking better led her to make different lifestyle choices, which resulted in her becoming healthier— inside and out.

The fact that Americans spend more than $33 billion a year on diets, supplements, and weight-loss programs each year[1] is a powerful testament to the fact

21

that we care about our health. We want to be thinner and healthier. However, given the increasing statistics and realities of illness, disease, and disability due to lifestyle choices, we must concede that most programs are not working. So, what's the answer? Give up on programs? Stop trying to change? Absolutely not!

STOP! Think First, Then Act

You can make healthier habits a part of your life. Programs can and do help. The trick is to start at the beginning. The problem is that most of these programs start at the wrong place. Most encourage buyers to *jump into action* without the appropriate reflection, assessment, and strategic adjustments. Smoking cessation programs have been guilty of this. Slap a patch on and quit. Chew gum and be done with your smoking habit forever. Sustainable success doesn't happen that way.

Our society's solution to resolving problems or breaking unhealthy habits is to get into action to fix the problem—quickly.

A client recently described always feeling stupid and slow because she's doesn't problem solve quickly. She knows she needs more time to think through problem-solving situations than others. (Therefore, she's not quick to action. Being surrounded by action-oriented people, she felt less sharp, less successful.) She said, "Someone will describe a situation or problem to me—they want immediate suggestions and action. I'll have to think about it for about an hour and all of a sudden, I get it." Her tone of voice told me she felt she was failing her people. I asked, "When you come back with your thoughts and ideas, do you tend to make fewer mistakes than others? Do you find that you see the overall implications of a situation better too?" She said in a lighter, relieved voice, "Actually, yes! That's why they want me managing wherever I work." Slower can be better. When you sense a need to go slower, give yourself permission to do so.

Our tendency to act quickly and think later sets the stage for the "Ready, fire, aim" syndrome we see in the world. The action response has been a part of the behavior-change science field for many years. When you set goals and want to develop new habits, you are striving for behavioral change. It would then seem natural to attempt behavior change as a first step. The reason that the same lifestyle goals (losing weight and starting and maintaining an exercise program) hit the top two on so many people's New Year's resolution list year after year is because what seems natural (getting into action) is not the answer.

The first step to change is **not to get into action**. The first step involves reflection and assessment. It's important right from the start to consider: (1) why you want to get into action, (2) how you will successfully do that, (3) with whom, and (4) how you will navigate the obstacles that will attempt to get in your way. I will come back to smart goal setting techniques later. Keep in mind, before you experience a lasting behavioral change, you need an attitude and/or perspective change. You need a cease-fire in activity to develop a plan to incorporate healthy, sustainable changes that will impact your joy, your energy, and impact in the world.

Getting Started

Whenever I begin coaching someone, I start with these two questions, "Why now?" And, "What's different about you or your circumstances that indicates it's genuinely time to change?" If that person doesn't have a specific response, we look to see if there is a good answer. *Without a clear, compelling answer to these two questions, successful change is almost impossible.*

While most people would say they have set goals in their lives, experience has shown me that great goal setting is a skill that eludes many of us. The reason? Most people decide upon a goal or goals to accomplish at one point in time and neglect these three critical steps.

1. First, they do not thoroughly evaluate what accomplishing the goal will require in time, energy, focus, or finances. They, therefore, set themselves up to be knocked off the path to success by extenuating circumstances.

2. Second, they fail to revisit the plan to achieve the goal on a regular basis. I have seen countless performance plans with goals clearly set for the next annual review at work that are not accomplished because the performance plans were not used on an ongoing basis as a guide to success.

3. Third, they don't tie their goals to a long-term vision of who they want to be, what they want to become, and how they want others to experience. If they do tie the goals to a long-term vision and obstacles occur, they are able to directly connect their choices and decisions to their goals. Recognizing the connection of their

immediate goals to their long-term vision provides encouragement to stick with their intentions and actions.

Create a Life Vision and/or Wellness Vision

Early one Monday morning, my mother broke an oath she made to herself thirty-four years earlier. She walked into a fitness club and signed up to take an exercise class. During her senior year of high school, she made a promise to herself that once she shed the gym uniform, she would never again make herself climb into workout wear.

However, here she was, choosing to begin an exercise program. No one was more surprised than I was as she came into *my* class!

Irene, my mom, had a new vision for herself. She wanted to be healthy and active as a grandmother in the years to come. She knew if she wanted to take better care of herself, she needed to get moving. She realized she did not have to do what she did in high school. She could start exercising with someone she would enjoy and in a class she felt she could successfully finish. Mom innately understood the saying, "Not fun, not done." That is one of the key attitudes to getting active and staying active for the rest of your life. You need to choose to participate in something you enjoy. And you can begin at any age. Men and women in their eighties and nineties have shown positive outcomes after beginning an exercise program. Your restrictions are determined by your personal health history and pre-existing conditions. While past challenges may alter the activities you engage in today, they do not preclude you from trying new things.

(You will do focused work on your exercise habits in chapter six.)

Beginning to exercise was part of a wellness vision Mom had begun to work on for herself. I have a life vision that incorporates my wellness; however, sometimes it helps to individually create a wellness vision when healthy habits have eluded you. You can create a life vision and/or a wellness vision. Your wellness vision is a subset of your overall life vision. I will describe and refer to life visions and wellness visions. You may be focused on your wellness vision if your primary goal is to get healthier. (You will find a wellness vision development exercise in appendix C. This exercise is followed by a goal setting and writing exercise that propels you to achieve your goals and ultimately your vision.)

What is a wellness vision? Do you have one? I'll bet you do, it just hasn't been articulated yet. A wellness vision is a clarifying statement about your health and well-being that can include the *outcomes* you want for your health, the *motivators* you have for pursuing healthy habits and for acknowledging *obstacles* that you intend to overcome. Recognizing the obstacles that will stop you enables you to create strategies to overcome them. Including into your strategies and plans your personal strengths and past experience will help you succeed.

Here is an example of a wellness vision written by a working mother: "To honor my priorities by spending fewer weekend and evening hours working, so that I will become physically fit, will lose forty pounds, and will have more quality time with my family." Notice how clear this statement is about what she wants. She mentions her desired outcomes and motivators. In her daily, weekly, and monthly planning, she can quickly evaluate what her obstacles will be (time, others' expectations, energy). She can then design a workable strategy incorporating her own work/life challenges. She may want to work out six days a week, yet may deliberately choose four exercise days and make a commitment to be active on a daily basis. In other words, anytime she can walk, she does. Instead of asking kids to run for things, she becomes her own "go-fer."

Taking time to create a wellness vision allows you to be honest, direct, and intentional about your objectives and reasons for wanting to become more disciplined in your daily habits. Wellness is both an attitude and a choice—a choice to be proactive about the quality of your life. Having a wellness vision enables you to be strategic in your approach to incorporating healthy habits consistently into your life. Most importantly, a wellness vision impacts your whole life—all of who you are and how you live.

The missing link for most people is the lack of a defined wellness vision and a plan to incorporate the required behaviors and attitudes into their daily living. People have visions for their lives that often include professional, as well as, personal goals. Organizations have visions for their businesses or associations. Why shouldn't you have a wellness vision for your overall health and well-being? Without one, next year you may be making the same New Year's resolutions you made a few months ago. Goals and dreams rarely fail due to a lack of commitment or enthusiasm. They die or dissolve because someone gives up on the dream for lack of a compelling vision that has a plan to achieve it.

Virtually every client I have worked with has recognized the importance of developing a consistent exercise program. Yet, eight out of ten struggle to exercise consistently. Just because we know something is healthy or smart does not guarantee we do it. As Dr. Edward Creagan, editor of the book, *Mayo Clinic on Healthy Aging*, said regarding exercise, "Nowhere is the gap wider between what we know and what we do." [2]

Exercise is a key ingredient in a wellness vision. God has designed our bodies in such a way that they renew, recharge, and become stronger, not weaker, *when used*. So often, people say, "I'm just too tired to exercise." Guess what? Exercise is exactly what they need! You can start slowly, you can start small—just start.

Any dream worth pursuing takes energy, tenacity, discipline, and fortitude. Without your health, none of these are possible. Billions of dollars are spent each year on strategic plans, corporate mergers, acquisitions, change initiatives, new products, and new business ventures; many end up sabotaged by the fatigue, burnout, and stress-related illnesses experienced by individuals and employees who have neglected their health. Families' lives are altered forever by the ill health of those they love. While there are many factors we cannot impact or influence, exercise is not one of them. You *can* get and stay active, especially when exercise is tied to a wellness vision.

Most people don't exercise because they *love to exercise*; they love the *results* of exercise. There are a number of ways to get that result; look to find one that works for you.

Mom has given up aerobic classes; however, she continues to walk the treadmill thirty minutes, three times a week. As a result, her heart rate, blood pressure, and weight have stayed just where she likes. *And*, she remains proud of her efforts, and I remain proud of her.

Setting Goals That Work For You

Goal setting is best completed when you have your vision created so the goals and vision work together. The vision describes the outcomes of the goals you set that will be achieved by the choices you make.

Part of your mission (I hope) in reading this work is that you are ready to set and achieve *effective* goals. With that in mind, you may read with special interest the summary of thirty-five years of research on effective goal setting from the September 2002 issue of *American Psychologist*.[3]

- ❑ When people have specific, difficult, measurable goals, performance is higher than when they are exhorted to simply do their best.

- ❑ Research now supports the conclusions that goals are best reached when (1) people make a public commitment to their goals, (2) leaders communicate an inspiring vision, (3) leaders/coaches are good models, (4) there is consistent feedback, (5) people are taught skills to help them succeed, and (6) the leader/coach expresses confidence in the person's ability to succeed.

- ❑ The major benefit of a team setting goals is not better motivation; it is that participants can think together about strategies to perform better.

❑ Success in reaching a team goal is more likely if the team goal is consistent with the personal goals of each team member.

An overview of effective goal setting suggests you need to be very clear about what it is you want to achieve by accomplishing a goal. You want benchmarks that help you easily identify when you've achieved your goal, along with indicators that you are making progress. Your plan to achieve your goal will include an honest and thorough assessment of what will potentially get in the way (or who may get in your way—consciously or unconsciously) and how you will strategically work through the obstacles and challenges you face. You will also benefit from working with others that clearly understand your goals and desires.

For instance, many people say, "My goal is to be healthier and more energetic." My response, "What does healthier mean to you? What would it look like in terms of your physical and/or emotional state of being? What will you do with more energy? And, if it sounds like a good idea now, what's gotten in your way for achieving it up till now?"

Thoughtfully answering these questions will allow you to more clearly and effectively set a goal and prepare for the challenges for achieving it. Many people have heard of the SMART acronym for goal setting, which describes in five letters that your goals, to be more easily achieved, need to be specific, measurable, action-oriented, realistic, and have a time frame for achieving them. I often refer to the A as being for "ardently desired." I'm cautious about encouraging action too soon. Again, the reflection sets the tone and direction of your action. Desire and "want power" versus willpower will fuel you when boredom, frustration, or fatigue threaten to take you off your path.

Thinking patterns and unwanted behaviors are often the driving factor behind unachieved goals and a dissatisfied life. Below you will find a list of examples from my clients. The following statements expose the reasons they believe they need to change themselves or their thinking. As you read through the list, ask yourself if you can relate to them. Check off the ones you can relate to, write in the margins, or pull out a piece of paper, making notes as you review these common challenges to setting goals in order to improve upon or change something:

- ❏ a lack of focus or discipline related to exercise, nutrition, sleep/rest needs
- ❏ a pursuit of perfection in everything versus striving for excellence
- ❏ never believing they or their efforts are good enough (this tendency has actually been identified by Dr. Valerie Young as the Impostor Syndrome and will be discussed more in chapter seven)
- ❏ fear of rejection, which prevents individuals from taking risks or dreaming beyond their current reality
- ❏ self-sabotage, which includes a variety of avoidance behaviors and poor self-talk
- ❏ addiction to achievement
- ❏ a general lack of contentment
- ❏ an inability or lack of awareness as to how to set boundaries and create consequences for not honoring them (by oneself or others)

- ❑ a lack of clarity about what is really needed and wanted in life
- ❑ a lack of permission from oneself to make one's own health a priority

The following example of three goals set by a past client Catherine were chosen based upon the challenges she could relate to in the list above.

1) I want to make a decision about my direction and vision for living a life that is congruent with my values, especially as it relates to my work. I will know I have done that when I feel passionate about my work.

2) I will give myself permission to take better care of myself, so that I'll be happier and more holistically healthy. I will know that I am doing that when I feel great about myself.

3) I will start developing a stronger faith walk with God, so that I will experience a stronger sense of contentment and less anxiety on a regular basis. I will know I am doing that when I stop living out of fear, and I am motivated by my desire to contribute to my community and society.

Let's look back to the second goal listed above. If this is your goal, you can take it to the next level. Determine one specific goal you could set that would support this overriding goal. What will be your motivators, obstacles, strategy, and outcome for following through? What strength of character or experience will help you?

Catherine's goals show how she responded to these questions.

Motivator—supports my value of taking care of my health.

Obstacles—not making the goal a priority; I let other priorities get in the way.

Strategy—planning and scheduling activities and meals for the week, at least until I develop the new habits.

Outcome—I will be taking care of my body, which will help my mind, reduce my stress, and make me feel happier.

Strengths—I am organized and persistent.

You will have the opportunity to begin writing out your goal statements, motivators, obstacles, strategy, outcomes, and strengths in appendix D.

What Really Helps You Make Behavior Changes

A helpful behavior change model is one designed by James Prochaska, Ph.D., and his fellow researchers. The model he and his team created, and continue to perfect, has been effectively used in behavioral psychology for years, primarily in addiction recovery. This model uses a stage-theory approach to goal setting and changing behavior. The model consists of Six Stages of Change.[4] You've probably heard that grieving has stages to it. Well, so does change. Action is a part of the change process; however, action is *not* the first step to change. Without starting at the beginning of the process, you set yourself up to fail.

The Six Stages of Change

When you understand the Six Stages of Change, you will find yourself effectively coaching yourself to better thinking and, therefore, smarter planning and action. The six stages are precontemplation, contemplation, preparation, action, maintenance, and termination. There is not a typical period of time for people to remain in any particular stage. As your attitudes and behaviors change and evolve, you move from one stage into the next, sometimes moving back again. You can have goals set in every area of your life and can be at a different stage for each of them. For instance, you could be in the action stage of finding a new job to remove or diminish stress in your life. In this stage you would be actively interviewing, possibly applying for jobs online, and/or networking. You could be in the preparation stage of change around exercise thinking it would be a good to find a place to work out. You could be contemplating calling the phone number you got for a well known personal trainer. Finally, you could be in the precontemplation stage regarding your marriage relationship. It doesn't occur to you right now that you and your spouse are detached living in the same house leading separate lives.

As you read through the stage descriptions that follow, consider what stage of change you are currently in for the various goals you have. It is not until you determine what stage you are in that you can create an effective, practical strategy to get to the next step.

Change is not a groupthink. It's an individual task. Each of us as individuals must create our own capacity for constant change. The better we understand change, the better our ability for working with it, and the better we will be in our life journey. Learning about what goes into change will enable you to be less apprehensive and more determined to make changes in your attitudes and habits.

STAGE 1. PRECONTEMPLATION
(NO INTEREST, NO INTENTION)

Precontemplators have no current intention to change. They may have tried to change a particular behavior in the past and given up, or they may deny the reality of the problem. They may be demoralized, having dismissed the possibility of ever changing. We all have people in our lives who are at this place. It is likely this stage describes us at some point.

STAGE 2. CONTEMPLATION
(BEGINNING TO SEE THE LIGHT)

Contemplators acknowledge they have a problem and are willing to think about their need to change. While they are open to information and feedback, they may remain in this stage for years, realizing they have a problem, but feeling unable to generate the energy to change. At this stage determining strong motivators for changing their behavior is very important. This stage may be the most emotionally and physically draining one because the needed change weighs on the person (physically and/or emotionally).

This is the reflection stage, the thinking stage, the no-action stage. Therefore, for the take-charge, Type A individuals, this stage is often skipped or skimmed through because Type A people like action. The contemplation stage requires slowing down, reflecting, and assessing, and has a process orientation. The reality is that this is the stage that prepares the way for the head and heart to connect on making lasting change. Remember, *it's better thinking that leads to better choices in life*. Just as we have behavioral habits, we also have thinking habits. These habits need to change before *lasting* behavior change will occur.

STAGE 3. PREPARATION (STARTING TO FLEX THE COURAGE MUSCLE)

People in this stage are on the verge of action. They are generally developing action plans and may even have made small changes. This is the stage when you ask others you respect how they balance their lives, incorporate exercise, or find time for hobbies. You look to others for creative ideas and solutions. You could call this the brainstorming and research portion of preparing for change. At some point, whether because of a personally established deadline or a crisis, you step into stage four, which is action. A cautionary note: You can get stuck in this stage of getting ready to get ready and not move on to action—ever.

STAGE 4. ACTION (USING THE MUSCLE)

People in this stage are following the action plan they developed. The better developed their plan is and the more attention they have given to the work of the contemplation and preparation stages, the more successful at change they will be. This stage is where all those small steps, small choices, and mini sacrifices make a huge difference. The combined impact of a positive attitude and small choices that fuel action and good choices sustain the changed behavior.

STAGE 5. MAINTENANCE (KEEP MOVING)

Maintainers continuously engage in their change process for at least six months. While the change feels more natural in this stage, overconfidence and life stresses can lead to relapse to old habits. Maintainers can also experience a major change in one area of life (a job and/or location change), which then impacts other areas of life (getting away from a consistent exercise program) that requires going back and beginning again in an earlier stage of change for that life area. The good news is that since you formed a successful habit once before, you usually need to spend *less* time in the earlier stages. You can also remember your previous success, which oftentimes provides the confidence and energy needed to try again. Positive living and healthier choices come more naturally.

Jodi considered herself in the maintenance stage of exercise. She loved her exercise program and life as a part-time employee and new mom. She had begun exercising to lose weight after her pregnancy. Two years into her regular healthy lifestyle, she and her husband moved. She was also four months pregnant with her second child. She found herself busy with the move and tired from the pregnancy and began cutting back on her exercise program. Finally, she just quit working out. Eight months after her second child was born, she realized it was time to get back into her old routine. Recognizing how recording her workouts helped in the past, she journaled her journey back to regular exercise. She continues to journal even though she is again in a maintenance stage of exercise. The process of writing keeps her aware of her choices, which fuels her motivation to live healthfully.

STAGE 6. TERMINATION (RUNNING ON AUTOMATIC)

In this stage, the new behavior becomes an integral part of daily life, so much so that the likelihood of relapse is essentially nonexistent. Some professionals question whether people ever reach this stage, although Prochaska and colleagues say it is possible for a small percentage of individuals. I consider myself in the Maintenance Stage of my healthy habits. I never want to take for granted the importance and impact of my daily choices.

As you set your goals and plan your action steps, whether to get healthier, grow your business, have more fun time with family or friends, begin a new career, or simply clean out your closets, don't forget to stop, evaluate, and start at the stage of change you're genuinely at for this specific area during this point of your life. You may be at Stage Four, ready to get into action to change your eating habits, yet at Stage Two for potentially changing your career or job situation. Being at different stages of change is okay—you simply need to take that into account as you move ahead in the areas of your life.

Thinking before leaping enables you to jump into action in a sustainable, practical way that will allow you to experience more success and less stress. By looking at change through the six stages described, you'll discover that being successful at making lasting change will become a natural habit that will open the door to new and more exciting habits year after year.

Think, Choose, Act, Win Model (TCAW)

Once clients are in the Contemplation and Preparation stages of change, I teach them the Think, Choose, Act, Win model I designed for getting into action and staying in action. Think, Choose, Act, Win is simple to say. It's easy to remember. There is one additional concept that is important—the concept of "The Wall." When you do your best to make changes and discover you hit the proverbial wall, your strategy doesn't work. (I resist the word "fail," yet that is what most people call it.) Without forethought and a plan for success (which includes the possibility for regrouping), surrender, failure, and frustration are the predictable outcomes.

The Think, Choose, Act, Win model is designed to take six to sixty seconds, and is intended to encourage you to make the *best choices* in the moment of decision.

You need to make decisions daily that impact your health in every dimension of life. By deliberately taking six to sixty seconds to pause before making a choice, you can change your life. Stop yourself before eating that glazed doughnut and ask yourself whether it's worth the calories, sugar, and fat. Reward yourself for not eating it—preferably a non-caloric reward. Stop yourself before you charge out the door on your way to work without your workout clothes. Consider whether it just might be better to take five more minutes to pack your stuff. Taking six seconds to bite your tongue and consider the positive way to respond to an irritating comment or rude individual could save you from misunderstanding, frustration, and ill feelings.

Let's take a closer look at how the Think, Choose, Act, Win model works.

STEP ONE: THINK

First, consider the choice. Think through and acknowledge the easiest answer to your question or choice. The easiest answer is the one most of us choose for that very reason—it's easy. Sitting and watching TV is easier than gearing up for a walk. Eating high-fat, high-sugar, and easily accessible foods is quicker than thinking though the best food choices for your body. Ignoring snide remarks from an adult sibling may seem better than confronting the issues behind the comments. Over time, these easier decisions create the build-up that leads to poor health physically, emotionally, financially, and interpersonally. What is the choice you need to make right now? Identify it. Take the time to think through what your best choice would be in the moment. For instance, will eating that scone fulfill your goal of eating wisely each morning? Would firing back an angry e-mail to someone support your commitment to be professional and take the high road when working with clients?

STEP TWO: CHOOSE

Next, choose by considering what would be the best choice. The best choice is the one that moves you closer to your goal(s). If you're striving to live a healthier, more connected life—the easy answers don't lead to the life you want. Quick eating usually means unhealthy eating. Do you find yourself eating quickly (and less healthy) frequently? *Every choice you make impacts another area of your life in a ripple effect.* Have your choices today taken you closer to or farther from your goals?

STEP THREE: ACT

Great intentions and good choices don't have meaning until they are put into action. Once you make a choice, act on it. The step that comes after *thinking* through a choice is *choosing*. Once the *choice* is made, *action* needs to happen. If the *action* gives you the results you want—you *win*. Sometimes your action doesn't result in the outcome you want, which suggests you've hit the proverbial wall.

Laurie scheduled her workouts for the next week and committed to her program on Monday, Wednesday, and Friday. She was going to walk for half an hour after work to unwind and exercise before jumping into the evening routine. On Monday, her daughter came home sick in the afternoon from school and wanted some extra attention. Laurie stayed home and skipped her workout. On Wednesday, a client requested a package be shipped overnight. By the time Laurie arranged for the products to go out, her window for walking was gone and she had to hurry home to get her son to soccer practice. By Friday, she was so discouraged and tired, she decided a glass of wine with her neighbor sounded more appealing than a walk. Strike three. Laurie hit the wall. In the past, she would have considered herself an exercise failure. However, through our conversations, she learned to reframe the skipped exercise sessions. After reflecting on what happened, she acknowledged exercising after work was not going to work for her. So, she and I figured out another plan that succeeded.

If a new strategy or plan does not work, strive to let go of anger, guilt, or frustration. Look to learn from what didn't work. Try a new plan, a new approach that could succeed.

When your good intentions are followed by positive actions (or choices), you continue to move forward closing the gap between what you want and what you are experiencing. Sometimes your strategy works. Sometimes, it does not. When it doesn't, I call it hitting the wall.

When You Hit a Wall

Hitting a wall looks and feels like failure. In practical terms, here is an example of how it may play out for you. After reflection and assessment (Step One, Thinking), you determine that this is the time to begin exercising (Step Two, Choosing). You decide to schedule exercise into your life after work two days a week and one time over the weekend. After two weeks, you have only exercised once during the week. You have hit a wall.

Go back to Step One (Think) about what worked and what didn't work. Maybe you determine trying to go after work is too difficult—traffic, late client calls, kids waiting at home, etc.—are too strong a deterrent for you to be consistent. Okay, re-think the situation. What else could you do? How about working out in the mornings? If you *choose* that, you do what you need to do to make time and get your exercise in before work. At this point, you act (Step Three) and find the new plan works. Success!

STEP FOUR: WIN

The *win* occurs when you make *intentional choices*, act on them, and successfully follow through.

Applying the TCAW Model of Decision-making to Your Life

> *"I recommend you to take care of the minutes, for the hours will take care of themselves."*
>
> Lord Philip D. Stanhope

The first step, think, is the most important and usually requires the most time and thought. The second step, choose, implies intention. Most people have great intentions. The third step, action, is the most challenging. This is the step of execution. The hope is that your action will result in the outcome you want, the win. However, hitting the wall isn't all bad either. Hitting the wall causes you to rethink and re-create your plan for success. You can make the changes you want. It may take more time than you'd like. That is why commitment to the process of change is so important. A good TCAW goal is one that is worthy of your time, energy, and effort. Only you can decide what is worth it. The TCAW model for decision-making and action suggests that the more thought and planning you put into the process, the more likely you are to succeed at achieving your goals and intentionally changing your life.

STEP ONE: THINK—THINKING EXAMINED

To think means you consider your options, assess the choices you've made in the past, and determine which provided positive outcomes and which did not. Think of the old journalism formula of five Ws & one H (who, what, where, when, why, and how). Reflecting upon who you really want to be is an important step in the journey to living the life you want.

Some of the questions you would use could be:

1. *What* is my goal?
2. *What* do I want to change?
3. *Why* do I want to change this?
4. *How* will I know I've been successful at accomplishing my goal?
5. *How* will I reward myself?
6. *Who* can support me in the changes I want to make?
7. *Who* can be a resource (information/facts)?
8. *Where* will I find support (people)?
9. *When* will I commit to this change?
10. *What* am I willing to give up?

11. *What* roles do I play in life that I need to consider?

I have found there is not only one set of questions that have impact on someone's goal setting, mission setting, and motivation for changing lifestyle habits and thinking patterns. Some people value evaluating the many roles they play in their life—evaluating what each role requires of them and whether their expectations are appropriate. For instance, an e-mail I received from a client said, "I am realizing that all my expectations of myself in the past with the multiple jobs, house chores, and baby duties were impossible." That realization was something to celebrate—because with that insight, my client was able to set more-realistic, less-stressful expectations. Not an easy task, yet, an important one. Setting realistic expectations for oneself is harder for people than they realize.

Here's an example of one of my clients reviewing the roles in her life along with what she determined she wanted to have, to do, and to be.

Example #1

Margaret is a respected certified financial planner. Some of her responses to the Vision/Mission/Goals exercises may spark your creativity or expand your thinking as you answer the questions in the appendix.

Life Roles: Margaret's challenge was to honestly evaluate her current roles and responsibilities in each area of her life. She needed to determine the roles that she would choose to maintain and those she could potentially eliminate or change focus on.

HER ROLES AS SHE REVIEWED HER CHOICES WERE:

- ❏ Wife
- ❏ Mom
- ❏ Mentor/coach
- ❏ Writer/trend spotter
- ❏ Observer/learner/wisdom seeker
- ❏ Musician/artist/creator
- ❏ Household financial planner (and portfolio manager)
- ❏ Team leader
- ❏ Dog trainer
- ❏ Customer care coordinator
- ❏ Volunteer

To determine how to best choose the roles she would continue and those she would let go of, Margaret considered what she wanted from her life. This is the list she wrote.

EVERYTHING I WANT TO *HAVE*:

- ❏ Meaningful and ever-growing relationship with God
- ❏ Conviction that I am following the course God has laid for me
- ❏ Meaningful and ever-growing relationship with my husband
- ❏ Happy, healthy, well-adjusted kids
- ❏ Close, nurtured, and nurturing friendships
- ❏ A bottomless well of spiritual and emotional energy
- ❏ A slice of time in every day just for me

- [ ] A slice of time in every day to revel in key relationships
- [ ] Funny, helpful self-talk
- [ ] Strong, healthy, lithe, well-rested, and well-tended body, mind, and spirit

Margaret also considered what she wanted to do and how she wanted to be. In other words, how she wanted others to experience her energy, attitudes, and character.

EVERYTHING I WANT TO DO:

- [ ] Try my best to live in Christ's footsteps—intentionally
- [ ] Teach, mentor, create, live, love, learn, leave a legacy
- [ ] Practice extreme self-care

EVERYTHING I WANT TO BE:

- [ ] Well-rested
- [ ] Fed for wellness
- [ ] Patient, loving, peaceful, centered
- [ ] Spiritually fed
- [ ] Financially prudent
- [ ] Intuitive
- [ ] A visionary
- [ ] A leader
- [ ] Organized
- [ ] Loyal, devoted
- [ ] Honest, fair
- [ ] Open-minded
- [ ] A deeply empathetic listener
- [ ] Emotionally intelligent

You may or may not relate to Margaret's list. Create your own list. What you write will help you decide upon your next steps.

Another way to think through what you want, or who you want to become, is to answer the statements, "I will be…," "I will have…," "I intend to…"

Example #2

Peg, a very successful saleswoman, wrote her list for the exercise, "I will be and I will have and I intend to if I am successful at being intentional in my life." This is what she wrote:

I WILL BE:

- More patient
- Intentional
- Self-nurturing allowing myself time for refueling/refreshing on a regular basis
- Developing other interests
- Pursuing new relationships
- Increasing my mental and physical health through regular exercise/yoga
- Having fun
- Seeking my joy!

I WILL HAVE:

- Closer friendships
- Clearer vision of my purpose
- A stronger spiritual connection to God
- Positive movement in my career
- Better self control (not giving my power away)

- ❏ Set boundaries
- ❏ My spending in check
- ❏ More responsibility at work

I INTEND TO:

- ❏ Make every day a great/good day
- ❏ Be happy
- ❏ Say good morning/hi/hello
- ❏ Take in good critical advice and learn
- ❏ Try to see the best in everyone
- ❏ Reward myself for a job well done
- ❏ Learn to self-coach
- ❏ Give myself kudos instead of relying on receiving them from others
- ❏ Worry less about others
- ❏ Read more
- ❏ Be attentive to my self-talk, altering it when needed
- ❏ Be the feisty me again
- ❏ Live intentionally
- ❏ Be a good mother
- ❏ Take care of myself—physically, emotionally, mentally
- ❏ Continue to learn/study and be a student of life
- ❏ Strengthen my relationship with my girlfriends, my daughter, family, co-workers
- ❏ Live, making intentional, proactive choices each day
- ❏ Thrive and not strive

- ❑ Be content with my life
- ❑ Learn Spanish
- ❑ Be exceptional
- ❑ Control my reactions
- ❑ Do the most productive thing at the time
- ❑ Experience my emotions
- ❑ Go with the flow—especially after I've done the best I can
- ❑ Be exceptional in sales or whatever my work is
- ❑ Make as many contacts/calls as possible every day
- ❑ Be me (which is requiring a little—okay, a lot—of work)

You can see by the lists shared above, you can be creative and have fun thinking through what you want to see come true for you in your life. Dream big. Imagine what you would really like to experience or bring to life.

Before you make a choice about a behavior you want to engage in, pay attention to these additional cues that help you make good decisions.

- **Gut reactions**. Trust your instincts about your situation, people, or circumstances.

- **Physical reactions**. Feel what your body is trying to tell you. Don't mask your physical manifestations of emotional responses to things or people by taking medications, overeating, spending, or drinking to make your physical or emotional responses go away.

- **Automatic or habitual responses you do not want to make.** Tune in to when you choose what's outside the box of *appropriate* options. For instance, if you've determined to drink alcohol only on weekends and find yourself having wine two or three nights a week, think deeply about what is going on for you and what better choice you can make.

After you have reflected and thought what you intend to change, the next step takes place. You need to make a choice.

STEP TWO: CHOOSE—CHOOSING EXAMINED

This is where powerful conversations begin. Change that *lasts* begins with positive self-talk or the intentional, purposeful filling of your mind with positive, inspiring, and transformational input. When your thinking changes, your beliefs (about both yourself and your circumstances) change. Beliefs influence your actions. When your beliefs align with what you desire, your actions (behaviors) begin to serve to fulfill your goals.

"If you don't take charge in your head, you'll never be able to take charge in your life." Kate Larsen

Follow-through makes the difference. You may decide during your reflection that going to bed earlier would be wise for you to do. So, you choose to go to sleep earlier. When you choose to change, you begin to take better care of yourself.

SELF-ABSORPTION OR SELF-CARE: YOUR CHOICE

You probably have had great intentions of taking better care of yourself. Good intentions don't necessarily result in great outcomes. Positive intentions are a good place to start. However, execution is our focus.

If you've been getting ready to get ready for too long, it's time to get honest with yourself. It's easier to be a martyr than mature. To be mature is to take responsibility for your choices. The outcomes of your choices are often out of your control. That's okay. Your responsibility is for the intention, motive, and effort. You need to give yourself 100 percent permission to take care of yourself from this day forward. Great self-care is NOT selfish. It's more selfish to continue being tired, cranky, less creative, resourceful, impatient, hurried, and harried. Your family, clients, and peers don't deserve the leftovers of who you are. Self-care that allows you to renew, recharge, and rejuvenate is not about self-absorption. It's about honoring the body, spirit, and mind God gave you.

STRATEGIES FOR SUCCESSFULLY MAKING CHANGE

The following strategies can help you make healthy choices:

- **Enlist a partner.** The journey will be more enjoyable and more fun with individuals or groups who understand, encourage, and support you in your efforts to make consistently wise choices. An accountability partner or support group will help you make changes more quickly and confidently. Your partner can be a professional (personal trainer, dietitian, physical therapist, chiropractor, support group, or coach) or simply a like-minded individual on the same path as you are.

- **Adjust your intensity level and remember to have fun in this process.** This one is for me too; I tend to be too intense.

- **Moderation is the healthiest springboard to a wonderful life.** Few things in life are black and white. There are many wonderful, pleasurable things in life that can be enjoyed in moderation—rich desserts, for instance. Being intentional about the quantity, quality, and frequency of any choice we make is important.

This chapter opened with the recap of my conversation with Mary Beth, a frazzled, fried, and fatigued professional woman. Mary Beth worked through the TCAW process coaching with me and with herself. She determined to live more intentionally throughout the year, making hundreds of small choices that she knew would make a big difference over time. And what a big difference they made. Read what Mary Beth shared in her annual review below and be encouraged to focus on your small choices that can make a big difference in your life.

What were the best and most important attitudes or behaviors you were intentional about this year?

> *"A happier person is not a person in a certain set of circumstances, but rather with a certain set of attitudes." Hugh Downs*

- Listening to my heart and making decisions based on my dominant areas of my life. Most importantly, the process I engaged in that led me to the decision to leave my position. For me, that was a great leap of faith and the most important decision I made this year.

- Giving myself permission to step out and take time to just be.

- Trusting my faith and praying for guidance and support during the year. My faith has grown stronger over the year, and I have a sense of knowing everything will be okay.

- Being intentional about checking my motivations for doing something and acting accordingly. I ask myself more questions.

- Building my relationship with my kids and being more involved and aware of what's going on with them. Being more involved with school and volunteering to help.

- Being part of the family and spending more time with the family–eating dinner together regularly, playing together, going to church together regularly.

- Being supportive and a resource for the people I worked with.

- I took more risks in this year—taking on my new role in HR and then ultimately leaving the company.

- Learning something new—I'm taking piano lessons and loving it.

- Taking care of myself—I am exercising regularly—five days a week, sleeping eight hours per night, and eating better.

- Getting a handle on my finances, putting together a budget, and living within the budget (still working on).

- Journaling—sporadically at first and now weekly

What would you love to say is different about you a year from now? Start making that happen now.

STEP THREE: ACT—ACTION EXAMINED

After you have reflected on your best choice in the moment, you step into action and do something or say something that supports your goal. The action step depends upon the outcome of those choices. When you make a choice and act upon it, you either experience success or you hit the proverbial wall. When you hit the wall, you want to give up or sink to the floor. Don't do it! You have discovered what doesn't work. Find a window in the wall by taking a new approach, try a different way. Be willing to experiment with various ways to make a behavior change successful. That's a win for you.

STEP FOUR: WIN—WINNING EXAMINED

There is actually not much to examine in this step. When you successfully make a behavior change, the thing to do is celebrate.

- Action is a part of the change process; however, action is *not* the first step to change. Without starting at the beginning of the process, you set yourself up to fail.
- For decades, our culture has focused on *looking* better instead of *living* better.
- Change is not a group activity. It's an individual task. You must create your own capacity for constant change.

- Every choice you make impacts another area of your life in a ripple effect.
- When your thinking changes, your beliefs change. Beliefs influence your actions. When your beliefs align with what you desire, your actions begin to serve to fulfill your goals.
- It's easier to be a martyr than mature.
- Your family, clients, and peers don't deserve the leftovers of who you are.
- Great self-care is NOT selfish. It's more selfish to continue being tired, cranky, less creative, resourceful, impatient, hurried, and harried.
- When you think better, you choose better. When you choose better, you get better results.

WORKINS

In your journal, write your comments, insights, and observations.

1. Have the choices I made today brought me closer to or farther from my goals?

2. What would I love to say is different about me a year from now?

3. Where do I pursue perfection versus excellence in my life? (Your answer may become more evident or clearer when you consider the question, "In what part of my life am I rarely, if ever, satisfied?")

4. Complete the exercise called, Real Versus Ideal, in appendix E. This exercise can help you focus on behaviors and attitudes you would like to change.

5. What would I have to do, to have, or be, to be content with that part of my life?

6. What does being healthier mean to me?

7. What would my health/energy be like in terms of my physical and/or emotional state of being?

8. What would I do with more energy?

9. What's gotten in my way of pursuing and achieving better health up till now?

10. Complete the exercise, What I Really Need in My Life Right Now is More…, in appendix F. Incorporate what you learn from this exercise into your vision, goals, and strategies.

WORKOUTS

1. It's time to add some great sayings to your mental arsenal of self-talk. The following attitudes and the perspectives implied will serve you well as you choose to live with energy, impact, and joy—the antidotes to frustration, fatigue, and frazzle. Try using the statements below as mantras you say to yourself. If you consistently incorporate them into your repertoire of self-talk, you will find your attitude and energy improving quickly. Select your favorite five statements and create sticky notes for yourself

that you can stick on mirrors, walls, and books that will frequently remind you to incorporate them. Say them out loud as often as you're willing to do so.

- No perfection allowed; excellence is my goal.
- I am a role model to those I live with and work with.

On some days, remembering your commitment to being a great role model may be the one thought that helps you make your best decision in the moment.

- I must be willing to give wholehearted permission to myself to succeed.

Giving myself permission to be honest about my desires, needs, and required behaviors is at the heart of my ability to grow and change.

- I will think of life as a journey. Progress is the goal.

If I only celebrate or enjoy my efforts when a goal is accomplished, I won't enjoy my day-to-day living. *Life is* about the journey; the goals just give me direction.

- I choose to change.
- I get to change or improve.
- I can do it; one step, one bite, one moment, one laugh, one nap, one conversation at a time.
- I choose to live in the moment/present.
- Schedule time with a friend, peer, or trusted confidante and share your vision, goals, and success strategies with them.
- Tell them what you need from them to be successful.

A Three

Keys to Living an Intentional, Joy-filled Life

How many people do you know who live joy-filled, passionate lives? I'll bet your list isn't very long. Isn't that a shame? We have been blessed with so much that it is truly amazing we struggle to be content on a daily basis. Myself included. Unless I stay aware of my self-talk and attitudes, I quickly submerge myself in the uncomfortable mode of comparing myself and my achievements with others. Yes, after more than twenty-five years of paying attention to my being intentional, I still need to stay on guard. With so many competing messages about success and passionate living, it's easy to forget that life is lived one small choice at a time. With each choice comes either, as Stephen Covey calls it in his book, *The Seven Habits of Highly Effective People*, a deposit or withdrawal from the bank of personal fulfillment.[1] You may find it surprising that it is the simple, often mundane, choices of life that leave us feeling either drained or renewed at the end of the day.

"Time is the coin of your life. It is the only coin you have, and only you can determine how it will be spent. Be careful lest you let other people spend it for you."
Carl Sandburg

The problem starts when we unknowingly accept others' definitions of success over our own (often unclear) definitions of success.

What is your definition of success? How will you know you're successful? Having a clear understanding of what success looks like and feels like, personally and professionally, will help you recognize when you're on track to achieve what you want.

The topic of success is complex and charged with emotion. Consider the following three principles of success, which are important to consider as you decide what success is and how you will pursue it.

Principle One: Success means different things to different people, yet most people don't take the time to define it specifically for themselves.

A lack of clarity in defining success and its pursuit is the driving force behind the burnout, disease, and dysfunction in our culture.

Principle Two: Success implies striving to meet some set of standards established, by some person or group. Standards are generally established, so goals, outcomes, and results have a benchmark for comparison.

If you haven't determined the standards that will work for you, others establish your standards for you by default.

Principle Three: Obtaining success always exacts a cost—it takes our time, energy, ability, and resources.

Actually, pursuing any goal costs something in time, energy, or money. The hope is that the cost is worth the gain to you and your family.

These three principles play out first in our minds through our beliefs, assumptions, and perceptions, and are heard through our self-talk (the things we say to ourselves that no one else can hear). Your inner voice will consciously, or unconsciously, guide your decisions and choices throughout the day. If you don't take charge in your head, you'll never be able to take charge in your life.

I believe we say things to ourselves in our busyness that actually sabotage our best intentions. Three of the most common are:

- I can get to where I want to go without a road map.
- What I'm doing isn't really hurting me. I could be worse.
- My family and friends know how important they are to me.

These self-sabotaging thoughts or self-talk statements are causing people to overeat, drink, spend, and neglect their health, family, friends, and finances. Read and reflect upon whether you are an unaware victim of these self-sabotaging thoughts or beliefs.

1. "I can get to where I want in life without a road map."

Whenever I drive somewhere for the first time, I take the time to get directions and preferably a map. Even when I think I know where I'm going, I often insist on having a map. I've discovered a generalized feeling of knowing where I'm going isn't good enough. My internal directional compass has malfunctioned since birth. After many years and miles of random, confused driving and misspent fuel, I now have a plan when going somewhere new. I walk into my office, sit down at my desk, and pull up www.MapQuest.com to print out directions. This web site is a simple, yet powerful tool in my toolbox for sane living. Wouldn't it be great if you could pull up your life map at www. MapQuest.com?

"Don't spend ten dollars' worth of energy on a ten-cent problem... There are millions of want-to's and have-to's in life. Ultimately, these pressures create stress only when your time and energy-spending decisions aren't consistent with your goals, beliefs, and values."

Dr. Donald A. Tubesing

Whether you're finding a physical location or striving to reach a new place in life, using a road map that is based upon *your* starting point and leads directly to *your* destination is a smarter, more efficient, and practical way to go. Yet, the tendency is to look to someone else who's arrived and follow their path to success. Think of professional people you admire and would like to emulate. Consider what would happen if you followed their paths (road maps) to success. What differences do you recognize between their lives and yours that would make their plans a good one for them but not for you?

What works for them—works for them. It is unlikely their exact approach to life and decisions will work well for you. It doesn't matter how earnest you are about achieving your goals. If your choices do not fit with your season of life, energy, and resources, you will not succeed.

It's easy to see why you could get lost, frustrated, or detoured when you least expect it by following someone else's life road map. Creating your own road map is the more efficient and effective way to design a plan that will lead to your life success. Your life journey matters, which is why it is so important to follow a map that incorporates all aspects of *your* personality, experiences, values, and needs.

2. "What I'm doing isn't really hurting me. I could be worse."

Do you say:

"I'd love to have more energy, but overall, I'm okay."

"Yeah, I should have something more nutritious than a pot of coffee for breakfast."

"I know I should park farther away and walk, but I'm in a hurry."

"Sleep is a luxury I can't afford. That's what retirement is for—catching up on all the sleep I missed out on when I worked."

"I'll see a doctor when I need one; check-ups are a chunk of time I can't afford right now."

"I know I need to quit smoking, but I always gain weight, so…"

Whew! How many things are you putting off right now because you're telling yourself, "It really isn't hurting me"? Deep down, you know better. With the accumulation of time and unhealthy choices, yes, you *are* hurting yourself. The good news is that there are many little changes you can make that will make a big difference in your health and in your life.

When you tell yourself, "I'm not that bad off. I could feel worse. I'm not hurting myself and besides, there just isn't enough time to do anything about it," at least acknowledge that you're also saying, "I am choosing mediocrity. I am choosing to risk my health over the long term, and I am reducing the quality of my life today. I am forgoing family time for something less important but more demanding." Giving yourself permission to take care of yourself is not an indulgence; it's a necessity. We unknowingly sabotage our health, success, and happiness by giving ourselves unrealistic, deceptive messages.

At times, you may serve a higher purpose by ignoring your personal needs in order to care for others. However, when putting off self-care becomes a *habit*, you drain or diminish the very energy you need to serve others.

3. "My family and friends know how important they are to me."

Another significant self-talk message that sabotages the health of your relationships sounds something like this, "My family, friends, and peers *know* how important they are to me." This thought assumes something that may or may not be true. This presumption can make or break the success of your relationships.

This message can do the most damage to your significant relationships because the translation your family and closest friends hear is, "I am so busy and overwhelmed, I don't have the time or energy to slow down and be truly present with you. But I know you understand and you'll be there when I have time to slow down." Well, they just may not understand. Without your investment today, they may not be there when you need/want them.

Think of three priceless, special people in your life. First, think of each one individually. When is the last time you gave each one your undivided attention? When is the last time you cut them short because of your busy schedule? Now think of them as a group. Do they know their value to you? How do they know? Actions speak louder than words. What do your actions say about your commitment to these important relationships?

Just by your presence you have the ability to transform lives all around you. However, being fully present is one of the greatest challenges we have today. For instance, take Bill who is the president of a national firm. During a recent coaching session Bill said, "Three years ago, I took my son to Canada on a fishing trip. I don't think I was actually there for one moment of it." He recalled that ongoing business challenges and problems kept him preoccupied throughout the trip. With new insight, he now calls this son once a week to stay connected. Conversations last from five to thirty minutes. They are both enjoying a different relationship because he changed his habit of not being present for the relationship.

By the way, physical proximity is not the answer. You may spend a great deal of time with those you love, yet not be present. "Being" is tough for the "doer." If you're a doer, you don't feel productive unless you're checking things off a list. Yet, our closest relationships grow most in those quiet, unproductive moments of being together.

"To hear, one must be silent."
Ursula K. LeGuin

Here's a challenge that will give you great insight into your "being" ability. During this next week, while you are talking to or listening to one of your priceless people, do nothing else at the same time. Stop doing dishes, reading the paper, scanning e-mail, etc. Notice how you feel. Notice how they respond to you both during your time together and afterward. If you like what happens, find more opportunities to be present with your priceless people.

If you have a financial planner, you may be familiar with what a portfolio review is. This is a report that enables you and your planner to remain updated with one another and track your progress with the financial goals you've set for the future. Family and friends don't provide a Life Portfolio Review—but what if they did? What if you were reviewed quarterly for your focus and energy given to your loved ones? What is the quality of your investment in your relationships? On a scale of one to five, rate your relationship proficiency.

Rating: One indicates a complete disconnect from an individual. A five indicates a close, connected, and rewarding relationship.

1	2	3	4	5
disconnected		growing		rich, rewarding

How can you know how your relationships feel to others? For example, the quality of your relationship can be reflected on your child's face that lights up when you walk in the door. You can tell when you have a deep, hardy laugh with a close friend. You can tell when you experience regular, comfortable intimate moments with those you're closest to. As University of

Colorado former football coach Bill McCarthy says, "You can tell the character of a man by the countenance on his wife's face." Does your face reflect joy or exhaustion? Satisfaction or unhappiness?

Recently I asked a client to describe his last fifteen-minute conversation with either of his daughters. He paused, searching his memory and finally said, "I don't think I have *ever* had a fifteen-minute conversation with them." His daughters are eighteen and twenty-one years old. He knows he loves them, but he needed help communicating that love.

Strengthening Your Relationships: Where to Begin

Begin to build closeness with simple questions. For example, do you know who your child's or grandchild's favorite teacher is? Why does this person have a special place in his heart? What's her best friend's name? What does he want to be when he's an adult? What has she learned about relationships that she thinks is important? What does he want to know about you when you were a kid? Use the same questioning style and technique you use for learning more about your current or potential clients with your family and friends. Listen with the same intensity and interest.

Another small choice that can make a big difference in your relationships is to arrange two-hour and one-hour dates. If you can manage a two-hour date twice a month with your spouse and a one-hour lunch or dinner with a close friend, also once a month, you will find that both relationships are amazingly recharged.

Busyness is the germ that destroys the health of your relationships. While each of your relationships requires varying levels of time or energy, each also requires your *undivided attention*. Five minutes of attention today could save you heartaches tomorrow. Those five- and ten-minute segments add up to strong, bonded relationship in one, five, or ten years.

Your relationships are what make you rich. Strong relationships require something more difficult to come by than money—time. Improving your communication skills and your connectedness to those around you will do more to further the health of your family and business than any other step you can take this year.

Ten Misunderstandings That Keep People from Living Intentional, Joy-filled Lives

In addition to negative self-talk and self-sabotaging statements, what else keeps you from being happy? Here are ten concepts that may get in your way or hold you back.

1. **Guilt is a consistent and strong motivator**. Guilt is a key inhibitor. "I feel guilty when..." You fill in the blank. When talking about failed attempts at lifestyle changes, this phrase is probably the most commonly used one. The message that feeling guilty is an appropriate, if not acceptable, reason for not following through on great self-care is wreaking havoc on our bodies, minds, and souls. Because you feel guilty does *not* indicate you care more about something or someone. It's likely the word guilt is not the true meaning of what you're feeling. Let's check this out. Write out on a piece of paper what guilt

means to you. Now, look at its definition and synonyms in a reference book and see if you really mean what you say.

The *Oxford Dictionary* defines guilt as: 1. the fact of having committed a specified or implied offense. 2.a. culpability, b. the feeling of this. Synonyms are criminality, blameworthiness, reprehensibility, censurability.

Now, ask yourself, is *guilty* the right word for what you're feeling? If not, what would be a better word?

How about the word responsible? I feel responsible for not getting there on time. Is that an appropriate question if you arrive thirty minutes late? Sure. What could you have done differently? Not shoved in one more errand that threw you off schedule or answered those three more e-mails? The next time the better choice (if not being late is a value for you) would be to leave more time between commitments, stop checking e-mail, don't take the call that voicemail could pick up, etc. Those are choices you can control. On the other hand, if a traffic accident occurs, you can't control that, so you needn't feel guilty. How would feeling guilty serve you? It wouldn't, so don't. (Letting go of guilt is easier said than done because feeling guilty is also a habit formed in life that you need to be replacing with a healthier, more appropriate emotional response.)

2. **Most people aren't trying hard enough.** Many people are doing the best they can with the level

of self-awareness they currently have. I believe people want to do their best, but false beliefs, lack of energy, lack of clarity and/or support hold them back. What isn't lacking is other people's requests for time and energy from you. A lack of self-care causes people to tolerate the things that drain their energy and vitality and diminish their self worth. What do you tolerate that drains you? After you create your list, decide which things on the list you're willing to eliminate. When will you take your first step toward resolution in these areas? Be specific about assigning a date and time to taking your first step.

3. **True success is immediate**. Immediate gratification is a problem. Discipline and sacrifice carry a lot of baggage in our culture. Recommitment to intentional living needs to take place *every* day, sometimes hour to hour. Our "delayed gratification muscle" is atrophied; for some it's torn. Surgery to repair it is necessary. How disciplined are you? Turn up your awareness on your own need for immediate gratification.

When you choose intentionally, using wisdom and insight as your guides, you minimize the chances of developing one of the most difficult feelings to live with—regret. Often, the only way I can make a final decision on something (because both or all choices are good) is to choose the action or words that leave the smallest window of regret possible. You have to decide for yourself what the best answer is for you and/or your family.

4. **Wealth provides financial health and well-being—contentment and peace of mind.** If wealth brought financial health and well-being, Americans and most Europeans would certainly enjoy an unprecedented level of contentment and peace of mind. Perhaps you recognize this is not the case. Despite the fact we are wealthier as a nation than at any other point in history, we still have a great deal of anxiety and stress that burdens our hearts and minds. Things have inadvertently become more important than health and relationships. Rarely would one admit to that. However, look at the rising rates of depression among teens and adults alike. Anti-depressants have become the second most common prescribed drug. Divorce rates run too high, with finances driving much of the discord in marriages.

   While you cannot control aspects of the economy, worldviews, and circumstances, you can control your attitudes and perspectives as they relate to finances and wealth. The place to start is by looking at your wants versus needs as discussed in chapter two in the section on goal setting.

5. **Contentment is a passé goal.** Contentment is a misunderstood concept. For many, it infers a settling for less. It suggests that achieving a certain, comparatively good, status quo is acceptable. When asked the question, "Would you like to feel contented on a more regular basis?" most people say, "Yes, I'd love that." However, with discussion, many realize they

associate the concept of contentment with stagnancy, mediocrity, or settling for less because contentment implies they're satisfied. Done. Complete. I suggest that being content is a wonderful state of being to pursue. Being content says you are grateful for what you have, you are calm and grounded in the now. You may want for more in different areas of your life; however, you recognize that when the time is right (and if it is right), you will have more, do more, and share more. To be content is to be at peace with life as it is now, yet always reaching to become stronger and healthier in body, mind, and spirit.

6. **If I slow down, I'll fall down—and never regain that fire-in-the-belly passion I need to succeed.** Slowing down scares some people because they fear if they slow down, they'll fall down and never get up. Their self-talk says, "If I don't drive hard, it will look as if I don't care or I'm not committed to the team." Or, "If I don't stay on top of this, I'll never catch up, and I'll just drown." For some women, they are afraid if they slow down and listen to what their bodies and lives are telling them, they won't like the answer. They don't have the energy or capacity to deal with what may become evident anyway.

Where can you slow down? When you review your typical day, you'll probably find many possibilities you've overlooked before. You may even determine, despite it being difficult to do, that slowing down your personal pace and reducing your commitments are the wisest things you could do. You may need to start with simply slowing down for a five-minute window of time before rocketing into your day. Later, you may decide ten minutes would be helpful. Slowing down for short periods of time can make such a dramatic difference in your mood, perspective, and daily choices that you won't want to miss that time anymore.

During my cancer treatments, I moved at a dramatically slower pace. This pace was partially because the chemo resulted in a great deal of fatigue and my body wouldn't move at my usual quick pace. It was also because I knew there was no need to rush. Whatever got done—got done. What didn't get done would be there tomorrow. I found peace in that. Cancer treatment is over; however, there is a piece of slowing down that I want to maintain in an ongoing way.

"The most precious thing under the sun today is a minute, and he who can do the most with it can demand the most."
Herbert Kaufman

7. **Soul-searching and reflection is completed during the four-year college process as you determine your direction for your life**. People don't really know themselves. Most of us grow into adulthood without ever taking the time to figure out who we are, what makes us tick, and what excites us or drains us. In other words, we often don't know ourselves well. It is important to identify personal interests, strengths, passion, and calling. The exciting world of work or a young family yanks us out of the self-learning stage before we're ready to make choices based

upon knowing ourselves deeply. Life circumstances also change us. Many women today haven't taken the time to incorporate life's experiences and new insights into their understanding of themselves. When's the last time you allowed yourself time for introspection? Does the thought of introspection excite you or make you uncomfortable? If it makes you uncomfortable, acknowledge that feeling and do it anyway. Make an appointment with yourself—and keep it. Spend time getting to know and enjoy yourself.

One of my clients discovered that she was so afraid to be alone, she sabotaged her best intentions by rolling from one mediocre relationship into another. This hasn't been a counseling issue; instead, it's been an eye-opening aha! insight into her patterns of behavior. She said, "I know the right or healthy thing to do, but my behavior sure doesn't show it." I guarantee that since Kirsten achieved this insight about herself, she won't ever be able to settle for a mediocre relationship without a small voice calling her attention to it. She may or may not act upon the voice, but she'll be aware of the impact of her choices. Ultimately, the choice is still up to her.

8. **In the workplace, results are more important than the people who get the results**. People connections are relegated to the end of the list of to-dos. The thing that attracts us to the to-do lists is the sense of accomplishment, completion, and results we experience when something gets checked off. This is one of those statements

that you probably get a visceral response to which says, "Of course that's not true." Yet, look at the world of work. What is it that gets rewarded? I would wager nine out of ten times rewards will be tied to revenues, not employee loyalty, passion, health, vitality, retention, etc.

In the early nineties, it was becoming more and more apparent that the health of employees was directly impacting productivity and profits in organizations. Yet, the majority of businesses would not consider sponsoring programs and investing funds into employee health. I recognized this would not happen until the costs associated with health care directly impacted the bottom line profits. In the early 2000s, the problem became glaringly obvious and corporate America began to invest in solutions geared toward prevention. Today, many organizations are striving to address the health needs of their employees. Happier, healthier employees provide the results organizations are looking for.

Results are generally achieved better with connected and contented individuals.

Connecting with people in the workplace provides challenges all of its own.

You can spend time with someone and not genuinely connect. Quality connection with someone happens in the quieter, slower moments and doesn't fall into the to-do checklist the way a doctor's appointment can. Does your need to check to-dos off your list get in the way of spending focused time with your spouse, kids, friends, or peers? Who needs some of your undivided attention? Will you make time for that person today (even if it means not getting something else done)?

9. **Knowing why you exist and what your purpose is, is critical for having energy and direction in life.** Most people have a vague sense of what they want. Part of getting to know yourself and understanding where your interests, passions, and fears exist helps you to get clear about what you want in life. Clarity about what's important to you at the deepest level allows you to make decisions that impact your mission in life. How clear are you about your life's purpose? If you chase a dream that is someone else's and not your own, you will be drained, frustrated, and discouraged. Discover your calling and you will feel compelled to be all that you can be. If you lack energy or enthusiasm for life (and you're not physically ill), think about how you have spent your time, energy, and money in the last year. Have your choices been tied to an intentional outcome or to merely getting by? What do you need to do about what you have just discovered, realized, or gotten clearer about? When will you do something about it?

Sheila was the vice president and general counsel (attorney) for an international firm, traveling outside the country regularly. She was also the divorced mother of a young daughter. She felt exhausted, disheartened, and stuck in her life. Over time, she developed migraines and a thyroid problem. She decided it was time to figure out what her true purpose was and what she needed to do to make that happen, even if it meant leaving her law career. Early on, we figured out her heart and passion for her work was gone, and she needed a dramatic change. She put together a plan and courageously resigned from her position allowing herself the summer months to figure out what she was going to do next with her life and career. She has since explored a number of career options that have excited her and reenergized her for life. Her energy, joy, and passion have returned. Had she not had the courage to evaluate what was working and what was no longer working in her life, she would still be stuck in her career and likely more ill and dissatisfied with life.

10.**Saying no to requests and challenging expectations is rude, selfish, and career sabotaging.** People don't know how to set appropriate boundaries. Recently, I had three coaching calls in a row with individuals who each described wanting other people's approval so much that they ignored their own need to set and keep their boundaries both at work and home. This challenge is a common one.

You need insight, skill, and practice to set boundaries with yourself and other people. When you feel helpless and/or frustrated with other people, you've likely allowed others to disregard your

"Boundary-setting skills are non-negotiable to creating the life you desire and are committing to change."
Kate Larsen

77

boundaries. You've trained them to do so by not establishing consequences for ignoring your boundaries. It's obvious that children need boundaries set with appropriate consequences for lack of follow-through or a disregard for the boundaries. Adults need the same thing. One of my favorite quotes that ties to this concept perfectly is, "Lack of planning on your part does not constitute an emergency on mine." Boundary-setting skills are non-negotiable to creating the life you desire and are committing to change. Do you set boundaries for yourself and others? What consequences for ignoring those boundaries have you established (and followed up with) during this past week? What boundaries do you need to set for yourself? How about for others? What consequences could you use to reinforce your expectations that your boundaries be honored?

On Your Own Path to Life Success

Once you've built the foundation of your life, you'll find it needs ongoing maintenance. Living a joy-filled, passionate life takes effort. However, this effort and energy is well spent. The greatest amount of vigilance is required to effectively manage your self-talk and attitudes.

By now, I hope you have a clearer understanding and picture of what success is for you. Hold that vision before you each day, and you'll make better decisions if you do. Creating a road map that is customized to your interests, values, family, career, faith, and finances is the smartest way to go. Carve out time for relationships that are important to you. Make time for health.

Many false beliefs sabotage people's success at living fully and living healthy. Seriously considering the ten misconceptions in this chapter will prepare you, strengthen you, and direct you to taking charge of your health and life.

TRAINING TIPS

- It is the simple, often mundane, choices of life that leave you feeling either drained or renewed at the end of the day.

- If you don't take charge in your head, you'll never be able to take charge in your life.

- Strong relationships require something more difficult to come by than money—time.

- Because you feel guilty does not indicate you care more about something or someone.

- People want to do their best, but false beliefs, lack of energy, lack of clarity, and/or support hold them back.

- Slowing down scares some people because they fear if they slow down, they'll fall down and never get up.

- You need insight, skill, and practice to set boundaries with yourself and other people.

- Busyness is the germ that destroys the health of your relationships.

- Discipline and sacrifice carry a lot of baggage in our culture.
- Feeling guilty is a non-productive habit.

Use your journal to write the answers to these work-in questions:

1. It is important to consider the standards you use to define success for yourself. Define success in your own terms in fifty words or fewer.

2. Write down five statements that begin with, "I will know I am (or will be) a success when..."

3. Answer the following questions:

   What's the price I'm paying for my pursuit of success or achievement?

   Taking a balanced look at the cost, I need to consider the following areas as they impact my life success overall:

   - Physical—what is the toll my pursuit is having on my body/health?
   - Emotional—do I have a sense of contentment in most areas of my life?
   - Spiritual—do I believe I am living out my purpose?
   - Interpersonal—am I being the person I want to be?
   - Intellectual—am I learning, growing, enjoying life?
   - Fun—how important is humor, joy, and laughter to me? Am I so intense I've

forgotten how to have fun? (A rare reader of this book would be the one who needs to get more serious about life and cut back on the fun.)

4. Fill in the blank: "I feel guilty when…"

5. Define what guilt means to you. With this definition in mind, does that change your statements above?

6. What is a better word than guilt for you to use?

7. A lack of self-care causes you to tolerate things that drain your energy and vitality.

8. What do you tolerate that drains you?

9. What are you willing to change?

10. Where do you need to slow down in your life?

11. What time of day would you be willing to intentionally slow down? (How will you remind yourself to take this time?)

12. When was the last time you allowed for some relaxed, purposeful introspection?

13. Does the thought of introspection excite you or make you uncomfortable? If it makes you uncomfortable, acknowledge the feeling and do it anyway.

14. Boundary-setting skills are non-negotiable to creating the life you desire and are committing to change. Do you set healthy boundaries for yourself? What types of boundaries do you set? What consequences have you instituted for yourself?

15. Do you set healthy boundaries with others? What types of boundaries do you set? What consequences have you instituted when your boundaries are broken or ignored?

WORKOUTS

1. Tell someone you trust about the insights, observations, and commitments you are making due to being more self-aware of your needs. (This may be the same person you shared your vision and goals with from the exercise in chapter two.)

2. Ask two people who know you well what they observe about your pace and schedule for life. (Consider what you want them to say. Write down here what you *want* them to say.)

3. Write down what you think they *will* say. (The person you're hesitant or afraid to ask is probably the one you ought to ask.)

4. What did they *actually* say? (Yes, come back to this later. Highlight this page or mark it so you remember to do so.)

5. Your take-away?

6. Ask three people who know you well what health behavior they would value seeing you engage in. (The person you're hesitant or afraid to ask is probably the one you ought to ask.)

7. Does your need to check to-dos off your list get in the way of spending focused time with your spouse? Kids? Friends? Peers?

8. Set one boundary this week. Record the outcome of the conversation that occurs and write down the consequence for an individual or yourself if the boundary is ignored or stepped over.

Four

Mantras, Attitudes, and Perspectives—M.A.P.s That Will Change Your Life

A few years ago, while reading the *Wall Street Journal*, I was surprised to see a sketch of a friend on the front page. An interview surrounded the picture. I called her to say, "Hey, way to go!" She said, "Well, that's my fifteen minutes of fame." You've probably heard Andy Warhol's often-misquoted statement. "In the future everybody will be world famous for fifteen minutes." His phrase, first shared in 1968, has come to refer to people who do something of dubious distinction or are involved in a minor scandal and manage to capture our attention for a while. For you and me, it usually means we receive acknowledgment on a grander scale than usual for our efforts, professionally or personally.

The question is, "At what cost do we pursue the accolade, the fame, or recognition?" How much of our time, money, energy, peace of mind, or relationships do we invest to achieve prominence? Obviously, not all fame comes at an unreasonable cost. However, it's important to look at our efforts on an ongoing basis to determine whether we are still working, creating, or striving in a manner that allows for sustainable success over a lifetime. Keep in mind that you and I define for ourselves what success means.

In an interview discussing finding balance in *Fast Company* magazine, John Perry Barlow shared a question he often asked himself, "How thin can I spread myself before I'm no longer 'there'?"[1] We live in an era of abundance in every way: material goods, opportunities, and activities, etc. The challenge is to manage our freedom and to strike a balance in the face of endless opportunity.

The Importance of Being Positive
Mantras

A mantra is a commonly repeated word or phrase. It is also described as a verbal formula repeated in prayer and meditation. In other words, it's thoughts that play in our minds, that you can intentionally focus upon to change your state of being, your perspective, or attitude. Mantras form messages either heard in the head (self-talk) or voiced out loud—consider a mantra as a mind formula. For instance, small choices make a big difference is a powerful mantra. An affirmation that you could use that personalizes this mantra would be, "I will make small choices that make a big difference." Another mantra is, "up till now." An affirmation using this mantra could be, "Up till now it has been too hard for me to make time for relaxation."

Attitude

For our purposes, attitude refers to a state of mind or a feeling; a disposition. Attitude implies an *emotional* response tied to a state of mind. Insight and awareness can adjust attitude.

Perspective

Your perspective can mean different things. Similar, yet different from attitude, it can mean a *mental* view or outlook. It also can be described as the subjective evaluation of relative significance or point of view between people, circumstances or situations. Information often changes your perspective.

Ten M.A.P.s for Change

The following ten mantras, attitudes, and perspectives (M.A.P.s) have the ability to change your life if you embrace them and create the habit of using them to direct your choices each day.

1. Small Choices Make a Big Difference.
2. Life Is a Journey.
3. Learning Never Stops.
4. Make Choices That Won't Lead to Regret.
5. Time Warps Work.
6. Scale Your Choices.
7. Make Gratitude Your Attitude.
8. Motives are the Key.
9. Build Reserves.
10. Reflective Writing is an Amazing Tool.

"As the dimensions of the tree are not always regulated by the size of the seed, so the consequences of things are not always proportionate to the apparent magnitude of those events that have produced them."
Charles Caleb Colton

1. Small Choices Make a Big Difference. People, in general, don't give credence to the mantra that small choices make a big difference. If they did, Americans would be the healthiest, leanest, most relaxed, and joyful nation on the planet. Wealthy—yes. Healthy, slim, and joy-filled—we're not. American culture focuses on achieving big or significant things, noteworthy, or newsworthy accomplishments that warrant getting everyone's attention. The small successes achieved, one choice at a time, go unnoticed. For instance, skipping snacking in the afternoons goes unnoticed until a couple of pounds drop off. Taking ten minutes in the morning to plan your day seems too simple until your stress level drops and you feel you are meeting your daily goals more effectively. You can find power in the ability to choose wisely and succeed on a smaller scale from day-to-day. I consider myself successful at the end of the day if I've had my quiet time, had a great workout, and been proactive with my current to-do list. On the days I don't manage to do all of these things, I look back and ask if I did the best I could for the day. Did I make all the small choices I intended to? If yes, I fall asleep with a grateful heart. If not, I make a commitment to myself to do some of those smaller things the next day.

I find it interesting to learn about the small choices others make that enhance their lives. Before giving a keynote speech or a workshop, I ask select audience participants to share their ideas. I ask these two questions: "What small choices do you make day-to-day that you notice allow you to live happier and more content?" And, "What small choices have you made that inspire and motivate you in your work environment?"

Ann, a workshop participant, gave me this response to those two questions. She said, "I have made my office space into a place I really like. I listen to good music; I have a warm old lamp; flowers; plants; pictures of friends; and my kitty, Vivien; pretty rocks I collected on vacations; and colorful art pieces that make me feel good. I spend a little money and get good pens and pencils that feel good in my hand, a good stapler, and hole puncher." She enthusiastically went on to say, "They make a huge difference in my sanity, as I use them a lot. I eat a good breakfast every day, and try to plan a day each week to go out and eat with coworkers—and not talk about work. I try to take a walk around the building (outside) at least once a day. I smile a lot, which is selfishly motivated because I like to get smiles back, but it works!" Notice all of the small adjustments that made the difference.

You make one small choice, consciously or not, each morning when you get up. You decide whether you are going to live with intention and awareness of your choices—or not. You can choose wisely and con- sistently one choice at a time. Every morning you put your feet on the floor, I challenge you to say, "Today, I'll be on purpose. I'll be intentional." That translates into a thousand little choices made all day that enable you to go to bed at night saying, "Today was a day well lived. Everything is not done, but what I did get done, what I did think, say, and do was with purpose and was congruent for me." Doing the best you can each day ought to leave you content. You cannot do better than your best. Strive to let go of the "that" which is incomplete and do your best again tomorrow.

Every choice you make today either brings you closer or farther from your goals. At the end of each day, consider where your choices took you today.

When crisis happens, you shift gears and cope, function, adapt. You do what it takes. It's the small choices, however, that define your life. It's the small choices that either refuel or drain you. For instance, skipping breakfast because you're in a hurry to get out the door, then grabbing a pastry from the cafeteria or staff desk, working through lunch, and having a vanilla latte at 3:00 p.m. all involve a number of small choices that add up to one very poorly fueled woman at the end of a day. Imagine what weeks, months, and years lived like that do to your health. (A 24-ounce vanilla latte has 350 calories, roughly 480 if you have whipped cream.)

Another place you make small choices comes in the words you use. Little comments you utter either build up or tear down those around you. Negative internal head chatter like the following will not help you succeed. "Geez, can she ever get anything right? What's his problem? I'm so sick of not being able to get anything done—this will never change. I'm never going to lose these fifteen pounds." The smart choice to make when you hear yourself talking this way is to ask yourself, "What is the truth in this situation? Am I really powerless? Do I want to get caught up in his negative mood? Is her reaction about me or about something or someone else? Am I receiving the brunt end of frustration caused by some other source? Is it true I'll never lose weight, or is it just going to take longer than I'd like?" Pay attention to and think through your internal chatter and challenge the truth of your comments. The result is you can change your self-talk and change your response—to your benefit.

Small choices about how you use time also count. Small blocks of time either get you fit or increase your potential for disease and illness. Twenty minutes of walking will do you more good than you realize. Taking the stairs instead of the elevator every day will help you lose weight, improve your lung capacity, and strengthen your legs.

There is power in the small choices you make each day. Small choices add up to a changed life.

2. Life is a Journey.

Life is a journey is a healthy perspective to develop. Each of us experiences the journey in our own unique way. Just as every runner in a race notices different scenery, connects with various people, and finishes with various times. The journey is important. Your journey matters because of what you notice, who you impact, and the legacy you leave.

In June 2000, my husband and I and another couple headed to Duluth, Minnesota, to run our annual half-marathon. I wanted to run this race differently than in the past when my only goal was to finish as quickly as possible. I wanted to look around more and enjoy the people more this time. The last time all I had on my mind was the finish line. I bolted out, with my head down, and just plugged along. It was Kelli, my running buddy, who commented on all the wonderful people and support along the way. After the race, she said, "Did you see that family that came out with banners and decorations for us? How about the small band of guys playing along the road, wasn't that just great? That one group with the blankets, chairs, masks, and cold beers were a stitch, weren't they?" Cold beer. Did she say somebody had cold beer? I missed that too!

I realized that in my focus-on-the-finish attitude, I skipped looking around and just ran to the end, and *then* I thoroughly enjoyed my surroundings. I realized a simple shift of looking up and around, even periodically, would have changed the experience for me. I suspect that I thought if I looked up and around, enjoying the run, I'd slow down too much and perform badly. In truth, slowing down would have made my experience richer.

So, this time I decided I was going to look around more. I was determined to search out cool people and things to tell Kelli about. When the gun went off, I ran with my head up, taking in the sights. Much to my delight and surprise at the race's end, I not only collected some great sights and stories, but I also improved my time by seven minutes!

Life is a journey. We can put our heads down and plow through all the responsibilities, challenges, and activities and miss the good stuff, or we can take a look around and enjoy the journey. Having fun along the path of life does not mean you lose all intensity. It simply means you know when to lighten up and when to put the blinders on.

I had no intention of winning the race. Only a small handful cared about my race time. So why did I previously miss all those sights and sounds? Because I didn't *choose* to look around before I set out. I chose to finish as fast as I could just so I could be done with the race. I was solely focused on finishing. I decided to expand my focus for the race so it became a richer, more fun experience. I needed to intentionally include looking around in my list of what I wanted out of the race.

View life as a journey. This is a great perspective to keep. If at the end of your life you want to be remembered for the difference you made in people's lives, you'll need to slow down and intentionally look to see where you can serve and have an impact. It takes time to connect with people on an intellectual and/or heart level. We tend to get caught up in checking off the to-dos because there's a sense of completion in that. Yet, the ultimate loss comes from not enjoying the journey made rich because of the relationships we share, nurture, and grow. Relationships grow deeper in the slower moments of life.

3. Learning Never Stops.

Learning never stops for the intentional, deliberate, proactive person. This perspective compels you to continue stretching yourself to grow and evolve. Ongoing learning implies results in ongoing change. They say there are two things you can count on in life: paying taxes and dying. There is one more universal truth—change happens. No one gets out of life without experiencing ongoing change. The fact is change is a guarantee. How well you cope with change will entirely depend upon your willingness to learn and put into action that knowledge. I have a notebook from a conference with the theme spread across the cover, "Knowledge is Power." I disagree. Knowledge is Power *only if* it's put into action.

I'll share a humbling insight with you. I prefer to be the one who knows the answers. Yes, I prefer being the expert. I feel very uncomfortable being the new kid on the block. I'm more comfortable knowing what's going on and how things work, and I love sharing that knowledge. Doing something new requires I show up without knowing the answers.

Growth, new insights, and new paradigms that impact your life can't happen until you step into a place of "I don't know." The more comfortable and accepting you can be about being in that place, the lower your defenses will be and the faster learning takes place. One of my sons needed help in his math. He absolutely refused to go to a tutor and look stupid. He struggled until he went to his dad and asked for help. He caught on quickly with a small amount of help and now comfortably admits when he doesn't know something, and he asks for help. Everybody is much happier with this outcome.

4. Make Choices That Won't Lead to Regret.

One of the ways to make a final decision to move forward or to make a choice about something is to ask, "Which choice will lead to the least regret?" For instance, on days when I've planned to exercise, yet have work demands in front of me, I get tempted to forge through the work and skip my workout. With sixty seconds of reflection I recognize that the benefits of my workout on my mind, energy, and stress level will help me get more done. Thirty to forty minutes of exercise gifts me with more stamina and peace of mind. Rarely has my commitment to work out versus get more work done resulted in regret.

Regret can occur at the end of a day, at the end of a relationship, or after a diagnosis of a lifestyle-impacted disease. Do what you can today to positively impact your health and relationships so you do not regret the way you have lived. I certainly experienced this when diagnosed with cancer. Quite a few well-meaning people made the comment during and after treatment that maybe the disease occurred to give me a chance to rethink my life and make different decisions. Actually, just the opposite happened. I was deeply grateful to discover that I had no regrets with my choices—I would live the same way given the chance.

5. Time Warps Work.

A simple trick to employ when trying to make a choice is to do a time warp. That means in that moment of choice, you ask yourself, "In ten minutes, when this chocolate chip cheesecake is gone (onto my thighs, no doubt), will it be worth it?"

"If I take on this work project, will it be worth it next month, for all the juggling I'll have to do to make it happen?" Admittedly, you often don't have a clear answer. Answer to the best of your ability with the information you have at hand, consider past experience, and trust your gut.

You're lying in bed an hour after your regular bedtime reading a great book. Self-coach by asking, "How will I feel tomorrow morning if I read one more chapter? Will it be worth it?"

"It will be a lot of work to get this degree, write this book, change careers. I'll be five years older in five years. Will this be worthwhile then?" (This is about measuring the cost to you emotionally, physically, financially, relationally, and spiritually.)

6. Scale Your Choice.

In a coaching conversation, I often ask, "On a scale from one to ten, how committed are you to this goal? Ten being 'absolutely committed, it's basically done' to one being 'I forgot the goal already.'" If the answer is seven or under, the client and I work to adjust the goal so their commitment level rises to an eight to ten. It is only at that level of commitment that lasting change will take place.

Have you ever requested something from people, were told they would handle it, and then discovered they dropped the ball? You realize they just said yes to get you off their back, to avoid conflict, or because they didn't want to admit their limitations. That's what you do to yourself when you commit to a goal with a seven or less. You're setting yourself up for defeat. Instead of setting yourself up, adjust your goal so you can experience a victory. Like most people, sometimes I have a hard time admitting to my limitations.

I recently did that to myself. I offered to follow up on a committee project, knowing my schedule was too tight, but I wanted to help. When it came down to the wire—other commitments, quite honestly, rated higher—I dropped the ball.

You may aspire to eat healthier each day, but your commitment to eat differently right now is at a five for any number of reasons. The question to consider is, "What would I need to adjust in my goal to shift my commitment to an eight or nine?"

For example, suppose agreeing to bring your lunch to work three times a week versus five times changes your commitment level to a nine on your commitment scale. If you ate better four or five times that week, it will be a bonus. You'll do your three times and experience a victory.

7. Make Gratitude Your Attitude.

When our son Christopher was eight, we were at the dinner table sharing stories from the day. We were talking about the fact that something may seem impossible, but really it will just take a little longer to accomplish. Christopher picked up on the topic of impossible and said, "I'll tell you what's impossible. Last night, I was saying my prayers, and I was trying to talk to God without saying 'thank you.' Now that's impossible."

Your attitude influences your perspective in any situation or relationship. Your perspective impacts your self-talk, which influences your beliefs. Your self-talk and beliefs are influenced by your intentional or unintentional incorporating of other people's influences, beliefs, convictions, and insights. Strive to influence your own perspective rather than follow someone else's. Make sure your perspective feeds your positive attitude and creates more energy for you. Judgmental perspectives foster negative attitudes that drain energy.

Choose to have an attitude of gratitude about all that you possess and experience. Being bitter or ungrateful never served anyone in a positive way.

When you're feeling your grateful heart has shriveled a bit, look up, look around, and get into action serving and helping those who may look at your life and think you have it better than they do.

Laura experienced a particularly difficult divorce. Unfortunately, even divorced, she continued to experience frustration and difficulty. Although she recognized she should be feeling grateful to be done with the divorce process, she couldn't let the frustration and anger with her ex go. She couldn't let it go, at least, until an eye-opening experience reminded her of how to be grateful for where she was in life and how she got there. A friend asked Laura to help distribute clothes to a group of women shopping at their community thrift shop. These women needed help finding clothes and outfits for job interviews. Laura was so taken aback by the gratitude of these impoverished women and their gracious spirits that she realized she was looking in the wrong direction to feel better. Instead of looking around at her circumstances, she decided to look up and be grateful. She became inspired that night to keep a gratitude journal. Each night for a month Laura wrote down three things—most often very simple things—she was grateful to know, own, notice, or experience. It changed her outlook, which changed her choices, which changed her life.

> *"Don't do things to not die—do them to live better, to enjoy life, and make the difference you were meant to make."*
> Kate Larsen

8. Motives Are the Key.

What is your motive for wanting to live wisely, choose intentionally, and to live on purpose? As you reflect on your dreams, goals, and commitments throughout this book, you will begin to identify ambitions, fears, insecurities, and hopes that powerfully drive your actions. The more aware you are of what drives you, the better you become at dealing with obstacles to your success and making better choices for yourself. So, why do you decide to exercise after work, but then skip it? Why do you promise to not add one more activity or project to your pile, yet find yourself saying yes to another request? Why do you stay at a company that you know does not honor your desire for a more balanced life?

When conducting coach training for health professionals, I help them sort out the most important types of questions to ask clients. A simple reminder that has helped many involves their examining their motives for asking the question(s) they ask. For instance, as a client tells a story or recaps a day or situation, questions naturally form in their minds. Here is a simple, yet powerful quality control check I suggest. Ask yourself, "Why am I asking this question? Is it to fulfill my curiosity, direct the conversation a certain way, or because I genuinely believe the answer will help the client?" The same approach would be great to use in your regular conversations with others. Staying away from gossip is smart. Not directing others to where you think they should go honors and respects them. Asking questions that reflect you're authentically listening and caring for what they have to share is a wonderful way to engage others. Have you considered what motivates you to do and say the things you do?

Six Motives That Make a Negative Difference

There are many motives that drive your behavior and choices; many professionals boil them down to wanting to avoid pain and increase pleasure. Some negative motives I commonly hear are:

1. I don't want to disappoint people.

2. I feel guilty spending too much time on myself.

3. I don't know where to start to make changes.

4. I lack self-discipline.

5. I have too much on my plate to slow down right now.

6. If I make the changes I believe I need to make, I'm afraid I'll be divorced, lose my job, alienate my kids, fail, disappoint myself—pick any one.

> *"What really traps us are circumstances, attitudes, expectations, and routines—at least these things are easier to change than people."*
> Kate Larsen

Your motive for living intentionally is not to hurt, but to help. Your intent is to become all you can be—to use all your potential and share your gifts. These are great motives. Your responsibility to others is simply to articulate your boundaries, goals, insights, and intentions and let other people's responses be their own. You don't have to own their reaction nor answer to them. Take a deeper look at these six attitudes or beliefs that can get in the way of you making those small choices that make a big difference.

1. I don't want to disappoint people.

I have never worked with someone who enjoyed disappointing others. I know those people are out there. However, they're not the individuals looking to grow, change, and positively influence the world. In other words, they're not in my workshops or coaching sessions. And they probably won't read this book.

If you have been overextending yourself, ignoring your own needs and boundaries, then, yes, you will now disappoint people by being motivated to take better care of yourself. People have relied on you because you've been willing to give so much despite your own needs (that they probably don't know about). Let's evaluate *why* you are disappointing them when you begin to care for you.

Sylvia found herself more and more frazzled and unproductive at work. Her coworker Bill had unknowingly become accustomed to her covering his mistakes. His addiction problem was becoming more apparent to her each week, yet she did not want to make the wrong decision on how to handle the situation. Finally, when her migraines became too frequent and her own work began to suffer, she set boundaries with Bill regarding his responsibilities.

Two months after she stopped covering for him, his addiction became apparent to those in the organization who needed to know and could act on his behalf. The company helped Bill get into treatment to achieve sobriety. Who knows how much longer she could have continued to cover two people's workloads? Sylvia found the cost to her physical and emotional health too high. Her commitment to quality work was compromised, so she took the risk of disappointing others—especially her boss—by not covering for Bill any longer. However, consider how much Sylvia sacrificed—her health, sense of accomplishment in her own work, time off, etc. when she did cover for Bill. You can probably imagine such a scenario yourself.

If you have been covering someone else's butt, doing their work, picking up their slack, and in other ways making life more convenient for someone else, they definitely will be inconvenienced when you stop. They may even have to face consequences for their choices. It will then be their responsibility to figure out what needs to be done differently. If you are handling your responsibilities, then your bases are covered. Maybe your boss, spouse, sibling, or friend needs coaching. Today could be the day you begin to practice letting go of worrying about what other people think. It is your choice.

2. I feel guilty spending too much time on myself.

If feeling guilty keeps you from taking better care of yourself, review why you are striving to develop new habits. Your reasons may be that you want to be more patient, more creative, and/or more calm. You want to be able to concentrate on other people or on your work more deeply and consistently. You want less stress-induced symptoms of fatigue and being overwhelmed. These are not selfish motives. They are actually quite wise. Taking better care of yourself is good for you *and* other people. With that in mind, feeling guilty does not seem to be an appropriate response to self-care.

3. I don't know where to start to make changes.

Sometimes the changes you envision for yourself are so large and all consuming (impacting so many areas of your life) that you give up before you start. Being overwhelmed does little for your creative juices. To say you don't know where to start can be a fair statement. The best place to start is to write down and describe where you are today in each of the areas of your life and where you would like to be.

The Life Inventory Wheel exercise is one commonly used by professional coaches. The areas of the wheel consider physical well-being, financial health, interpersonal relationships, intellectual pursuits, career aspirations and direction, spiritual health, and personal development (hobbies, self-growth). The difference between your reality (what you are currently feeling, experiencing, achieving) and what you would like to have or feel is called the gap. Your goal (and mine) is to narrow that gap—not in one day, or one week, but at a pace that will help you make it stick. The Life Inventory Wheel found in appendix G can give you an idea of where to start after you've spent time clarifying your direction and personal vision.

The goal will probably look pretty big, so break it down into parts. Defining a clear, compelling vision statement for yourself will help you move toward what you want to experience and achieve. A compelling vision statement states what you want your life to look like. This statement can act as a compass directing you to your true north— your purpose in life. As your wellness vision focuses on your health, your life vision focuses on your whole life. Your wellness vision is a subset of your life vision.

4. I lack self-discipline.

It's not self-discipline you lack; it's commitment. When you are deeply committed to something, self-discipline is not the issue. Choice is. When you catch yourself saying, "I lack self-discipline…" acknowledge you are also saying, "Therefore, I'm not responsible for this choice."

Usually, when clients refer to their self-discipline, they're referring to choices around fitness and food. As mentioned earlier, billions of dollars are spent on dieting—each year. The kicker is that diets don't work. There is no quick fix. A healthy, smart way of eating (versus a diet) requires self-discipline about what goes in your mouth. Fat rollers, blasters, and reducers don't work—at least not for the long haul. Intentional choices and smart actions do.

5. I have too much on my plate right now.

If you're too busy to take time for your life, you're too busy! You only get one shot at this life. You get one body. One life. If your life is that full, allow yourself a longer period of time to adjust your priorities. If you have a heart attack tomorrow, were diagnosed with cancer next week, or lost a child to a sudden death, your life would change. *You* would be changed by your loss. If you recognize your plate is too full, why not make changes now—before a crisis? Don't wait. You can find time for what is most important to you. If your health is important (if it is truly a core value), you'll *make* time. You will never find a more perfect time than now.

6. If I make the changes I believe I need to make, I'm afraid I'll be divorced, lose my job, alienate my kids, fail, disappoint myself—pick any one.

This is probably the toughest barrier to overcome when committing to change. Kathy and I were talking through her intake session questionnaire. She was delightful. Kathy's personal trainer had referred her to me. I heard her desire, enthusiasm, and hope that she would begin to make the changes she felt called to make for a long time.

I noted, however, that whenever we talked about supportive people in her life, her husband of nine years was never mentioned. She became agitated when I asked directly about his support for her. A moment later her tension dissolved, and I heard sadness and resignation more than anything else. No, she couldn't count on him. As a matter of fact, she quietly and tearfully admitted, she was afraid if she really committed to all that we talked about, she would end up divorced. She wasn't describing wanting selfish, irresponsible outcomes. She just didn't know where to begin or how to progress without burning bridges.

Kathy and I agreed that her relationship with her husband needed work and that she would put energy into it later on as she became better at her own self-care. She really didn't have the physical and emotional reserves to deal with her marriage at that time. It was deeply important for her to be able to say out loud her greatest fear was in becoming an intentional woman, and she needed the skills to move ahead wisely.

What is the greatest fear you need to voice—out loud—to enable you to move forward with your commitment to be intentional and purposeful in your life? Take the time to write about what you fear, desire, and are grateful for in your life. Or talk with someone about these things. Articulating the random, often unnoticed, thoughts that tug at your heart, mind, and soul will help you become clearer about the steps you need to take to close the gap(s) in your life between what you experience and what you want to experience.

9. Build Reserves.

Having reserves reduces stress. Reserves of what? Reserves of everything! My stress is lowered when I know I have reserves of intangibles, like energy, and reserves of tangibles, like gasoline. Whenever the orange fuel light pops on in my dashboard my eyes flip down to the lower right side of the dash and there it is, that little orange fuel light that says I better stop soon. If you're like Jack, my husband, you're thinking, "Yeah, so?" He can drive for days with his fuel light on. My tendency is to want to pull over to the first station I see to maintain my reserves. Running out of gas would not be the end of the world but a real hassle I'd like to avoid. And it's relatively easy to avoid. Just stop and refuel.

Does that sound like something that has application to life? Absolutely. Do you need to stop rushing through life, fatigued, yet driven by overwhelming demands? If your body, mind, or soul is screaming for you to stop and take better care of yourself, do it. Your personal orange light is on. Many of your daily choices are driven by economic motives. Evaluate your financial reserves and examine what you need to do to create better reserves financially. Building financial reserves allows you more freedom, while reducing fear in your choices.

10. Reflective Writing Is an Amazing Tool.

I began journal writing in the third grade. I came home from a trip to Evansville, Indiana, in love. Since love was a totally new experience, and one I did not feel I could safely share with my mom and dad, I decided to share it with myself. I pulled out a small leather accordion style index card case that was held closed with a brown string that looked like a shoelace. Inside I wrote the story of meeting Gary, a boy I met that I had an immediate crush on.

I continued to journal through college; then I just stopped. A couple of years later, I wondered why I stopped. After reviewing my journals, I realized I had only taken the time to write when I was down, overwhelmed, scared, or angry. In my need to always appear happy and together, I chose to write my negative thinking and self-doubt in my journal. That left me feeling down and depressed. It became a Pavlovian response. As I grew healthier and more content with myself, I unconsciously avoided journaling because it no longer served a positive purpose. With that insight, I chose to record both the ups and downs of my life. Journaling then became a tool. You can choose how to use journaling as you take charge of your health and life.

Using a journal is also an effective tool for dealing with anxiety and fear—two of the most powerful obstacles for making and maintaining changes. Here's an example of how Peg used journaling as a tool for relieving stress effectively. An e-mail she sent me said, "You had challenged me to writing down things that are making me anxious and what I am doing to handle them better…Keri [her nine-year-old daughter] is going away with her dad this weekend, and I'm feeling anxious about it. After writing about that and asking myself how else I could look at the situation, I realized it is a good time for me to refuel, and it gives me a chance to build on my other relationships with friends and family. Besides, I can't change who Paul [her ex] is or what he does, so why would I put my own precious energy into worrying about it? My goal is to be the healthy parent. I immediately felt more grounded once I wrote that and sat back to reflect about it. Stress attack aborted!"

The adage that "whatever gets measured, gets done" is true. So a number of years ago, I created a journal for my clients to use to initiate and maintain change in. The goal was to raise their level of awareness around the choices they made that either enhanced energy and positive relationships or diminished energy and destroyed relationships. If you're aware of an unhealthy or unproductive choice you are about to make, and take six to sixty seconds to think through a better choice in the moment, you can then choose differently and change your life—one choice at a time. Journaling your thoughts, actions, and observations is an amazingly powerful activity to do.

Harnessing the Power of a LifeWalk Journal

To make journaling simple, yet powerful, I created a lifestyle journal for clients that enables them to track their food and exercise choices and note what impacted their choices. For instance, did they have a better workout when exercising with a friend or on their own? Did they more consistently exercise at a certain time of day? How often did they eat for nutritional reasons versus emotional ones? How well and for how long did they sleep? What did they laugh at on a given day? Just being aware that a space in their journal calls for a comment on laughter in their life causes many to raise their level of awareness around fun and levity. Most people are too intense.

Each day also allows comments on best choices made. After journaling all of these choices over the course of a month, clients could go back to review the implications of their choices and the influences impacting them. This reflection enables them to fine-tune their habits, making more and more positive choices throughout their days. The journal is a quick, simple, yet powerful tool for creating lasting behavior change.

In *The Will to Believe*, the well-known author and philosopher, William James, wrote, "If you can change your mind, you can change your life. What you believe creates the actual fact. The greatest revolution of my generation is the discovery that individuals, by changing their inner attitudes of mind, can change the outer aspects of their lives."

Your attitude and perspective matter. The mantras you incorporate into your thinking will fuel your energy for change. They will make a big difference in helping you stay on track to making the positive choices that impact your life.

TRAINING TIPS

- We live in an era of abundance in every way. The challenge is to manage our freedom and to strike a balance in the face of endless opportunities.

- Every morning you put your feet on the floor, I challenge you to say, "Today, I'll be on purpose. I'll be intentional."

- Doing the best you can each day ought to leave you content.

- Every choice you make today either brings you closer to or farther from your goals.

- Small blocks of time either get you fit or increase your potential for disease or illness.

- Having fun along the path of life does not mean you lose your intensity.

- It takes time to connect with people on an intellectual and/or heart level.

- Learning never stops for the intentional, deliberate, proactive person.

- The more aware you are of what drives you, the better you become at dealing with obstacles to your success and making better choices for yourself.

- Your responsibility to others is simply to articulate your boundaries, goals, insights, and intentions and let other people's responses be their own.

- It's not self-discipline you lack for making and sustaining change; it's commitment or compelling motivator.

- If you're too busy to take time for your life, you're too busy!

- If your health is important (if it is truly a core value), you'll *make* time. You will never find a more perfect time.

- Intentionally directing and monitoring your M.A.P.s will enable you to continue to make choices in your life that help you take charge of your health and life.

- Judgmental perspectives foster negative attitudes that drain energy and divide people.

WORKINS

1. What's the truth regarding your health, relationships, work circumstances? Are you powerless? Do you have options? What are they?

2. Do you get caught up in others' moods and mindsets? Do you give them the power to ruin your day?

3. What are three of your most frequently stated judgments? (e.g., "This whole process is ridiculous." "Going to this will be worthless." "I'll never be able to do this.")

4. How did this perspective develop? Was it based upon experience or others' perspectives?

5. Who nurtures a negative attitude in you by agreeing, contributing negatively, and judging others? (This relationship would be worth reconsidering and potentially letting go of, or you could intentionally choose to spend less time with this person or group.)

6. Life Inventory Wheel exercise

Fill out the Life Inventory Wheel in appendix F. Rate yourself in each area of your life on a scale of one to seven. Look at each area on the wheel and determine what you would like your number to be in each area of life mentioned. For instance, if you currently rate your physical well-being at a three, think about what it would take for you to rate yourself at a five or six. Are you willing to pursue accomplishing or attaining those things that will close the gap between what you are experiencing now and would like to? If not, let the anxiety, frustration, or guilt go. Use your energy to change the attitudes and behaviors you are ready to work on. If you are ready and committed to get into action—do so!

WORKOUTS

1. This action item will require both thought and action. While this workout is the shortest list of workouts for any of the chapters, it will keep you just as busy as many of them. As you go through your days this week, pay attention to your thoughts and choices. Notice when you're

rushing and ask why you are in such a hurry. Is it necessary? The action is to notice, remember, and write down what you hear yourself saying to yourself; jot down insights. Examine how your choices impact your energy, family, and work interactions and mood.

2. After four chapters, you have probably made some commitments to change thinking and behavior habits that will reduce your stress and increase your energy. Use the Progress Report for Stress Busting and Energy Building page in appendix H to evaluate and track your progress.

Five
Food: Friend or Foe

Everyone's on a diet, yet people are getting fatter. Obesity is called a disease, yet health insurance doesn't cover treatment. Administrators and teachers advocate eating healthier snacks and beverages at school, yet the vending machines that line the halls are filled with candy, high-fat snacks, and liquid sugar filled with chemicals, dyes, and additives. A handful of states have begun implementing more rigid and healthy guidelines for what is available to students in school. (The challenge is that schools get kickbacks from the supplier companies providing funding that many schools say they cannot do without.) We're told we eat too much, yet portion sizes keep getting bigger at home and at restaurants. How ironic. It's no surprise we tend to eat to fix our cravings versus fuel our bodies. While storms in the food industry are brewing due to lawsuit fears and the significant rise in heart disease and diabetes in this country, nationwide change will take too long for you to wait for it to become easier to eat smarter.

The truth is that if you want to have energy, you want to weigh your ideal weight, you want to sleep well, you want health for the long term, then you *will* eat well. How you fuel your body impacts everything in your life. Food needs to be your fuel, not your fix for boredom, anger, fear, or anxiety. Nor can it be your first choice as a friend to celebrate or reward yourself.

Dietitians and doctors alike will tell you weight gain and loss are based upon a simple formula: Expend more calories than you put in and you'll lose weight; take in more calories than you burn off and you'll gain weight. The quality of what you eat makes almost as much difference as the amount you put in your mouth.

In this chapter, you will learn (or be reminded of) behavioral and attitudinal steps for eating wisely. You will have the opportunity to use the Think, Choose, Act, Win model for decision-making and gain a more hopeful perspective about the choices you have with your eating. The power that is within you—the power of choice—will either support or sabotage your great intentions to eat wisely.

Begin today to educate yourself so that you can make discerning choices and not be fooled by the marketing gurus of food companies around the world. Be more alert, more informed, and more in control.

The two challenges the majority of my clients have when it comes to smart eating are confusion and fatigue. They are confused by all of the conflicting reports, information, and diets available. Each report or diet espouses wonderful, if not conflicting, results. Busy, nonstop schedules also leave many people fatigued, prompting them to eat whatever is easy and available at the expense of good nutrition. You have to have energy to follow your plan, and the stamina and determination to stick with your healthy eating resolve. It's hard to go against the flow of the culture and your kids who have strong opinions about what they want to eat. And, if they're like most kids, whole grains and vegetables don't make the top ten list.

Eating healthfully definitely goes against the flow. Recently, we were with a group of families talking about raising kids. I commented, "Jack and I assume we're goofing on something, and we'll just hear about it when the boys are thirty." One of the adults turned to Jamie, our second son, and asked, "Okay, Jamie, what one thing do you know you're going to be saying when you're thirty about what your mom and dad did wrong?" He responded, "Food! We have to eat way too healthy. It's not fair!" While I would love for my kids to say I'm a great cook, I'm more likely to hear about the torture of the way I made them eat as kids. (Actually, I pray that's their worst comment in the years to come.)

Obesity: A Serious Concern

One out of three Americans is obese, twice as many as three decades ago, and enough for the Centers for Disease Control and Prevention to declare obesity an epidemic. Obesity is defined by your body mass index, or BMI, a calculation in which one's weight in kilograms is divided by the square of your height in meters.[1] If your BMI is twenty-five, you're overweight. If it's thirty, you're obese. Over forty, you're morbidly obese. The human body is composed of a variety of different tissue types. The so-called lean tissues, such as muscle, bone, and organs are metabolically active, while adipose, or fat tissue, is not.

Scales, up till now, can't accurately determine the lean-to-fat ratio of that weight. An individual can be overweight and not "over-fat." A bodybuilder, for example, may be 8 percent body fat, yet at two hundred and fifty pounds may be considered overweight by a typical height-weight chart. Therefore, these charts are not a good indication of your ideal body weight for optimal health, much less for athletic performance.

You can discover your own BMI at http://nhlbisupport.com/bmi/bmicalc.htm. The best way to learn your body composition is to have it measured. The gold standard of body composition analysis is called hydrostatic weighing or hydrodensitometry. However, because hydrodensitometry is time consuming, cumbersome, and complicated, most physiologists turn to skinfold measurement as an acceptable alternative means of assessment. The American College of Sports Medicine states that skinfold measures, when performed by a trained, skilled tester, are up to 98 percent accurate.

The bottom line is Americans need to seriously address their weight issues. Being overweight is associated with four hundred thousand deaths a year and an increased risk of heart disease; type 2 diabetes; and colon, breast, and endometrial cancers. This statistic is not just true of Americans—there are now as many overnourished people as undernourished around the world. Due to the epidemic of obesity among both adults and children, it's critical to learn how to make the best possible eating decisions. The University of Arkansas for Medical Sciences reported there are now

127 million Americans who are overweight. And there's another 60 million who are obese and 9 million who are morbidly or severely obese. That translates into 64 percent of adults over the age of twenty who are now overweight or obese. About 15 percent of all adolescents and children are now considered to be overweight. All of these weight issues are based upon body mass index.[2]

My goal is to encourage and challenge you to make intentional decisions about the type of foods, the quantity, and quality of the foods you eat. I call this philosophy tactical nutrition or strategic eating. Eating smart is just one of the strategies you can chose for living healthier.

Tactical nutrition or strategic eating doesn't just happen. You need to plan your meals because our culture is geared toward quick eating, food-fix eating— satisfying whims for flavors and textures, not to increase your vitality and energy. Being tactical means you've considered your choices with a strategy.

Creating a strategy requires you have a goal in mind. To stick with your strategy when the going gets tough requires a deep level of commitment and perseverance that only comes with an internal motivator that's connected with your core values.

Eating smart does not have to be boring, torturous, or impossible. To make good decisions requires information, a certain attitude, and self-awareness. You need to be willing to learn, to patiently work a process, to be open to testing new foods and recipes, and to develop a healthy perspective about the role of food in your life. Eating better happens one bite at a time, which is why your mantra of "small choices make a big difference" is so helpful when it comes to healthy eating.

This concept is critical because studies have shown losing weight isn't the biggest problem for people; the greatest challenge is maintaining the weight loss afterward. The maintenance stage is the toughest. Research conducted by the National Weight Control Registry shows that 20 percent of their losers maintain their weight loss for a year or more. They have the largest database of people who have achieved this goal. The average amount their participants have lost is sixty pounds, and they've maintained that loss for five years or more.[3] Admittedly, the numbers still show that at least 80 percent are regaining their weight. The top two suggestions shared by successful weight loss maintainers are that small choices make a big difference and exercise is critical. (No surprise there.)

The truth is I have neither the time, energy, nor inclination to count calories, weigh food, or scrutinize every morsel I am going to eat. If that's true for you—be encouraged because there is hope.

To change anything in your life is a matter of the heart. When I speak of heart, I am talking about that which motivates you, that which you have passion for, that which you desire; and that which inspires you from *your* innermost being.

One of the goals most of my coaching clients have is to improve their eating habits. The majority of individuals who eat well today do so because of a crisis at some time in their lives. Far too many people are not changing their familiar eating habits until they've lost their health to illness or can't tolerate the fatigue associated with unhealthy eating any longer. The dependence on diets, quick fixes, and quackery needs to end. It's frightening to see how many people refuse to trust common sense and practice personal discipline when it comes to eating.

Does this scenario sound familiar to you? You decide on Sunday that this week you're going to start, and stick with, healthy, smart eating and end on Saturday shaking your head and asking, "What the heck went wrong?" What happens between good intentions and action is the difference between success and failure. What happens between the two will lead to either being healthy and fit or struggling, frustrated, and overweight.

The Challenge of Emotional Eating

Eating healthfully and eating to lose weight are not necessarily the same thing. There is a different mindset and motivation behind each. Their intention may appear similar, but I'll bet you recognize the difference between the two. People fail at diets and permanent weight loss primarily because their goal is skewed—losing weight versus being healthy. Eating healthy tends to naturally lead to weight loss. Emotional eating is a well-known saboteur of healthy nutrition. Unrecognized and/or unmet needs are key triggers for eating. If you've attempted and failed numerous times to lose weight, yet feel a heartfelt desire to succeed, it's possible—and even likely—food isn't the issue. Food is just the bandage that masks something else.

Food has a way of impacting the body and emotions, which can, at times, feel like a balm. Food may provide comfort, relief, or relaxed feelings. For some, food becomes a physical way to stuff down emotional frustrations and anger. Identify the times you eat for emotional reasons. In the moment of choice, you can self-coach, consciously questioning the benefit of a food or drink against its impact (e.g., in calories, guilt, sluggishness, or the adrenaline rush).

If you stop for six to sixty seconds before taking that first bite or first sip, you'll make better choices day by day. Those daily choices add up over time. Coaching yourself around food choices is also healthy emotionally because it decreases self-recrimination and increases self-satisfaction. Self-coaching is also an empowering skill to develop.

Most people recognize when they are eating emotionally. Some laugh and shrug it off, while others express an intense desire to change their habit of emotional eating. Which response do you have to your emotional eating? If you were to catch yourself, even once a day, and *not* eat something due to boredom, anger, fatigue, or anxiety, do you think that would make a difference at the end of a week? A month? Are you curious enough to try? One pound is equivalent to 3500 calories. How about cutting down your calories by 500 a day. After one week, that would equal one pound. Look at the calories in what you drink as well as what you eat. You will find ways to cut out those extra calories.

While I only touch lightly on this topic here, keep in mind that using food as a self-medicating or escape device is serious business. You may find it helpful to reflectively consider some of your emotional eating habits. What emotions or times of the day trigger unplanned eating?

My client Bill commented, "I've noticed that when I'm not feeling really good about me or I'm not excited about my work or life, I begin to crave sweets again. Sweets also represent fun. So, when I crave them, I know that either I'm falling off purpose in my daily life or I'm not having enough fun." He then said, "If I figure out what is missing (fun or passion),

I get back on track by filling the need versus filling my mouth."

What are some ways you could handle these emotions without overeating or eating compulsively? I received an e-mail from Donna, who said, "This weekend I asked myself why I kept on going for the unhealthy food instead of the healthy food. I figured out that the reason was because every time I was hungry I asked myself, 'What am I in the mood for?' Dumb question. I am always in the mood for something sweet. I started asking myself, 'I'm hungry. What would be healthy for me to eat?' Somehow, I knew cookies weren't the answer, and I actually started looking for something healthy to eat. What is exciting is that I'm figuring this out myself!"

Understanding Your Food History

It's important to recognize the messages you received as a child about food. I can't remember any specific messages about food itself, but I do remember meals were generally stressful. We all had our assigned seats. My dad was incredibly unpredictable, and it was often a war of wills around the table. Meal times were more stressful to our health than the foods we ate.

Do past messages about starving children in other parts of the world cause you to clear your plate even when you're not hungry? Do you nibble on leftover food from your kids' plates as you're cleaning up? Was love expressed through food, so it has a nurturing message for you? Has it become simply a habit to sip, sample, and taste foods while you cook? Remember the calories of everything that goes in your mouth, whether anyone sees you or not, count.

Take time to identify issues in your life and/or your past, which are harming you today. What ways can you care for your emotional health without involving food? You may be able to accomplish this on your own; however, if this is your challenge, I encourage you to seek the guidance of a professional. When one of my sisters struggled with bulimia, she went to campus counselors for support. She discovered a shocking number of fellow students were experiencing the same problem. Getting professional help, I believe, saved her sanity, and possibly her life.

My mother's return address label reads, "Hand over the chocolate and no one will get hurt." Mom is not alone in her love of chocolate. Have you thought of some other ways for dealing with the emotions that cause you to grab chocolate? Okay, for a moment think about a recent situation that triggered your eating chocolate. Pretend for a moment you're in that situation again right now. What could you do differently that wouldn't involve chocolate calories?

Begin today to get clear about what you want your eating to do for you. Assess how you can make that happen one choice at a time and then get into action. Choose a thirty-day window to commit to making small specific change. What are three goals that will prepare you? For instance, one woman I know who lost thirty-five pounds spent a month finding ten healthy recipes her family would eat. (And, I assume, she then made the food using those recipes.)

You want to eat smart for your health, energy, weight, or any number of positive reasons. Most people I meet are informed about better or best choices to make, but don't make them on a consistent basis. *Consistency is where the magic happens.*

If health is a high value for you, you *will* eat smarter on a consistent basis. And you will do what it takes to figure out what will work for you.

Think of the last food or drink you had that you *knew* wasn't a wise choice, but you had it anyway. What trade-off did you get for health, energy, or reserves? Was it comfort, relief, boredom, or peer pressure? Then decide if you'll do that again. You may decide it wasn't worth it.

People go on and off diets. Changing your eating habits is not about going on a diet, because a diet is temporary. A diet you go on and off of, but healthy eating isn't a choice that is meant to be short term. It's meant to last a lifetime—one day at a time, one choice at a time. Slips will happen, adjustments will be made, you will rethink your choices. Eating smart will become a part of you.

Balancing Needs and Wants: Everyday and Sometimes Foods

Years ago I saw a nutrition tape that shared an idea about explaining nutrition and eating to kids, which I loved and have adapted to use with my kids as well as my clients. It's great because it's so simple. The simplicity lies in the question you can ask yourself before eating or drinking, "Is this food an everyday food or a sometimes food?" Your answer will help you quickly decide on the merits of the food choice.

My plan for eating is based upon balancing my everyday foods and my sometimes foods. When the kids were young, I wanted a way to describe strategic eating without attaching emotional good/bad labels. So, we taught the boys about foods we need to eat every day (everyday foods) and foods that were fun, tasty, or pleasurable that were either low in nutritional value and/or high on disease-promoting properties. We called the second group sometimes foods because they were fine to have periodically or sometimes as a smaller part of a healthy diet.

A second question helps me evaluate when to eat sometimes foods. I do the scale test. On a scale of one to ten, is this food worth the calories to me. One means "Yuk!" Ten equals "To die for/yummy!" I only eat "sometimes foods" when they score a seven to ten on the scale. If a food or drink only registers a six on my taste bud scale, why would I take in the calories, fat, chemicals, guilt, and remorse it offers? Cheesecake is a four to me, so I don't bother. Betty Crocker Supreme Brownies are a nine! (A ten if they have a perfect texture.)

One of your motivators for eating more wisely could be because you are a role model for your children. Kids watch what you do; they don't care much about what you say. I'll never forget the morning after Kiel, my oldest son, had been to his first professional baseball game. He was four. After driving his truck around on the kitchen floor for a while, he switched gears and began a new game. I was washing dishes and heard Kiel circling the kitchen island calling out, "Potato chips, potato chips, come and get your chips. Mom, do you want some chips?" I absentmindedly answered, "No thanks, hon." Silence. "Broccoli, broccoli, come and get your broccoli. Mom?"

Kids learn a lot from what we do, little by what we say. What are you role modeling for your family when it comes to fueling yourself for health and vitality?

Winning, whether in sports competition or life, takes discipline. Discipline requires energy. When your energy—emotional, spiritual, financial, physical, interpersonal, or intellectual—stores are low, you don't have what it takes to consistently win. You simply don't have the energy to use self-discipline. Don't kid yourself. There are no shortcuts to intentional living or intentional eating.

You need to plan your meals and snacks, even for a short period of time. Let me emphasize this isn't a moral issue. Eating habits have a great deal of emotional baggage attached to them; however, not eating well does not make you a bad person. You may be a frustrated, tired, overweight person, yet not a bad person.

Accidental eating is frequently blamed for sabotaging diets. If you don't plan–even generally plan—how you will eat, then what you eat is by accident. An accident, by its very definition is something that happens by chance, through a mishap or is an unexpected happening. Most people eat by chance. The decision as to what to eat is determined by this unspoken, often unconscious process of elimination.

Eating the Right Way

Eating the right way simply means you set a standard for how often, how much, and in what manner you will eat. Eating the right way suggests eating wisely, keeping in mind the balance of foods you have consumed over the course of a day or week. Eating the right way implies you listen for body cues for hunger versus eating according to the clock.

Research shows that when you eat out with friends, you tend to eat more and to take in more calories.

Knowing that is a strong possibility, I attempt to be more intentional about what I'm eating, how fast, and how much.

Are you sitting when you eat—at a table or in the car? Frequently eating on the run doesn't allow the body to relax and enjoy the flavor and texture of the food.

Eating with family members makes the mealtime more conducive to relationship and bonding time for couples and families. Family meals are also frequently recommended as one of the most powerful rituals families can adopt. Whether your family consists of just you, you and your spouse, you and your spouse and kids, or you and your kids, mealtime can be wonderful for the body *and* soul. However, getting everyone in one place at one time can be more challenging than planning the meal itself. Designate nights or mornings for your time together. This step may be your first one toward healthy eating as a family or couple.

Small Choices Make a Big Difference

Genetically, we are prone to enjoy and crave fattier foods. Family meals tend to be richer and creamier or fried and crunchy. When you think of a favorite family or fun food, I doubt you think of broccoli and carrots.

Snacking on and enjoying healthier foods seems to be an acquired taste. Actually, I think the toughest challenge my clients have is eating enough vegetables to make a positive difference. Most adults haven't lost the kid mentality or preference around avoiding veggies at all costs.

It's one bite, one snack, or one skipped meal at a time that impacts your energy, weight, and health.

Each choice counts. Each choice adds up. For instance, the negative choice is having a double espresso (that keeps you up for three extra hours that night) with a friend after work instead of a decaf flavored tea or coffee. The regrettable choice is the filet you ordered at 8:30 p.m. during a business dinner that kept your insides churning all night. And it's the simple chocolate bar and a soft drink at 2:30 in the afternoon that created the energy slump at 5:00 p.m., when you were about to prepare dinner, that leaves you wanting to serve what's easy and not necessarily healthy.

Weight is not gained in clumps (with the exception of cruise vacations and holidays). Weight is gained one bite or one sip at a time. While genetics can play a factor with weight challenges, the simple fact remains. When you take in more calories than you expend, you gain weight. When you expend more than you take in, you lose weight. As a general rule, people are eating larger portions, more frequently, of foods that are not nutrient-rich. They are also less active than ever before. The result: weight gain. I hesitate to chase the gene theory. Let the scientists do that. You take responsibility today for what's going in your body and what you are doing with your body.

A word of caution: Because we are each unique, it just may be that your body doesn't metabolize certain foods properly and you need to eat differently. For instance, for a number of reasons, you may not be able to have dairy foods—they just don't serve your body well. Alternative nutrition and supplements will be important for you. That is the exception versus the rule.

Using the Think, Choose, Act, Win (TCAW) Model to Eat Healthfully

Let's look at how you apply the Think, Choose, Act, Win model to healthy eating. You can coach yourself to rewarding choices. The TCAW model incorporates reflection, brainstorming, planning, and strategizing about potential obstacles, practice, adjustment, and celebration.

Whether the decision is about what to eat, what exercise class to take, or whether it's time for a quiet break, the following process will help you make the *best* choice in the moment. The Think, Choose, Act, Win model was described in detail in chapter two. We will take the model here and plug in the goal of healthy eating.

1. Think

First consider the choice. What eating decision are you trying to make? Are you planning your meals for the week or merely deciding what to have for lunch? Are you beginning to focus on healthy eating because a child is gaining too much weight or has a family member been diagnosed with diabetes? Are you tired of being tired and recognize you would benefit from cutting down on caffeine and sweets? Whatever your reasons for strategizing your eating plan, decide what you need to do differently. Even if you don't know *how* to do it, decide *what* you want to change first.

2. Choose

One of the secrets to lasting change is change that is accompanied by attitude shifts. You need an attitude shift that gives you the mental strength and fortitude to resist temptation and stand strong in your resolve to change. That shift is accomplished with positive self-talk and the intentional, purposeful filling of your mind with motivational, positive input. Prayer for strength and support isn't a bad idea either.

Aside from internal motivation, you need information to make a choice. Get the information you need to make an informed choice. Then make your choice. What information do you need most to make better food choices?

Write down the aspects of nutrition that confuse you. Is it reading labels or understanding what to believe in the paper about new research? Are you curious about supplements and vitamins? How about how much calcium you really need? What throws you off? Knowledge isn't power; action, based upon solid knowledge, is.

3. Act

You either eat something or you don't. You have a cup of coffee or fresh orange juice. You stop and pick up some fresh produce or you stop at a fast food restaurant. Making a choice doesn't mean you've acted. *Acting is a separate step.* I can decide to work out after work today and still drive straight past the health club on the way home. I can choose to order first at lunch so I'm not influenced by everyone else's choices and then somehow end up ordering last and ordering differently because of it. Choosing (intention) and acting (execution) are two different things. Act on your choice. In your action, your knowledge becomes power.

4A. Win

Good choices (small wins) are those that support your good intention. I've never worked with someone who didn't want to be excellent. You win when you intend to eat well and then you actually do. You win when you decide to get more sleep and then you actually do. You win when you decide to work out and you do. Celebrate and cheer for yourself when you make great choices then act on them.

4B. Wall

Sometimes, despite your best intentions, you hit the wall, you mess up, binge eat, skip eating, overindulge, splurge—it happens. When you hit the proverbial wall while trying to eat better, dust yourself off, regroup, and recommit to putting smart food in your mouth the next time you eat.

You hit the wall when you don't eat all day because you're working so hard that you forget to eat. You hit the wall when you have three cups of coffee, a latte, and a diet soft drink all on the same day. You hit the wall when you hit a plateau in your weight loss and nothing seems to be changing, so you eat the junk you have successfully avoided for two months. When you hit the wall of frustration, I want to suggest another alternative to slumping to the ground and giving up. *Find a window in the wall!* Get up, determine what has worked and what hasn't worked so far in your intention to be healthier, and find another way through to the other side.

Hitting My Own Wall

I, quite honestly, didn't pay a whole lot of attention to my diet until my twenties. Before I was twenty-six, I ate almost anything I liked. And the foods I liked—I ate a lot of. I do, however, remember when I started wondering if what I ate did make a difference. I had begun teaching exercise classes and was amazed as I watched my manager (and mentor) run circles around me, despite being fourteen years older. She pointed out the huge holes in my diet and encouraged me to eat for performance and energy. It was at that point I began to monitor and alter my eating. I started to tune into my own eating habits. The first thing I looked at was the glaringly obvious saboteurs of good health. For instance, the Cheetos on the couch while watching the taped soap of the day needed to stop. Then the Sara Lee Almond Butter Ring coffee cake that was polished off each Sunday morning by Jack and me had to be replaced. I began using real roughage for salads. (Going from iceberg to romaine, endive, and spinach was, as Jack said, like eating the grass clippings, so I mixed iceberg in with it.) Next I looked at the menus at restaurants with more educated eyes and used self-restraint.

Some people think I was born with a different set of taste buds and have always enjoyed whole grain oats for breakfast, wheat germ and endive for lunch, and tofu burgers for dinner. Let me describe my background and lifetime eating habits before we address yours.

My eating (diet) history is probably similar to many adults of my generation. I grew up eating mashed potatoes loaded with butter, white bread, meatloaf, hot dogs, bologna, salami, corn, peas, carrots, ice cream sandwiches, hamburgers, tuna casseroles on Fridays, grilled cheese, macaroni, ravioli, Spaghettios, pork chops, chicken, and fish sticks (I thought fish came out of the lake square and breaded.) These foods comprised 90 percent of my diet.

In college I worked for Poppin' Fresh Pies (now Bakers Square) and in a bakery, decorating cakes and icing donuts. Yes, I had sugar and fats to my heart's content. I look back now and am awed by the fact I survived that period without having an angioplasty.

When Jack and I married, my favorite Mexican food was a platter of nachos (for myself) or a chimichanga. My favorite fish was deep fried shrimp. My Chinese of choice was sweet and sour chicken, fried rice, and fried egg rolls. My favorite egg dish was cheese omelets, the more cheese, the better. Finally, my favorite Italian food was lasagna (second in heart attack possibilities only to Fettuccini Alfredo).

I was an adult before I ever tasted broccoli. Fresh fish was also a new adventure. As you may be able to tell by this brief description, the seeds of healthy eating were not planted from birth.

Willpower or Wantpower: It's Your Choice

I actually don't believe in willpower when it comes to making different choices. It's *wantpower* that causes you to choose or act differently. It's the importance of getting the head and the heart to connect on a goal. With willpower, it's just the head that's engaged. Lifetime dieters have more willpower than other human beings on this planet.

Sometimes you might have to say no to sugar, salt, and processed food so you can lower your blood pressure, reduce your triglycerides, or just because you know it's healthier for you. I'm a moderate. I'm not a purist. I believe most foods in moderation are great. You don't *have* to change your eating habits.

You *get* to. When you get to do something, it implies choice, intention, purpose, and empowerment versus *have* to, which implies restriction, surrender, deprivation. Consider how these two perspectives can change your energy and attitude about eating for your health and vitality.

People who don't give thought to their eating habits don't care enough about their health or are genuinely naïve to the impact food has on health and energy. Notice, I didn't say, "They don't care about their health." I've never met anyone, kids included, who, when asked about their health, haven't said, "Yes, it's important; yes, I value it." But I have met many who only give it lip service.

Six Tips for Developing Smarter Eating Habits

To make the *best* choice in the moment or over the course of a week, examine these six tips for being able to Choose wisely *after* you've completed the Think part of the model so you can Act upon your decision.

1. **Assess where you are in relationship to food and drinks.**

Consider what you would like to do differently. How would you feel and perform if you altered your eating habits? What is it that you would like—more energy, less fatigue, a leaner body, better sleeping patterns? Think about who you know who eats the way you think you would like to. Who could give you encouragement and good ideas? Make a follow-up list of people to call, web sites to visit, resources to read. When you read or hear something that sounds too good to be true—it probably is. Skip that information or product. Evaluate research that is quoted by how

135

many people were in the study, what university conducted the study (with accredited and known univer-
sities usually providing more accurate information).
Investigate who funded the study or research. Results
from a study funded by a company that benefits from
the outcome causes me to look for an additional study
that achieved the same results.

2. **Spend time in the awareness stage** *without*
making changes.

Begin raising your level of awareness around food
choices and alternative options you haven't exercised
yet. What do you notice about your energy when you
eat certain foods and after you drink certain drinks?
Listen to your head chatter—that voice that whispers,
"It's only *one* cookie, or one mocha or gooey snack."
Challenge your thinking. What message is that
thought giving you? Do you agree with the message?
If not, replace your self-talk with more positive, encourag-
ing, true messages. For instance, "Yes, it is one small
cookie, and it won't be worth the calories." "Yes, it is a
party, and I would rather not regret eating this kind of
snack. I choose not to nibble."

3. **Prepare to incorporate the changes into your**
busy life.

Write out a shopping list, especially for those items
you have not normally been buying such as broccoli,
romaine lettuce, green and yellow peppers, Boca
burgers (soy meat substitute), and bottled water. If
you routinely buy applesauce with sugar, you may
want to write down applesauce—natural or no sugar. Begin to look at labels for the number of grams
of sugar, fat, fiber, and protein in foods. Check out
the number of spoonfuls of sugar in packaged pre-

sweetened flavored oatmeal versus natural one-minute oatmeal. You'll be surprised. Even if you still choose to buy the highly sweetened foods, at least you're doing it intentionally and not falling victim to ignorance, low energy, or habit.

4. Develop a support system.

Classes, friends, and professionals can all make a difference in your success in choosing purposeful, healthful eating. Friends may help bring you to one level of positive change. Courses and classes can advance you further, and a registered wellness coach and dietitian can help you fly to success. Ask friends what cooking and nutrition classes they've taken. Open your eyes to the information all around you every day in magazines and newspapers—reading with a discerning eye, of course.

Who will support your better eating/drinking habits? Who will sabotage you (intentionally or unintentionally)? What boundaries will you need to set with the people who sabotage you?

5. Plan your choices. Plan your meals. Plan your snacks.

In our fast-food culture, healthy eating *only* happens through intentional choices, which means they have to be planned. Planning is more important than ever on some occasions like on vacations, during the kids' sports season, at the beginning of school when everyone's schedules are being jostled around, during holiday seasons, and when eating out. Gosh, it looks like planning is pretty important year 'round.

After working with Kim, a client, for a number of months on her health habits, she finally surrendered one session and said, "One thing has become very clear. Unless I take the time to plan my eating, it just won't change." Bingo!

6. Keep a Food Journal.

Yes, I am once again suggesting journaling. No other tool has been better for assessing and reflecting about eating habits than keeping a log of food choices. Many of my clients use my LifeWalk™ journal to keep track of their daily lifestyle choices. You can use any journal that allows you to write what you eat, when, and why you eat it. Jot down how you feel physically and emotionally when you eat and even an hour or two later if you remember. The pattern you notice may be helpful.

Keeping a food journal allows you to see the interconnectedness of your health-related choices. Deb, a former client, kept track of her lifestyle choices, which included eating, exercise, sleeping patterns, and relaxation. She noted that when she ate poorly, her workouts weren't as good. She also noticed her sleeping suffered at those points, as well. This awareness helped her to begin making small adjustments and new choices in every area of her life. She started with her food selections.

It's important to assess how well you fuel your body for energy and health. Your fuel is the foods and beverages you put into your incredible machine—your body. Start by doing nothing. You don't need to change anything, just notice (be aware of) how and why you make the choices you do. After noticing time (or period of raising your awareness), ask yourself what you would like to do differently. Decide if you are ready and willing to make those changes. Act on your choice.

The Importance of Small Decisions

Small choices do make a big difference. Dan, a participant in a seminar I was leading, shared this story with me about his one small choice that made a big difference for him. The previous year, I had led a leadership program that Dan had attended. As the seminar began, I asked, "What habits have you changed or added since our program last year that have made a difference?" Dan answered, "Well, you said to make small choices, the ones that we could reasonably make. So, I decided that I could reasonably turn down french fries with my lunches. I started ordering fruit or coleslaw with my food instead. In the last year, without really changing anything else, I lowered my cholesterol twenty-eight points and lost five pounds." One lunch at a time!

Walk

If you could do something that would only take ten minutes here and there in your day—ten minutes that would increase your energy, help you focus, clear your head, and release the tension in your head and neck muscles—would you carve out those ten minutes? Research has proven that walking ten minutes three times a day makes a big health difference. Doesn't ten minutes seem less daunting and more doable than an hour or even forty-five minutes? Ten minutes is better than none. Start walking.

Wake Up

Sleep is another area where small changes can make a huge difference. When you get busy, where do you find more time—from your sleep time? I had one client who continued carving out sleep time until she was getting up at 4:30 a.m. each morning to juggle her day. My first assignment for her was to force herself to stay in bed until 5:00 or 5:30 a.m., even if it meant giving up some workout time. She still marvels at what a difference this change has made in her patience and energy level. (So does her staff.) Figure out how to make more time for exercise. Go to bed earlier and wake up more refreshed.

Water

Drinking water is a good example of a small choice that makes a *big* difference. My friend and neighbor, Raleigh, is six foot seven inches, two hundred fifty pounds. He loved a certain green soda. Whenever I saw him he was drinking one, even on the treadmill at the health club. I lovingly reminded him that he might want to consider cutting down on the green stuff, but alas, he enjoyed it too much.

Raleigh felt lethargic and tired all the time, despite working out daily—and drinking twelve to fourteen cans every day for the boost! He knew better; however, he ignored his body's warning signs that something was amiss.

The picture changed when Raleigh developed a kidney stone and experienced the worst pain of his life. He was told to reduce or take soft drinks out of his diet and drink lots of water every day. Several weeks out of the hospital he told me, "I can't believe what a difference it makes. My skin is clearer, I have more energy, and I'm sleeping better than I think I ever have, plus I don't have constant heartburn."

Now Raleigh and I greet one another in our cars with a toast of our water bottles.

Drinking water is one of those little things that make a big difference in your energy and health. Do it *before* you experience a kidney stone or other health challenge.

One of my favorite skin and food stories comes from my sister who moved in with us for a while after college. We didn't have soft drinks at home, so she ended up drinking a lot of water. She was amazed at how her complexion cleared up.

A safe bet is to drink eight 8-ounce glasses of water a day. An easy way to keep track is to drink three 24-ounce bottles of water (or any of the other large containers of bottled water). Now, don't scream, but also keep in mind that for every dehydrated beverage you have like coffee or soft drinks, you need to replace it with one to two glasses of water. If that tip just sent you over to the "I quit" side, start small. Just try having the bottles or containers of water around and drink what you can. Anything more is better.

Every so often, I see articles or book reviews saying Americans don't need to drink as much water as is typically recommended, and I groan. The number of people who over-consume water would be so few and far between, I'll venture to say, "Just drink more water!" Besides, it makes more sense to fill your stomach with water than unhealthy snacks and foods.

Be aware of chemicals and dyes in foods.

When I see colored holiday bread, I no longer think, "Oh, how fun!" Instead, I think, "*Great, more color dyes in kids' stomachs.*" I realize I sound like the Grinch himself. If your kids rarely eat processed, dyed, or chemical-laden foods, some colored bread certainly isn't going to hurt. Enjoy it. On the other hand, think about whether that choice supports your positive eating choices. Rethink the use of chemicals and fake foods, like Olestra, Olean, and Aspartame. (Note: Splenda appears to be a safe sugar substitute. Use with moderation.) None of these additives have ultimately helped to reduce the weight of Americans. Many of these additives have, at the least, questionable, if not worse, dangerous side effects.

The Bottom Line

We have to eat. Foods will either fuel us to higher levels or drain us and leave us dragging. The choice is up to you. Assess your goals, needs, health and support systems to prevent hitting the proverbial wall. Evaluating these things will keep you from giving up when the going gets tough. Reflecting and strategizing this way will create more success, which helps you reach your highest potential. The benefits of this thoughtful effort include staying healthy and active and the potential of avoiding the medical system. This would be an important success, considering the fact that the medical system will likely be overwhelmed beyond capacity in a few short years. We still don't know how much of our weight gain is driven by genetics versus habits. However, you can take control of your day-to-day choices and benefit from greater energy, better health, and the pride of choosing well.

If you are willing to coach yourself on a consistent basis, you will Think before you Choose, you will Act, and then you will Win.

Serving Sizes: Smaller Than You Think

The American fast-food and restaurant culture has influenced the amounts of food we eat by altering our perspective of the quantities we should eat. Even nibbling on the kids' plates or switching from a small serving to medium or large makes a difference. Fifty extra calories a day can add up to five extra pounds in very little time.[4]

If you want to reduce your calories and eat less (therefore, lose weight simply by eating fewer calories), then you need to be able to recognize what healthy portion sizes are. It is also helpful to know how nutrition dense or healthy a food choice is when selecting a meal. The best resource I've seen on this comes from Dr. Howard Shapiro's book, *Picture Perfect Weight Loss.*[5] This book visually shows healthy portions and types of food to eat. Full-color images show the comparisons of calories from one plate of food to another, so you can clearly see your food options and the trade-offs you make with your selections.

A study published in the Journal of the American Dietetic Association shows that portion sizes of many popular restaurant and packaged foods have increased substantially during the past twenty years. Researchers from New York University compared portion sizes to federal standards and found that most marketplace portions exceed standard sizes by as much as eight times. The researchers also found that portion sizes of many foods and beverages nowadays are two to five times larger then when the item first became commercially available.[6] You and I need to check the actual serving size listed on the packaging of foods to not fall victim to under-assuming the calorie content and quantity of a serving.

While writing an article one day, I was sitting in a coffee shop. As I looked up, I noticed a table of three women having coffee and sharing some pound cake and strawberries. What struck me was that the woman who was talking was also absentmindedly eating the cake. She had a whole piece of pound cake piled high with strawberries and whipped cream, and I don't think she actually tasted any of it. What a shame to have the calories without the sense of pure enjoyment accompanying it.

TRAINING TIPS

- Adopt the attitude of eating healthy for a lifetime, but do it one day at a time. Anything else is too overwhelming.
- Eat for the right reasons in the right way.
- Small choices make a big difference; every bite you eat makes a difference.
- Consider whether you eat to fuel yourself or fix an emotional response to something.
- Moderation is the mantra.
- Recognize each pound of weight lost and every dietary adjustment made are personal successes. Only make adjustments you are willing to maintain.
- When you pass on a pastry or fried appetizer, instead of feeling deprived, be proud of the fact you chose not to eat it.

Weight control, as everything else in life, is about perspective.

- Proactively evaluate messages you received about food as a child and the messages and beliefs you would like to maintain as an adult.

- You get to eat healthfully in a culture that has a plethora of fresh food choices.

- Fresh fruits and vegetables are everyday foods, and are good sources of protein and fiber.

- *Fresh, live foods feed live people.* If fresh foods only stay good for a few days, why would you want to eat a food that can sit on a shelf for one to two years and not go out of date? Reduce or eliminate processed foods.

- You don't have to be a dietitian to eat well; however, you do need to learn how to discern healthy choices from self-sabotaging ones.

WORKINS ►

Write your reflections, insights, comments, and answers in your journal to the following questions:

1. More focused than a health history, an eating history reviews what food has meant to you and to your family over time. What is your eating history? What messages about food did you get or not receive?

2. Have you decided, as an adult, which messages make the most sense to you and fit with your health goals? If not, consider doing so now.

3. Think about what you've eaten so far today. Have they been everyday or sometimes foods? How would you like to eat differently the rest of today?

4. Up to now, what excuses have you given for weight gain or poor physical condition? In what way have you *not* taken personal responsibility when it comes to your eating?

5. What do you need to be intentional about as it relates to food? What do you need to get honest about in the area of food?

6. How often do you eat for physical versus psychological reasons? How often do you ask yourself what you're in the mood for instead of what your body needs?

7. What are your favorite comfort foods?

8. If you could change your food preferences, what would you change them to? Are you willing to fight to do that?

9. Do you plan your meals? What helps you plan your meals? (What strategies, tools, kitchen appliances, web sites help you?)

10. Do you plan your snacks? Are you willing to? (Strategic snacking requires your time and thought.)

11. What eating habits are you teaching your family?

12. What are three changes could you make in your diet today that would improve your energy?

13. What tactics do you use to stop, reflect, and choose more wisely? Will you strive to remember the Think, Choose, Act, Win model for eating decisions?

14. How would your life improve if you had more energy? Do you believe your eating habits influence your energy level?

15. Are you willing to recommit yourself each morning to the importance of each food/beverage choice all day?

16. Do you sit down when you eat? Do you taste your food? In other words, how often do you eat in a distracted manner?

17. Who sabotages your healthy eating goals?

18. What family food rituals do you share at home? Which do you want to develop?

19. What habits do you want to teach your children so they do not struggle with food choices when they are adults?

20. How much caffeine do you eat (chocolate) and drink each day?

21. How much do you/your family spend eating out per week?

1. Plan your meals, snacks, and be aware of nibbling so you are eating intentionally and not accidentally. Begin today—no matter what day of the week it is.

2. Eat sometimes foods sometimes and in moderate amounts (so you don't feel deprived). Buy the mini size portions of foods. (I love Halloween time; the candy comes in my favorite sizes.)

3. Eat slowly. Enjoy what you're eating; taste it, savor it.

4. Use time warp to your advantage. Go out ten minutes in your mind and look back on this moment—ask yourself, "Will this be worth it in ten minutes?" In other words, make a conscious choice.

5. Journal; it will raise your awareness of choices.

6. Order your groceries online. It stops impulse buying, saving time and money.

7. Buy bottled water and put it where you will easily reach for it in your office, car, or home.

8. Shop the periphery of the food store, buying foods in the aisles only when necessary. Buy 80 percent of your food from the fresh food departments on the outside of the aisles and 20 percent from the processed food sections.

9. Read labels. For every four grams of sugar or simple carbohydrates you get one teaspoon of sugar. In most fruit-flavored yogurts, you get six to eight teaspoons in a small container. Is that a worthwhile way to spend your calories and get your nutrition? It's up to you. What food/drink ingredients surprised you this week?

Aside from internal motivation, you need information to make a choice. Get the information you need to make an informed choice. Then make your choice. What information do you need to make better food choices?

Fitness: Privilege or Pain

For more than twenty years, health profession-als ranging from the U.S. Surgeon General to personal trainers serving clients throughout the country have raised the call to get Americans more active. The results are discouraging. More than 60 percent of adults do not achieve the recommend-ed amount of regular physical activity. In fact, 25 percent of all adults are not active at all. Inactivity increases with age and is more common among women than men and among those with lower in-come and less education than among those with higher income or education.[1]

With obesity rates climbing steadily, it's critical to get the message out to people—you don't have to exer-cise to be healthy. You need to be physically active. You need to move! That's not just semantics. Physical activity *includes* walking, biking, swimming, *and* gar-dening, doing laundry, washing the car by hand, shop-ping, and more.

People are also missing, misunderstanding, or ignoring other important messages about exercise. As you become proficient at self-coaching, you will want to pay attention to some of the messages shared in this chapter. A wellness vision is essential. Do what you enjoy, and take it slowly. You can begin at any age. Awareness and good intentions are not enough—execution is the solution. Understand what fitness means and how it is achieved. Become informed about what fitness means for you and your family. A marathoner may not actually be fit. Surprised? In this chapter you'll find out why this is true.

Wellness visions were discussed in chapter two, but I will revisit some of the concepts here as I begin to discuss exercise and active-living principles and habits.

A wellness vision is developed out of your life vision, much as a marketing or sales department's vision is developed based upon the overriding corporate vision. Exercise is a core element of most people's wellness vision. The reason is simple: exercise, or being physically active, makes a positive difference in every area of your life. You may already be convinced of this rationale.

Before moving into an action phase of exercise, stop, and consider what you want exercise to do for you. Most people don't exercise because they love exercise; they love the *results* of exercise. You can get desired results in a number of ways. You will need to look to find one that works for you. A smart place to begin is by creating a wellness vision. You learned how to do that in chapter two.

Navigating the Gap

You know it would be healthy, positive, and rewarding to exercise. The greatest challenge I've seen toward incorporating consistent exercise into a busy life is the problem of the gap. The gap is the greatest distance in the world, and it's about eighteen inches long. It's the gap between the head and the heart. It's the space that exists between "I know I *should* exercise" (in my head because it makes logical sense) and "I *want* to exercise" (the heart's desire). Until you can get your head and your heart to agree to agree, exercise does not become a consistent lifestyle behavior.

In a seminar I was giving at a software firm I asked, "What's the difference between commitment and conviction?" John raised his hand and said, "One's in the head, and the other's in the heart." That's it. When you make the commitment to exercise (or sleep more, eat more wisely, or take time for relaxation, friends, hobbies, etc.), you need to also develop the conviction that the time, hassle, and creativity required to incorporate it into your life is a must, a necessity, a critical part to personal and professional success. *At that point*, you have the ingredients for a head and heart connection that inspires, transforms, and energizes your efforts.

One member of my walking class said she was proud of herself for being so consistent coming into classes. I asked if coming regularly was a new habit. Her response was telling, "I've had a membership for two years. Last year I didn't come in at all. In January, I said to myself I'm just going to come in four days a week and exercise. It didn't matter how hard or how long—I was just going to show up. Basically, I made the decision and I've stuck with it." She made a decision and acted on it. There is a distinction between when you're playing with the idea of exercise and *deciding*, regardless of the challenge, you are going to work out.

A client once started our coaching call by saying, "Self-discipline is born out of desire. I strongly desire to have a better attitude about exercise." That comment was the springboard to connecting her attitude and her actions.

Exercise Motivation—The Multi-level Approach

Try this solution to finding ways to get motivated to stay active and healthy for the short term and long term; it's a **two-level motivational approach** to exercise. Each day or each time you are in the moment of choice (that would be the moment you decide whether you *will* or *will not* exercise today), ask yourself what your short- and long-term reasons would be to follow through on your exercise intention. I'll share some ideas to stimulate your thinking.

Choose one short-term and one long-term goal to start or stay moving on a day-to-day basis. What motivates you on Monday may not inspire you on Thursday.

SOME POSSIBLE SHORT-TERM REASONS:
- ❑ a shot of energy
- ❑ rid stress from the day (which brings *all* kinds of benefits)
- ❑ relieve arthritic stiffness
- ❑ boost your mood/self-esteem
- ❑ get a better night's sleep
- ❑ spend time with a friend or group of friends

- ❏ get your creative juices flowing
- ❏ help you focus more clearly
- ❏ relieve constipation
- ❏ avoid spending money over the lunch hour
- ❏ improve your quality of life—especially during perimenopause

YOUR LONG-TERM GOALS MAY BE TO:

- ❏ lose weight without losing muscle mass
- ❏ lower bad (LDL) cholesterol level
- ❏ increase good (HDL) cholesterol level
- ❏ improve functioning of your heart
- ❏ prevent the development of osteoporosis
- ❏ control your blood sugar levels (to avoid or minimize the complications of diabetes)
- ❏ reduce the need for certain medications
- ❏ avoid illness overall (exercise boosts your immune system)
- ❏ minimize or prevent life-draining diseases such as cancer, diabetes, and heart disease
- ❏ role model healthy lifestyle choices to children
- ❏ strengthen your respiratory system
- ❏ increase your quality of life as you age
- ❏ enhance your sports performance

Select your short- and long-term goals for staying healthy and start moving.

Put Exercise into Practice

The phone call came on a Saturday night. Becky, said, "Kate, I just want to thank you for kicking me in the butt. (Figuratively, of course.) I told you how I still had unpacking to do from my move and couldn't seem to find the time or energy to exercise. You said, 'Get moving anyway. The boxes will be there when you get back, and you'll probably have more energy to put everything away.'" Becky went on to describe how she thought about our conversation all day. That evening she went out for a walk, and the next day she worked out on a stationary bike and climbed the stair stepper. She said, "I feel so energized and good I had to call. I did get a lot of the unpacking done!"

Becky focused on her short-term goal of having more immediate energy. Her long-term goals were to maintain a healthy weight, avoid osteoporosis, and remain patient, loving, and creative in her job. The combination of remembering her short-term purpose and long-term goals made the difference.

Getting Started

Start at the beginning. Remember the Prochaska Model for Change in chapter two? Evaluate what stage of change you are in as it relates to exercise. While getting into action is the goal, staying with it is the bigger objective. So, begin by creating a foundation for a lifelong habit to develop. You'll work on your goal to create a new habit one *day at a time*. With a proactive, patient approach to change, it will not be an overwhelming proposition.

While I enjoy sweating and moving my body, I'll be honest—my favorite part of exercise is the part when I'm done. I love the feeling of being finished, knowing I've done something good for my body. I enjoy knowing I've followed through on a personal commitment (which is great for self-confidence and self-esteem). I've relieved my body of stress and tension and usually found the opportunity to connect with some friends.

At a conference where I presented, a participant came up to me to talk. She said, "I saw you present here five years ago. I was inspired to get active then and I have stayed active. However, today you mentioned that it's hard for you to exercise. Is that really true?" I was stunned. She was actually amazed I said that getting out to exercise was often a challenge for me, and frequently, still a mental game. I realized I always need to tell people that, *"Yes, it's hard to exercise."* Yes, it takes my energy, tenacity, and determination, and, oftentimes, a stubborn drive to be consistent with my exercise program. I've got a hectic schedule, too, three kids' schedules, a husband, a home, and a business that could keep me busy 24/7. And aside from all of that, I'm postmenopausal.

Historically speaking, most energy produced for calorie burning was muscle-generated effort involving manual labor. Our physical exertion came from the daily tasks of living. The end of the workday provided the first opportunity of the day to relax from physical labor. Today, the end of the day is the first chance many have to *get* active. While times have changed, our bodies haven't. We still need to use our muscles to maintain their strength and efficiency.

The large and small conveniences of modern life demand that an active lifestyle is a conscious choice. Performing a variety of activities during the day accumulates and creates overall good health. There is a difference between exercise and activity. Different guidelines determine what you do and how much you do based upon whether your goal is to be healthy or physically fit. Most people would benefit from being more active in general. Taking the stairs, gardening, parking farther away, etc. are simple examples of activity that are healthy for the body. The national goal is not to make everyone fit. The national goal is to get people active.

As a part of my follow-up from cancer treatment, I am involved in a study that requires me to wear a pedometer every few months to track the number of steps I take during my average week. I have been quite surprised at the results of measuring my activity level this way. I'd highly recommend it for everyone—active or inactive. If 10,000 steps is the recommended amount of movement we need per day, then tracking your steps this way is an easy way to monitor your activity level. You will find it very revealing.

Many people are confused about how much they have to do and what they need to do to be healthy and fit. The primary components of a smart and effective fitness program include cardiorespiratory work, muscle strengthening and conditioning, flexibility, and a healthy body composition. Understanding the four key components of a healthy exercise program described in the next section will enable you to make better decisions about what your daily schedule should include. The information will allow you to consider which behaviors you're willing to engage in. These concepts create the foundation for designing a safe and effective exercise program.

Before describing the components of a healthy exercise program, I will share the definitions and distinctions between physical activity, exercise, and physical fitness.

Physical activity is defined as bodily movement that is produced by the contraction of skeletal muscle and substantially increases energy expenditure. Translation: You use your body to get things done, from walking to and from the car, to lifting the groceries, to gardening in the backyard to making two runs to the laundry room instead of one.

Exercise is a subclass of physical activity, which is defined as planned, structured, and repetitive bodily movement done to improve or maintain one or more components of physical fitness. This movement is the type you typically associate with exercise.

Physical fitness is defined as a set of attributes that people have or achieve that relate to the ability to perform physical activity. The more physically fit you are, the healthier you typically become. Intentional, planned exercise is the best way to get fit. Physical activity is the greatest way to minimize the atrophy and inefficient functioning of your body systems and metabolism. In other words, at the very least, avoid living a sedentary lifestyle. Look for ways to make sure you are moving—even if you're not sweating.[2]

> **Note**: Medical experts recommend that if you are a male over forty-five years old or a woman over fifty-five years old, you get medical clearance and follow-up, including maximal exercise testing. You should undergo essential screening components in physical conditioning programs for adults, especially if you

are at increased risk of cardiovascular events. Being screened before beginning an exercise program is especially important if you have known cardiac, pulmonary, or metabolic disease. My suggestion would be that if even without some of the above issues, if you have a family history of cardiac problems, make sure you get a doctor's clearance to get active.

Components of Physical Fitness

Being fit overall includes four components: cardiorespiratory health, muscle development, flexibility, and body composition. The first three categories involve activities for making your body healthier and stronger. The last concept of body composition is a healthier, more accurate way to judge your weight and define your goals. Most often, the goal when designing an exercise program is to make it fun, interesting, challenging, and effective without increasing your risk of injury or frustration.

Two other aspects of physical well-being include improved stability and balance. Often overlooked, good torso strength and body awareness are important to avoid injuries from falls or from pulling muscles caused by lifting or turning inappropriately. Improved balance and strong bones are positive outcomes of regular exercise. Yet, unless Americans habits change, by 2020 one in two American's older than fifty years of age will be at risk for fractures from osteoporosis and low bone mass. A report, published in 2004 by the U.S. Surgeon General Richard H. Carmona, M.D., warned that ten million Americans over the age of fifty years have osteoporosis.[3]

Bone diseases can lead to a downward spiral in physical health and quality of life, including losing the ability to walk, stand up, or dress, and can lead to premature death.

Some of the other findings in this report state that "About twenty percent of senior citizens who suffer a hip fracture die within a year of fracture." The financial implications are enormous. The Baby Boomer generation is just beginning to hit their sixties and already the direct care costs for osteoporothic fractures are eighteen billion dollars a year. I know that the post chemo drug I am on now for five years is known to leech calcium from my bones, so I will be very diligent and intentional about maintaining a consistent exercise program that encourages bone strength, good balance, and eating habits that provide nutrients that support calcium absorption.[4]

Cardiorespiratory exercise improves your heart and lungs. Also known as aerobic exercise, it involves the use of the largest muscle groups in the body—the legs. Aerobic work also involves working vigorously enough to increase your heart rate for a period of twenty minutes or longer. Biking, swimming, walking, jogging, rollerblading, and cross-country skiing are all aerobic activities. While chasing toddlers may feel aerobic, you need to keep your heart rate up in your training zone for a minimum of twenty minutes to have it qualify as being aerobic. You may have heard of working in your target heart range. This is a measure of your heart rate that is often used as a fitness indicator at rest and during submaximal exercise. To improve your aerobic (the heart, lungs, and circulatory) system, it is recommended you exercise at 60-85 percent of your heart rate as calculated by the "Heart

Rate Reserve (HRR or Karvonen formula)" method. The intensity of exercise that provides enough of a stimulus to improve the aerobic system is monitored by the Training Heart Rate (THR) range. The threshold for improvement is towards the lower part of the range (60 percent) for older, sedentary populations and towards the upper part of the range (85 percent) for younger, active ones.[5]

CALCULATE TARGET HEART RATE ZONE

To perform aerobics effectively, you need to calculate your target heart rate zone. To do this, subtract your age from 220 to find out your maximum heart rate, so if a person is thirty years old then:

Maximum heart rate
220 - 30 = 190 beats per minute

Then multiply your maximum heart rate by 65 percent:

190 x 65 percent = 123.5 beats per minute

123 beats per minute will be the lower range of the zone.

Now work out your higher range by multiplying your maximum heart rate by 85 percent:

190 x 85 percent = 161.5 beats per minute

The example reveals a target heart rate of **123 - 161**. When exercising, the heart rate should be within your own range at all times. To burn more fat, you should exercise within the lower range. Exercising at the lower range enables the body to take up enough oxygen so the cells can utilize stored fat. If you work out within the higher range of the zone, you will burn more calories; however, most will be in the form of carbohydrates and less total fat.

You can check your heart rate while exercising by gently placing your index and middle finger on the inner part of the wrist. Now count how many beats in ten seconds, starting with zero and multiply the number by six. However, I recommend using an automatic heart rate monitor so you can concentrate more on exercising.[6]

Muscle development includes two components: muscle strength and muscle endurance.

1. Muscle strength involves the lifting of weights or resistant muscle work (the amount a muscle can lift with a single exertion is indicative of sheer strength).

2. Muscle endurance work requires muscle contractions to be held and repeatedly worked. Muscle strengthening activities can be for specific body parts (calisthenics, push-ups, abdominal curls, tricep dips) or general strength building (walking, housework, gardening).

Weight training is also referred to as resistance or strength training. This type of exercise uses the body's muscular system to move against an opposing force. This force can be created in various ways using machines, free weights, exercise balls, Dynabands, natural body weight, and even running. LifeWalking (the type of powerwalking I've developed and taught for more than twenty years) involves strength training because of the isometric muscle contractions involved in the movements.

Flexibility involves the stretching and strengthening of muscles and areas surrounding joints. It includes muscles from neck, shoulders, back, chest, arms, hips, legs, shins, and ankles. Growing stronger but less flexible is a normal part of the growth process; remaining flexible requires effort. Activities that help increase flexibility include yoga, karate, ballet dancing, and Pilates.

F.I.T. Principles
—the Customized Approach to Fitness

Three principles of fitness are important to understand if you decide to move beyond being active to becoming fit. F.I.T. is the acronym that describes how to design a workout program. F = frequency, I = intensity, and T = time. How frequently should you be doing an activity, how intensely should you work, and how long should each session be? Another important question is: When should you increase your workload or go to the next level?

Let's answer these questions for each of the components of overall fitness.

FREQUENCY:

How often you exercise depends upon your goals and current level of health. Most basically healthy individuals would benefit by getting out and walking, swimming, or biking four to five times a week. You do not have to push yourself to sweat and/or gasp for air. That is a measure of intensity. The basic goal is to get you more active overall. Keep in mind that if you are over forty and have not exercised regularly, you would be wise to get a doctor's clearance. Better safe than sorry.

Cardiorespiratory fitness: The Center for Disease Control and Prevention (CDC), the American College of Sports Medicine (ACSM), and the U.S. Surgeon General have all recommended people accumulate at *least* thirty minutes of exercise on most days of the week. In 2002, the Institute of Medicine (IOM) recommended that people get a minimum of sixty minutes of moderate activity on most days of the week.[7, 8] Thirty minutes a day of accumulated movement is important for general health. To become more fit aerobically, it's best to exercise in your target heart range three to five days.

Muscle Strength and Endurance: Two to three days a week with a focus on specific muscle work is appropriate. Each strength-training day should be followed by a day of rest, giving the muscles time to rebuild and rest. You can strength train or do other activities that use opposing muscles or muscles that didn't get worked the day before.

Flexibility: Flexibility can be developed or maintained in two ways. One way is to incorporate it into your day, whether at your desk, in your car, or at home. You can even go online these days and find sites that feature desk exercises you can do on the spot. The other way is to participate in a class, a video program, or self-led stretch with the intention of focusing on flexibility. Stretching exercises should happen throughout the day and at the beginning or end of the day.

Every thirty minutes get up from your desk and move around. Do shoulder shrugs, pull your shoulders up to your ears and let them drop, roll your shoulders in a circular fashion, and stretch your arms above your head. Reach your arms behind your back and clasp your hands together. Feel the stretch across the front of your chest. Breathe evenly throughout.

INTENSITY:

The concept of intensity boils down to deciding how hard you want to push yourself. Some days you may decide to go for the gold, sweating and challenging yourself physically and mentally. Believe me, high-intensity exercise requires as much of your mind as it does your body. (Of course, low intensity exercise can too if you hate to exercise.)

Cardiorespiratory: Work within your target heart range or, better yet, work hard enough that you can't sing (because you need that extra air for breathing, not singing), yet not so hard you can't talk, either. Your perceived exertion is an accurate way to monitor your effort. (An exception is at the beginning of an exercise program when everything seems very hard.)

Muscle Strength and Endurance: Using weights, body bars, and resistance bands to work muscles requires more instruction and guidance. Rent videos/CDs, buy books, or work with a personal trainer to get set up on a program that's right for you. Slow controlled movements with proper body alignment are most important when using weights. Early in my fitness career, I hated having the mirror right in front of my face when teaching (or taking) a class. Today, I see the mirror as a partner in my workout because it allows me to correct my stance or movements when I see I'm out of alignment.

Flexibility: Hold stretches in their positions for thirty seconds each, if possible. Longer is better for allowing the muscle time to relax and stretch further without injury. Intensity is determined by your range of motion. Never push beyond what is uncomfortable. A little ache is okay; pain is an indicator to stop.

TIME:

How long you exercise depends, too, on your goals. Duration of the activity is another word frequently used when talking about the time involved with exercise.

Cardiorespiratory: Twenty to thirty minutes each session is a healthy time frame to start with getting active. You need seven to ten minutes for the warm up and cool down, and the work happens in the twenty or more minutes you are in your target heart range. When you are first starting to exercise, ten-minute increments of effort count. You can start slowly for short periods of time. Focus on what you *will* do, not on what you think you *should* do. If you know you'll walk for ten minutes, walk for ten minutes. If you think you should walk for forty, yet don't actually believe you can do it, you'll skip the whole walk. The key idea to keep in mind is to just get started.

My preferred amount of time to exercise is frequently different from the allotted time in the day. Like you, I work with the time I have. Some exercise is better than none.

Muscle Strength and Endurance: You can address muscle strength and endurance as they relate to time in two ways. One way describes the speed of movement, the other how long you should lift during your exercise time. This portion of the chapter is about how long versus how fast, although I'll comment on both.

For most people, you will see results if you lift weights two to three times a week for twenty to forty-five minutes each time. You will simply alternate the muscle groups that you work. Time takes on a different twist when you talk about muscle strength versus endurance. When you are working on muscle strength, you take the time you need to find your movement. Therefore, the time involved is much longer because the execution of moves is slow and methodical.

Endurance moves can be quicker, but should not be sloppy. You will usually do more repetitions of moves at a quicker pace with a lighter weight when you are working on your muscle endurance. For instance, you may work your shoulder muscles with lighter weights at a slightly quicker pace, therefore, the time involved will be shortened compared to the slow, purposeful moves of a bench press done with a heavy bar and weights.

You can even adjust muscle work without weights. For instance, doing push-ups to a very slow count works the muscles differently than doing them to a quick pace. Neither way is right or wrong. Each way accomplishes different goals for you. (If at this point, you're overwhelmed, please know that personal trainers are expertly trained to work with you on topics such as these.)

Flexibility: Again, speed of movement versus how long you should stretch are two aspects of time in relation to stretching. It is safe to say any amount of time spent stretching every day is a good thing. Generally, the more time spent, the better. Fifteen minutes is a fair amount of time to stretch. You will find the favorite amount of time that instructors like to teach a stretch class, as in yoga or Pilates classes, is sixty to ninety minutes. This is partly true because the slower you execute your stretches, the better. Since most people do not see the warm-up and cool-down stretch times as important to their workouts, any and all stretching you can add to your life, the better.

When should you progress to the next level of frequency, intensity, or duration? When you can execute moves without undue fatigue, and maintain proper body alignment, which indicates your body is safely ready for more of a challenge. You will recognize your readiness to change your exercise routine when you feel inspired to strive for more results or when you select a new goal to pursue.[9]

Body Composition

Earlier, I referred to the concept of body composition as being a better measure for weight than a scale. Body composition refers to how much of your weight is fat and how much is muscle. The more muscle, the better for both health and attractiveness. Muscle takes up less space, so you can weigh more, yet look lighter than someone else who weighs less on a scale. More muscle means more fat-burning capacity. More muscle means less exertion and effort on the part of your joints. It also means that the muscles that were intended to do the work are doing their part.

The Number One Culprit Sabotaging Your Exercise Efforts

The number one culprit preventing you from exercising is not your weak muscles; it's your de-conditioned mind. Your attitude is the first thing you need to tackle if you're looking to get active in life. The question of the day is not, "Do I feel like exercising today?" The question is, "What will I do to be more active today?" This is where the beauty and magic of Nike's slogan shows its brilliance. "Just do it." Don't ask whether or not you feel like going (for your exercise time); just get off your duff and go. Ten minutes into your effort, you're allowed to ask if you feel like doing this. At that point, if you still don't want to be on that treadmill or out for that walk or stretching on the floor, stop. At least you got ten minutes in and that's better than nothing.

Ten, twenty, or forty minutes of exercise are well worth the ROI (return on investment) on guilt. Companies talk about a financial ROI for their invested dollars. You can look at your ROI on guilt versus invested time on exercise. When I exercise, I get the return of no guilt because I exercised for the day. Thirty to forty minutes of exercise gives you twenty-four to forty-eight hours of relief from guilt. What would that be worth to you?

If mental fitness is your challenge, let's look at how you can inspire yourself in the moment of movement (or not).

Mental Fitness To Boost Your Physical Fitness

These ten mental fitness techniques will help recharge your workouts and commitment to living healthier. While these tips typically fit when associated with exercise in its traditional sense, they can also inspire and guide you during all your daily activities and endeavors.

1. Overcome Distracting Thoughts.

With limited time to dedicate to your physical fitness, it's important to focus on the purpose of your workouts. Never discount the precious few moments you can devote to a workout. Say to yourself, "Okay, I only have forty-five minutes, twenty minutes, or ten minutes, I am going to completely give it to myself and concentrate on this effort."

Take note of your movements in the mirror (or the windows in the gym). Don't criticize; observe and improve. Inspiring music can promote greater effort and intensity. Although reading or watching the TV during a workout may be a welcome distraction on some days, evaluate the difference your favorite music makes in your workout.

If you read while you exercise, consider putting the book or paper down for one to two sessions this week and focus on your breathing, your effort, and your body's response to your work. You may be surprised how much more you can put into your workout when you are more focused. I had a client put down her book for two out of four of her weekly workouts. She did this for two weeks and was amazed at the difference in how she felt at the end of each workout. She hadn't realized how much more slowly she moved while reading. While multi-tasking is great, sometimes you may find it rewarding to focus on one activity at a time. Your workout may be one of those times.

Distracting thoughts often pull your attention away. Pull yourself back into focusing on your movement, rhythm, strength as many times as it takes. The first fifteen minutes are always the hardest to concentrate. Avoid running errands and checking off to-dos while you're exercising. Be fully present in the moment, whether on the equipment or in a class. After you have yourself invested and working, you can let your creative juices flow. Just remember to come back into the present moment often enough that you can monitor your alignment and effort level for an effective workout.

2. Examine How Your Body Feels.

While you bend, stretch, run, walk, swing, and move, pay close attention to any signals your body may be giving you. Ask yourself: How steady am I lifting this weight? How rhythmic is my breathing? Am I breathing? (Many people hold their breath, forgetting to breathe properly.) Do I feel stiff or loose? Am I more tired or energetic than usual? Adjust your workout accordingly.

Monitor your progress. You will discover results you might otherwise take for granted. Structured methods for doing this include a health club's computer tracking system, working with a personal trainer, or your own journaling. Simple ways to evaluate change are to ask yourself questions. "Is this muscle stronger? Am I able to squeeze tighter? For longer? Can I do more reps with less fatigue? Stretch further? Relax deeper? Ride harder? Balance better?

3. Visualize Achievement.

Visualization allows you to see yourself doing a movement correctly or perfectly. Envision yourself stretching and reaching with full extension and perfect body alignment. If you work out at a club, look at yourself in the mirror, not the teacher. If you exercise at home, use a mirror to assess your moment. Visualize yourself picking up and lifting that heavier weight with confidence and strength.

Imagine fat and stress running off your body with your sweat. Imagine your heart pumping more blood, rushing it to your muscles to help you speed up and work stronger. Imagine your lungs taking in more oxygen and your blood system delivering it quickly to your muscles. Feel the power surge within you.

Your rehearsals and images should be objective, positive, and success oriented. You can create your own internal video and audiotapes. Take pride in your efforts.

4. Visualize For Motivation.

To stay motivated, try creating fantasies that focus on your activity. For example, you're playing in the Super Bowl, at Wimbledon, running the last mile of the Boston Marathon, or riding in the Ironman competition. Imagine you're swimming across the lake to your favorite getaway island. During the last three blocks of my exercise run, I visualize myself coming into the last quarter-mile of the Grandma's half marathon my husband and I run each year. I always think about how I want to finish that race, and I pick up the pace for that last few blocks. And I have been able to do that at each race in Duluth.

With every breath, imagine energy being drawn in and surging throughout your body. As you cool down, hold your stretches and image all tension leaving your body. Use the mirrors as your partner, not as a tool to criticize yourself. Very few people notice anyone in the room except themselves and the teacher. (Many are too concerned about how they look to even look around.)

Focus on your footsteps, a tree in the distance, your breathing, or your contracted muscles.

Don't compare your body, efforts, or fitness levels to anyone else's. *Compare you to you.* What progress have you made? Celebrate any improvements you've made.

5. Create Positive Self-Talk.

Negative thoughts can defeat your best efforts—listen in to what you say to yourself. Negative thinking drains energy and enthusiasm. It sabotages your commitment level. Thoughts that hinder your performance include, "I can't do this," "I'm too fat," "I'm too out of shape," "I'm too old, too young, too... (fill in your own limiting thought)," "I'm so slow," "I've tried this before, and it never worked," "I've never tried this before, and I'm too intimidated," "Who am I trying to kid anyway?" "I don't want to look stupid."

Quiet your brain's negative chattering! Instead say, "I can, I am, I will. I can do this one step/day at a time. I am stronger. I will stick with this program. I have the power to choose."

6. Encourage an Attitude of Relaxed Awareness.

You can initiate a meditative state clearing your mind of distracting thoughts, yet remain aware of what your body is doing. Creative energy is freed up during repetitive movement because the critical, analytical left side of the brain gets bored quickly and, metaphorically speaking, checks out. When that happens, the creative right side of the brain can play without restriction. Many people report coming up with all kinds of creative solutions and ideas during this kind of workout. (Running, biking, group cycling, treadmill walking or running, Body Trek, Body Peak, and Nordic Track exercises are examples of repetitive movement.)

7. Get Moving.

When you become more active, remember what your goal is. It's probably to improve the general quality of your life and health. You want to live with more energy, a peaceful spirit, and less stress, disease, and guilt. It really doesn't take much exercise to feel a difference in yourself. Develop the mental self-talk that celebrates *any* effort you exert. If you park farther from the office and walk, don't mumble about how "...feeble that walk was. I should be walking a couple of miles, not a couple blocks." Acknowledge any extra activity you incorporate into your day—including getting out of your chair to turn the TV channel versus using the remote.

Avoid the temptation to use your children as "gofers," getting things around the house or doing chores. You can bring the groceries in or put the boxes of fall or summer clothes in the basement. *You* do it. That's physical activity. Older people often are sabotaged by others' best intentions to help them out when they are denied the opportunity to lift, move, or carry things they could, and should, for their own well-being. Moving freely and with strength is a gift, a blessing.

8. Some Exercise Is Better than None.

So often people say to themselves, "I only have twenty minutes; that really isn't enough time to make a difference." If you believe that, I challenge you to a twenty-minute ab workout. Or, try twenty minutes of stretching. How about twenty minutes of walking the stairs in your home or office? Every bit of activity counts. Challenge the self-talk that says small or short doesn't count. It does. Any activity time adds up, and it does make a positive difference. Your small steps *will* make a *big* difference.

9. Visualize Yourself Already There.

Can you picture the joy and vitality you will have if you become more active and energetic? Can you imagine having enough energy into the evenings to actively participate in activities outside of work or for your evening clients? Envision success with all of your senses. How will you walk, talk, dress, and live differently with more energy and vitality after you have made exercise or regular physical activity a natural part of your life?

What is your motivation for getting active? The best reason (and longest-lasting motivation) is because you love yourself and respect your body and your health. All the reasons in the world will not motivate you to exercise unless they are personally significant to you. Exercise is a great deal; its cost is low when you consider its high rate of return. Just ask anyone who has lost his or her health for any period of time.

10. Not Fun, Not Done.

The saying used to be "no pain, no gain." Today it's "not fun, not done." Exercise doesn't have to be drudgery to be effective. Start an activity you enjoy, and you'll be more likely to stick with it. Also, ask yourself what it is about an activity that you don't like. There may be an easy solution to make it more enjoyable. One client decided walking wasn't really all that boring once he began listening to motivational tapes and radio channels he liked.

Choose activities you like, not those you *wish you liked*. You will stick with your program for longer with more energy. Appreciate not only the physical benefits derived but the mental benefit as well. The mental benefits alone are worth the physical effort.

You can overcome the challenges to exercise. Your mental attitude opens the door to unlimited fitness possibilities in your flexibility, strength, and endurance. Stay committed and use these mental exercises to keep you on track. Physical fitness is a gift and privilege. Realize your full potential both mentally and physically.

A Word on Genetics and Family History

Statistics from medical professionals and gerontologists have said that fully 75-80 percent of our aging is dependent upon our lifestyle choices. You are not doomed by your parents' genes and family history. Yes, you may be predisposed to certain conditions. However, I believe in the OSO concept of disease prevention. You have the ability and opportunity to impact the possible **O**nset, **S**everity, and **O**utcome of diseases or conditions you may be predisposed to experience.

Sixteen weeks after I had my second son, Jamie, I went in for the recommended blood chemistry workup. The doctor called with the results. You probably recognize that it's not good when the doctor calls with your test numbers. He said my cholesterol levels were strikingly high. Knowing my health habits, he said he'd like me to contact my parents and ask them what their cholesterol numbers were. He wanted to determine if my numbers reflected a genetic disposition to high numbers.

Sure enough, my dad's numbers were "something over 300." My dad has a slight build and would never appear to have a clogged heart. Apparently, I have a predisposition to higher cholesterol numbers. I was so grateful I had been eating wisely and exercising up to that point because I believe it kept me from starting on medications that I would need to take for a lifetime. (As a side note, my dad chose not to change his eating or exercising habits and seven years later had a triple bypass. He's still alive and doing well.)

Another genetic influence in our family is a predisposition to alcoholism. Because we've been aware of the increased likelihood that at least one of us would be susceptible to the disease, each of my siblings and I have been cognizant of the signs and symptoms of a potential problem. This awareness led my brother into sobriety and a different life as a young adult. Thankfully, because he was proactive, his body and his life have now been saved from the ravages of a devastating illness. And we have been spared the fear, pain, and disappointment that haunt other family members.

We also have had cancer and heart disease shorten and impact our lives. My paternal grandfather had multiple heart attacks, one of which killed him. My maternal grandmother had a brain tumor. My spunky aunt and godmother died of breast cancer at the young age of forty-five. Jack's paternal grandmother died a brittle diabetic. His uncle died of a heart attack in his fifties. His mother passed away due to complications of her multiple sclerosis in her late fifties.

"God heals, and the doctor takes the fee."
Benjamin Franklin

It's true that you and I can choose to make healthy lifestyle choices, specifically exercise, and still have a devastating disease impact us. However, its onset will likely be delayed. Its impact and severity will be positively impacted by having a healthy body weight and strong immune system, and the outcome will likely be better because you have already developed helpful habits that support your recovery or changed life. The mentor of a friend of mine developed prostate cancer. Doctors actually believe he has a better-than-average chance for recovery because he practiced preventive medicine by staying physically healthy and discovering the cancer early. Regardless of the amount of time Steve may have, his quality of life *now* is better than it ever would have been had he not been faithful in his exercise and nutrition habits.

Once you determine that making the time for exercise is of value, you need to next examine your self-talk. Think of the Think, Choose, Act, Win model. In the Think phase, you are examining why it's important to make time to exercise. You figure out how you can best prepare to get going and maintain your new habits. You decide upon the self-talk that will encourage, motivate, and inspire you. You then choose where to start. The critical step comes next in your action.

Remember it's one thing to choose to exercise, and it's another thing to do it. For example, if you realize you haven't exercised in two days (and you have a goal of four days a week of workouts), you need to think about that. If you find yourself saying, "I haven't exercised in two days already. If I don't go today, I'll blow if for the week because I'm so booked tomorrow. Oh, man, I've got to get ready for the meeting tomorrow. I can't take any time today. *Stop*. If I don't exercise today, I'm going to feel guilty, sluggish, irritated, and disappointed in myself—again. That's just not worth it. I will call Peg and ask if she can meet me at lunch for a forty-minute walk. I need to take a break in the day anyway to clear my head and refocus. Visiting with her will be fun. Besides, I'll take care of two things at once—social time and exercise. I'll pack some fruit and eat that when we're done. Better put a water bottle in my briefcase/workout bag too."

Can you see how thinking it through makes all the difference? Did you recognize the plan of action laid out and the dismissing of excuses that supported the ultimate goal? Did you hear the creativity and flexibility in that self-talk conversation? Did you see that in the end you win with this type of reflection and action?

Taking a Step Back

Systems are used to give structure to a workout. They apply the best possible combination of repetitions, sets, rest, volume, and intensity to achieve the desired outcome if you are weight training. There are many different kinds of systems and a lot of them give similar results. If your goal is cardiorespiratory improvement, distance, speed, and variety are important factors to consider. Personal trainers are smart partners because they help you design the systems used in your workouts, taking into consideration your medical history, physical limitations, personal workout preferences, equipment availability, etc.

If you cannot or choose not to hire a personal trainer, then it is important to be familiar with the terms and concepts used in fitness training. I've given you a good overview here.

Exercise is a Privilege

Do you have a should list? These items would be behaviors, attitudes, actions that you should be doing. Think of something you recognize you should do.

What do you think of?

When I ask this question in seminars, the top two responses are, "I should exercise" and "I should eat better." Try this perspective, it's not that you should exercise, you *get to* exercise or be active. Being able to get up and be active in any way is a privilege. "Use it or lose it" takes on a whole new meaning when you relate it to your body's ability to move.

Ryan is one of my greatest heroes. He is the son of a dear friend. Ryan was born with a condition called spina bifida. Among his complications and challenges is the fact he is confined to a wheelchair. He always has been and always will be. He has a positive spirit that would melt your heart and inspire your feet to move.

He cannot get up and walk. *You get to walk.* He doesn't have that choice, but you do. What a privilege it is to walk, run, bike, swim, and stretch. Now I don't believe for a moment that guilt is a motivator. **Awareness is**. If you were more aware of the privilege of being able to exercise, would you do it more often and more regularly? I'd like to think you would. So, the next time you are deciding in the moment to not work out because you don't have time, consider again, what will happen if you don't make the time. You may lose the privilege.

As a nation of people, we are very fortunate to be able to take time to exercise or get active. In the US, Canada, and Europe, we have more health club opportunities, videos, CDs, books, and time. Yes, time! In many parts of the world, people still are making time for the bare essentials of life. You and I have the privilege of being able to take time to walk from our cars a bit farther away or exercise some-where with other people. How blessed we are.

A Final Note of Caution

I cannot close a chapter on the topic of fitness and neglect to address one of the biggest negative factors affecting people's workouts. If you have this mental tendency, you will sabotage your best efforts at getting and staying active. You will either injure yourself or give up your routine all together. What nemesis do I refer to? The habit of comparing your efforts or results to someone else's. The moment you look around to compare yourself to someone else, you will become frustrated or disappointed. Guaranteed. The reason is you unfairly compare yourself to others that are very different from yourself. It's similar to comparing apples and oranges—it's not a fair or accurate assess-ment. Look at those who put in more hours, money, or effort because their lives and/or motivators are dif-ferent from yours.

I have worked with women who are in fabulous shape. They look wonderful; they have enviable train-ing statistics, endurance, and performance. Some attri-bute their physical success to the fact they don't have children (some expressing great sadness over their inability to do so); others do not have jobs that prevent them from spending time in a gym. Some women use exercise as an escape from the difficult parts of their life. Others are simply wired for fitness; they've got good genes. Some natural born athletes have found joy in their physicality. And that's great. However, that may not be you. So, *their* programs don't matter.

What matters is whether you are honestly doing the most you can with the body God has given you. Are you striving to be the best you or the best somebody else? I encourage you to take the small steps you need to get healthier and stronger, given the parameters of your life—during this season of your life. Do that, and you can celebrate your efforts with a healthier body and smarter attitude.

TRAINING TIPS

- With obesity rates climbing steadily, it's critical to get the message out to people—you don't have to exercise to be healthy.

- Most people don't exercise because they love exercise; they love the *results* of exercise.

- Having a wellness vision enables you to be strategic in your approach to incorporating exercise consistently into your life.

- Any dream worth pursuing takes energy, tenacity, discipline, and fortitude. Without your health, having energy for tenacity and discipline is difficult, if not impossible.

- You *can* get and stay active, especially when your daily choices are tied to your wellness vision.

- Until you can get your head and your heart to agree to agree, exercise does not become a consistent lifestyle behavior.

- There is a distinction between when you're *playing* with the idea of exercise and *deciding*, regardless of the challenge, you are going to work out.

- Evaluate what stage of change you are in as it relates to exercise. While getting into action is the goal, staying with it is the bigger objective. So, begin by creating a foundation for a lifelong habit to develop.

- The large and small conveniences of modern life demand that an active lifestyle is a conscious choice.

- Being fit overall includes four components: cardiorespiratory health, muscle development, flexibility, and body composition.

- The number one culprit preventing you from exercising is not your weak muscles; it's your de-conditioned mind.

- Ten mental fitness techniques help recharge your workouts and commitment to living healthier.

- Your decision to exercise or not will play a greater long-term role in your life than genetics.

- Being able to get up and be active in any way is a privilege.

- Comparing yourself to others is the first step to defeat and failure.

Think about what you want exercise or increased physical activity to do for you. Be intentional; make time for reflection. Look at your schedule right now and decide when you will take twenty to thirty minutes to answer these questions in your journal.

1. Is health and wellness a part of your life vision? If not, you can skip the rest of these exercises and move on to the next chapter. If yes, start with creating your wellness vision described in chapter two. The following questions will help you fill in the blanks for these statements:

- the *outcomes* you want for your health,
- the *motivators* you have for pursuing healthy habits,
- the *obstacles* you intend to overcome,
- a *strategy* to overcome those obstacles.

2. What is true about your health?

These are some of the physical and emotional impacts of inactivity (check any that are true for you):

- fatigue,
- lack of focus,
- inability to relax (even when you want to),
- headaches,
- heartburn,
- back and neck pain,
- excessive weight (and the resulting physical and emotional baggage),
- general impatience, quick to anger.

3. Which of those short- and long-term benefits of exercise would I like to experience?

- What do you want to be different or true about your health six months from now? One year from now? Five years?
- How would your life benefit if you got active?
- Do you have the energy you want? If not, why not?
- Are you able to relax?
- Do you believe that being physically active will help you be more creative?
- Would you be more patient?
- Would you sleep better if you were more active?
- What habits (conscious or unconscious) have you developed that sabotage you or hold you back?
- Who do you associate with that holds you back?
- Who could you spend time with who would actually encourage you to be active?
- What small steps could you begin with today?
- What risk do you need to be willing to take?
- What outcomes, results, or benefits would be worth the price of making the time to exercise?

4. Get benchmark measurements

- Types of benchmarks: blood pressure, cholesterol/ratio, weight, and blood sugar numbers.

- Get regular check-ups, immunizations, screening tests (especially breast, prostate, and colon cancer).

5. Find out what it would take to get physically stronger or healthier given your health history and interests. Start by exploring university and government web sites on health. Read articles and newspaper reports to monitor what is happening in the health and wellness areas. Talk with others, asking what has helped them. Interview or hire professionals like personal trainers, dietitians, professional wellness coaches, chiropractors, massage therapists, etc.

6. Decide what small steps you're willing to commit to (consider the cost of *not* making the commitment six months, one year, or five years from now). Can you live the way you are today in a sustainable way five years from now?

7. Pursue the resources, tools, people you need to make exercise happen in your life. Who can you hire, consult, or partner up with to become successful at making exercise a regular part of your life—one day at a time. Get their phone numbers or e-mail addresses and contact them within the week.

 **WORKOUTS**

1. Call your doctor today and set up an appointment to get an exam; get a full blood workup so you can review your cholesterol levels, triglycerides (especially important for women), get your pap smears, mammograms, and other tests that would help you monitor and benchmark your health over time. Consider bone density testing, FSH hormonal testing, and thyroid tests.

2. Tell one or two other people what you are ready to do. Who will you tell?

   1._____

   2. _____

3. Read one article—no matter how long or short—a day on exercise or active living. (Set up your computer to quickly access a website that has good information for you each day.)

4. If joining a health club would be helpful for you, gather information on different clubs. Put a deadline for gathering the information on your calendar along with a second date for when you will make the decision. If talking with someone else about the decision is important, set up a time to talk between gathering and deciding. Schedule a deadline for information gathering. After that date, make a decision to join or not to join.

5. Look for second-hand exercise equipment at garage sales. Look in your phone book for new and used equipment stores in your area to get the best deals on the tools you'll need.

6. Buy a tape, CD, or video this week that will inspire you.

7. Start one step at a time: park farther away, take stairs, do your own fetching, stand up straight—you'll be surprised how much effort this takes.

8. Each morning or week, pick at least one short-term and one long-term benefit of getting active. Write them on a sticky note and place the note on your bathroom or rearview mirror.

9. Put a pedometer on your hip and begin recording your steps for two weeks. Use the information on how much you move/walk to improve your activity incrementally.

Seven

The Care and Feeding of Family and Friends

A s I write this chapter, my mom is visiting from out of town. I'm working to juggle ongoing responsibilities to clients, kids, and being with Mom. How I end up choosing what to do in the moment, frequently, boils down to putting my relationships first. Taking the time to create memories that count is a powerful motivator for me. Yes, that means much is left undone. On the other hand, I will not have regrets about how I should have gone to the pool with Mom and the boys or I should have taken advantage of her visit to do some extra shopping. When life and responsibilities press in on me, I ask the question, "What choice will lead to the fewest possible regrets?" I realize the more positive approach would be, "What do I want to do?" or "What would be more fun?" My personality is too intense, my style too results-oriented. So, what motivates me to shift gears most often is a preoccupation with creating positive memories because time passes too quickly.

> *"We are shaped and fashioned by what we love."*
> *Goethe*

During the editing of this book, I re-read the above paragraph and thought about my cancer. While I am, I hope, in remission—what if I had a more aggressive form of cancer? What if I had died? Wouldn't those memories have had more meaning than whatever else I may have checked off my to-do list? I'm delighted to be here to say yes!

It seems the older I get, the faster time goes. If it feels that way to you, I wonder if you're making different choices day-to-day because of the insight.

The preoccupation of achieving personal success and prominence in the world is one the greatest threats to the family. Am I getting my due? Am I shoving every possible outcome into each day? Am I proving myself above a shadow of a doubt? Understand I am not referring to working adults whose work is based strictly upon financial need. I'm referring to those people who are stressed, strained, and dissatisfied with life because of their own crazy scheduling choices. I'm referring to those people who are stuck in some area of their lives, yet are driven to distraction ignoring or minimizing their need to change.

Many working professionals' fear of not appearing focused, committed, and available in the workplace is a prominent driving force, especially for working mothers, despite their wanting to take better care of themselves. Organizations are attempting to get more done, with fewer people, in a shorter amount of time with less energizing downtime than ever before. The opportunity for connecting with others seems to have diminished—the desire has not. Robert Putnam, a Harvard political scientist, has suggested that the American people are becoming increasingly disconnected from friends, family, neighbors, and society.

His book, *Bowling Alone*, draws from data from several large-scale social surveys. Based upon his expansive research, he states, "Television, two-career families, suburban sprawl, generational changes in values—these and other changes in American society have meant that fewer and fewer of us find that the League of Women Voters, or the United Way, or the Shriners, or the monthly bridge club, or even a Sunday picnic with friends fit the way we have come to live. Our growing social-capital deficit threatens educational performance, safe neighborhoods, equitable tax collection, democratic responsiveness, everyday honesty, and even our health and happiness."[1]

I believe some of the impact this disconnect is having on our culture is reflected in the emotional and mental state of many in our nation. I suspect it is seen in divorce rates, teen suicide rates, depression, and sleep deprivation.

Making the Best Decisions for Your Family

How do you make the best decisions for yourself and your family while fulfilling your responsibilities to your clients, employer, or peers? Can you make good decisions for each one at the same time? It often feels like taking care of yourself requires forgoing something important at home or at work. A great place to start when striving to make a choice is to consider the legacy and memories you want to make. What legacy do you want to leave? What will be important for others to say about you after you've left—whether it's after this life, after a move to another state, after you've left a former employer, or left a committee? Who do you want to be remembered for as a person?

(This legacy is different from our cultural tendency to be remembered for what you accomplished.)

As you consider your legacy in these terms, recognize the memory you create in other people's minds happens throughout your life—not just when you die.

Consider how you want to be remembered by family and friends. I don't mean at the end of your life, but at the end of the day, at the end of each year. I had the unique and unexpected opportunity to learn of my legacy, up till now, when I was diagnosed with cancer. I also experienced the true joy of connecting with long-lost friends who took the time to call me. (Why do we wait until a crisis or death before we tell those we love their importance to us?)

How do you choose to live? Make it easy for others to think of you the way you want by adopting attitudes and behaviors that support your hoped-for legacy. Do you want others to remember you as:

- ❏ a great cook/chef
- ❏ unusually patient
- ❏ always on time
- ❏ a health nut
- ❏ relaxed
- ❏ fun-loving
- ❏ intelligent and curious about learning
- ❏ a wonderful musician
- ❏ someone who watched your kids' favorite shows with them
- ❏ an outdoorsman/woman
- ❏ inspiring

- ❑ authentic
- ❑ faith-filled
- ❑ diligent about solving problems (reflecting persistence and creativity)
- ❑ _____ (others of your own choosing)

The list could go on and on. The point is that all people want their family, friends, and peers to remember them a bit differently. If you aren't clear about what life message you want to leave with others, as with many other things, the message you leave will be someone else's—predicated upon their life perspective, fears, strengths, experiences, and choices.

The top five characteristics or qualities I want to be remembered for by my family and friends would be:

1. I loved God and wanted to reflect His love, tenderness, and spirit to everyone I dealt with every day. That I had an eternal view of life versus temporal.

2. I loved Jack (my husband) and treated him with respect, loyalty, and devotion.

3. The kids came next (after God and husband); they didn't rule the roost, yet made our home rich and warm. They were unique, special, deeply loved, and appreciated.

4. I served others, yet did not do so to the detriment of my health or emotional well-being.

5. I honored and cared from my body and health through personal discipline and wise choices.

Among my peers, clients, and associates, I want to be remembered as, or for:

1. I loved my work and enjoyed what I did.

2. I genuinely cared about individuals and was a great listener.

3. I remained curious and open to ongoing learning.

4. I served others with integrity, consideration, and honesty.

5. I was a wise steward of the financial rewards of my work.

How about you? What do you want your spouse, kids, family, or friends saying about you? What kind of memories are you creating about yourself, your values, your heart, and desires?

If clarifying your values and vision is important for living the life you feel called to, communicating those values and that vision with others is the next most important piece of the puzzle. Knowing what I want, yet being unable to communicate it, can prevent me from successfully living out my values and vision. (For the most part, we are not effective communicators as evidenced by the divorce rates and turnover in the workplace.)

The problem is most people don't really know what good communication looks, feels, and sounds like. Two sayings fit most appropriately here: "Mean what you say and say what you mean," and "You have two ears and one mouth for a reason." God has a set of natural laws designed for healthy human relationships just as He has for nature (e.g., thermodynamics, gravity, entropy). One of the truest and most natural laws of relationships is that we want to be heard—truly heard. That would mean at both a head and heart level. How well do you listen?

I'll never forget co-presenting at a convention where we asked the audience to participate in an exercise designed to heighten their awareness of listening with intent and focus. While participants were having their conversations, my co-facilitator signaled me. After working with just one of the audience members, she suggested I add an additional recap question to the program we had not used before. She shared that this person had looked up after her turn at the exercise with tears in her eyes and said, "I've just realized I don't think I have ever *really* been heard." The question we then asked the group was, "How many of you realize today you are not really heard in your lives?" Too many people raised their hands.

One of the most important and challenging skills of professional coaches is the ability to listen so intently and so deeply that their own agendas and desires are of no consequence to the conversation. This skill is important because for as long as you hold onto your agenda or your hoped-for response, you don't genuinely listen to the other person. You are either waiting to give your response or calculating it in your mind.

Learning to Listen

How do you genuinely listen? There is a significant difference between listening and hearing. Yet, we use the words interchangeably. In the simplest of terms, to hear is a physical response to stimuli. To listen, though, requires focus, intentional hearing, and the use of conscious or unconscious filters to process what the physical body is hearing. To listen involves the head (intellect) and the heart (beliefs). Listening takes hearing to a deeper level because it looks for what is said and what is not said and puts thoughts, impressions, and interpretation together.

During training sessions for health professionals on coaching for behavior change, we often say, "Listen until you don't exist." That statement means listen so deeply and in so focused a manner you stifle your own internal head chatter and silence your ego needs, opinions, and perspectives so you can better hear those of your client. That's true of listening to children. Most of us have an automatic response to behaviors or comments our kids make. For instance, when one of our boys was in a particularly challenging phase of life, I felt an automatic anger response to what I perceived to be excuses. I know I did not listen well when I was already reacting before I had gathered all of his thoughts and explanations. As I learned to listen better, an amazing thing happened. He unconsciously recognized my shift, and made shifts himself that allowed for less tension and overreacting—on both our parts.

Good communication requires that the listener clarifies they heard what the speaker intended. Yes, I heard the words, but did I get the message? For instance, "Hi, Mom, I'm sorry I'm so late. Katy's boyfriend was in an accident and she was really upset. I didn't want to leave her." If I simply *hear* the message, I note that she was late, and she had some excuse for it.

Bottom line, she was late, didn't call, and is in trouble with me. If I *listen*, I hear that she knows she was late and acknowledged the fact. I also assume (my perception and translation), that Katy was shaken up and didn't want to be left alone. Next thought (perception) is I'm so glad my daughter has a tender heart and did the right thing. My response would then be, "That was a considerate thing you did for her; however, you left me wondering where you were. You should have called. Please do so, whatever the reason, in the future." Boundaries set, expectations clarified, and fight avoided. Relationship left intact.

How well do you listen? Do you:

- ❑ focus on the person in front of you during a conversation?
- ❑ recognize your own ego needs and filters that may taint the message or your perception(s)?
- ❑ intentionally put aside your stuff for the moment?
- ❑ clarify what you are hearing—make sure you repeat back what you think you heard?
- ❑ purposefully listen for emotion beyond the facts?
- ❑ reflect back the emotion you believe the person is experiencing?
- ❑ give physical and auditory signs of listening? (Lean in toward the person, provide good eye contact, and briefly comment as you track with that person, such as, "Wow." "No kidding." "How scary.")

> ❑ remain aware of your language? (Get rid
>   of "Yes, but…" The word "but" negates
>   anything stated before it.)
> ❑ speak your truth lovingly? (Keep in mind
>   that it's just your truth.)

Nourishing Relationships

Relationships, like our bodies, need nourishment. Our
bodies benefit from vitamins, minerals, and supplements. For relationships, those nutrients look like
quality time, quantity of time, an un-preoccupied
mind, a relaxed spirit, and/or a non-judgmental filter.
Time spent together interacting—not just physically
in the same place—nourishes our relationships.

**Don't be afraid to structure your connection
time with your spouse.** As difficult as it is for others
to make time for friendships, it appears even more difficult to schedule time with partners. It's easy to see
why you have to set up dates with friends; they don't
live with you. It is less apparent that you need to set
dates with those you live with because you would
think you would automatically get time together. Surprising numbers of us do not make that time at home;
therefore, we miss deep connection and genuine fun.
Romance is an intentional wooing of another's heart
and mind.

Newsweek magazine had a cover story titled, "No
Sex, Please, We're Married. Are Stress, Kids and
Work Killing Romance?"[2] In it the author acknowl-
edges that passion ebbs and flows in the healthiest of
relationships. However, a surprising number of couples reported that they were not having sex as often

as they used to. Many fell within the numbers of what psychologists call sexless marriages.

The revealing take-away from this article is that far too many of us are not taking the time to romance one another. Yes, communication counts; yes, making time for dates counts, as does, having sex—even when you're not in the mood. You may be surprised how in the mood you get when you commit to intimacy in your marriage. Many people want to be in shape physically and recognize they need to exercise to get fit. Therefore, instead of asking themselves if they're in the mood to work out, they just do it. The same can be said of becoming sexually active or involved with your spouse. Don't ask if you *feel like* it; romance your partner anyway. You may be surprised by your spouse's receptivity to being romanced and the resulting connection you experience.

Nurturing your love relationship will require some planning. Any activity that requires time and energy requires some level of planning. When our kids were young, we hired the teenager next door to commit to Thursday nights and Saturday mornings to our family. She came faithfully for seven years. Jack and I then had the time for our dates. You may laugh, or choke, but what we always did was go work out together and then head out to dinner or coffee. Uninterrupted conversation time was all we needed. We were recharged and renewed—both physically and emotionally. I realize that may not excite you. Here's the great part; you *get to* figure out what will recharge and rejuvenate your relationship. If exercise doesn't do it, what will? Now, call the sitter and make your reservation.

Expectations and Marriage

Floods of books have recently come out addressing the need to tend to the passion and sexual side of marriage. Perhaps the problem is not marriage itself, but our expectations for our partners and ourselves. If we look to magazines and TV programming to define what marriage should look like, we're going to be in trouble. TV and magazines sensationalize most aspects of real life. Talking and laughing nurture relationships and romance. Shared values and goals help glue a man and woman together. Those things on their own are too boring. Too simple. So, our culture complicates our lives by heaping unrealistic expectations upon our psyche.

The truth seems to be that we are too tired, too overwhelmed, and too out of shape to handle the challenges of an intimate relationship. We need to be careful not to use the busyness of our lives to protect us from real intimacy. Real intimacy requires true vulnerability and honesty. These qualities require emotional energy. It's understandable to see how the distance happens. Yet, the best gift you give your children is a genuinely loving, secure, and real marriage relationship.

In years past, self-sacrifice to care for one's children, husband, and even community was not only expected, but also respected. Today, the most respected sacrifice focuses upon those who tend to further individual careers, image, body, or self-aspired-to goals and dreams. To sacrifice your current desires for a higher value really isn't honored the way it once was. While many changes in our cultural psyche can be considered positive, this change is not one of them. Why? Because it would appear that in our desire to not be taken advantage of, used, or left behind professionally, we have—as a culture—put personal goals above the good of the whole. One lament I hear often is how motherhood is not respected or recognized as an honorable profession. I am not suggesting that one or the other (motherhood or full-time career work) is better. What I am suggesting is that individual women and men need to decide what will work for their households. Somebody has to take the lead and have the energy and commitment to do so.

I know of no one who, when getting married, plans to divorce. Till death do us part really is the hope and intent. However, as so many have found, lifelong marriages are frequently not the case. So, where do we draw the line between striving for personal achievement and accomplishment and family responsibilities?

The answer is not simple, nor is it the same for every person reading this book. A number of factors play into the answer. Every woman needs to consider a number of factors before determining what will work for her and her family. Three aspects stand out for me. One is self-awareness, the other is energy, and the third is the resources and support you have available to you. The more aware you are of your ego needs, strengths, weaknesses, fears, energizers, and giftedness, the healthier the choices you will make when it comes to how you spend your time, energy, and money.

Energy is the second factor for deciding how much you can handle with or without children. Because another woman can pull off working full time, being in choir, exercising regularly, and serving on local committees, does not mean her successes set the standard for yours. Figuring out what works for *you* is a process. Try different approaches to juggling your life that will enable you to create your ideal life. Then patiently, persistently, and creatively pursue the attitudes and actions that support that dream.

The third consideration is the resources and support systems available. A woman with a supportive, informed, and flexible husband is far more likely to have simpler options or choices in how she designs her life and choices. A disconnected, absent, or distant spouse complicates one's choices. Single parents have the greatest challenge of all.

Keep in mind that people on the outside cannot *see* the cost personally to the very busy and apparently successful. Some people just have more natural energy. It's dangerous to assume you should be able to accomplish the same number of activities as those around you. My sister and I used to chuckle because when we would talk about our days on the phone, she would be fatigued just *hearing* what I was doing between 6:00 a.m. and noon and laughed about the fact I would have been bored to death if my schedule was as routine as hers. But, you know what? Those schedules fit our personalities and lives at the time.

Husbands and wives need to be able to share their most important values, needs, insecurities, and fears without fear of ridicule or indifference. By understanding your partner's insecurities, frustrations, and sensitivities, you can work together to fill in the gaps or provide extra support where needed. That solution does not mean allowing yourself to be stepped on or taken advantage of. It means that if one person has a greater need for quiet or organization in the home, the other person can intentionally look to provide those spaces of quiet or organization at home. Doing so may mean spending money on having someone outside the home help.

One of the most surprising intake sessions I had with a client was one in which the client came to coaching to work on being less stressed and fatigued. She wanted to figure out how to best lay out her goals for her kids and career—striving to make the best decisions given her current situation. After she shared her hopes and expectations, I asked a simple question. "Kendra, I know that you are married, too. Do you want to involve or include him in your life plan?" (Since I make no judgments about how or what a person should do, I avoided any assumptions and asked the question.) She suddenly sat back and exhaled loudly. A stunned look crossed her face and she said, "Oh my gosh. I hadn't even realized I was doing that. I have gotten so accustomed to managing it all, I didn't even think about Dave. I can't believe I did that. Of course, I want him to be a part of this! He is huge. I want us to be a team in this."

The surprising twist I just referred to was that while Kendra came to the session with a specific outcome and goal, she left with a new vision. Her vision to recreate her life with her husband, working as a team, in their changed season of life became a focus for her written vision. They now had two children and busier careers. Teamwork became her personal mantra.

If you've been running hard and juggling a great deal for a while now, one of the first things to do is stop and consider the path you're on and if it's the one you want to be on. Part of being successful in life is knowing you are on the right path, even if you go slow at times or take detours. Finding your way back to the path you are called to is a blessing. It may require a sabbatical. It may require quitting a job to sort through things. What you don't want is for it to require you becoming seriously ill, having a spouse walk out on you (or vice versa), or dealing with an adolescent who cries out to you for help through drugs, delinquency, or pregnancy. Be proactive. Don't wait and have circumstances cause you to need to be reactive.

Stress and Relationships

I think much of what we call stress is, more specifically, anxiety. Anxiety more clearly articulates the emotion elicited when our bodies and minds respond to life in a stressed way. Understanding how anxiety is a serious health and relationship drain is important to improving and strengthening every relationship in your life. Think about it. How do you act when you're stressed out? I doubt patient, helpful, compassionate, and creative come to mind. When you say you're feeling stressed out during a hectic day, you are really saying you have too many demands being placed on you. You're feeling anxious about whether you can cope with it all. You don't want to fail people at work or home. Sometimes, the frustration is knowing you have to choose who to disappoint this time.

Robert Gerzon, psychotherapist and author of *Finding Serenity in the Age of Anxiety*, describes anxiety in three different ways: natural, toxic, and sacred.[3]

Understanding these types of anxiety as he describes them may be helpful for you, especially as you strive to incorporate the Think, Choose, Act, Win model into your decision-making repertoire. Thinking about how you want to respond will enable you to avoid being a victim of your stress/anxiety. Most often, anxiety is triggered and fueled by fear—the fear of the unknown or worst-case scenario thinking. The more you can learn about, plan, or strategize about handling a challenge, the better.

Natural anxiety is a positive energy that warns you of actual danger and helps you take advantage of opportunities and achieve your goals. (Think fight-or-flight response.) Toxic anxiety is the kind we usually think of, which is negative, draining, and self-defeating. This kind of energy results in worry, insomnia, illnesses, and depression. Sacred anxiety encompasses the kind of anxiety we all experience as we look at what it is we are here for. When you ask yourself the questions, "Why am I here?" "What is my purpose?" and "What am I called to do with my life, my skills, and my gifts?" It is at this point you are addressing what is called sacred anxiety. It is about contemplating the meaning of life and death. That is a positive and appropriate anxiety because pursuing answers to these questions allows you to choose a life of meaning and fulfillment.[4]

When you take the time to figure out what kind of anxiety you are experiencing and consider what you can do in the moment about that anxiety, you begin to take charge of your stress—specifically, your anxiety. When you do that, you will respond better to those around you who need your time and attention. Instead of snapping because your fuse is short, your nerves are fried, or your resources are diminished, you can ask for what you need and engage with others in a more productive, effective way.

We enter our relationships with the positive memories and negative baggage of past relationships. Your awareness of how you deal with anxiety, insecurity, stress, and fear will either support or sabotage your most important relationships. Habitual ways of responding to people can surface without intentional monitoring of thoughts and behaviors.

Sarah e-mailed one morning and wrote, "More pain…and yes, more gain. Craig and I had our usual breakdown arguments at bedtime last night when the kids wouldn't go to bed. Only this time, as painful as it was, I swallowed my pride and offered to talk about it. We talked for over an hour! Each time we do that lately it is so painful at the time but it goes to a new level. A better level. I kept reminding myself about the goal I had set earlier yesterday and kept telling myself that it was worth the pain of admitting I needed to change too. Whew."

You and your spouse may have developed some negative communication habits or unrealistic expectations over time simply by not paying attention to what was happening, or because you simply haven't made a strong, fulfilling marriage a high priority. Marriage requires energy, patience, time, and flexibility—qualities rarely left over at the end of busy days. You need to *make* the time, *create* the energy, and honestly *pursue* the relationship to keep it alive.

Handling anxiety well improves every aspect of your life. When you handle your responsibilities, other people's expectations, and your schedule in a way that allows you to take of yourself, you respond more positively to other people. By itself, that allows for fewer fights, disagreements, and misunderstandings. Think of the last time the house was chaotic, you were running late, and a child made a simple request. Did you respond with patience and grace or did you unnecessarily snap at your son or daughter?

Friendships—One of Life's Healthiest Supplements

Spending time with friends is a wonderful remedy for anxiety. Cicera said, "Friendship makes prosperity brighter, it lightens adversity by sharing its gifts and anxieties."

When was the last time you had that spark of recognition—that unspoken knowledge that you had found a confidante, friend, and like-minded spirit? What did that look like and feel like? For me, it was the front cover picture of a young attorney and her four boys. I was speaking to a chamber of commerce group and wanted to get to know something about their group, so I requested recent newsletters. There she was on the front page—a young, professional woman juggling work and life with even more males in her home than mine. More testosterone than I had at home—a frightening thought. To this day, Amy helps me when my anxiety rises or my frustration hits a boiling point due to messy rooms and forgotten homework. She is also the friend I can be transparent with, laughing at my quirks and brainstorming about my dreams.

Girlfriend Power

A confidante is a critical support person to have in your network of resources. A confidante means having a best female friend who knows you and loves you anyway.

Do you have a confidante, a friend who knows you so well you don't have to explain much to have her understand you or your circumstances? You need this kind of person in your life.

This is my unsophisticated soul-mate friend check-list. Do you have a friend who meets these criteria?

- ❑ Can finish my sentences and keep up with me when I don't finish any of them.
- ❑ Understands my jokes and stories.
- ❑ Appreciates news in the context of my life—including all of the implications and nuances of a broken-down car or a hus-band out of town.
- ❑ Is comfortably entwined in the mundane details of my life.
- ❑ Three-minute recaps are enough to main-tain the connection.
- ❑ Gives and takes of herself over time; sometimes I do the listening, sometimes she does the listening.
- ❑ Lightens my load with an understanding smile or a hearty laugh.

Four Requirements and Four Reality Checks for Friendships

The phone rings at 7:00 a.m. on Thursday. On most mornings a call at this time would alarm me. Not today. Since it's 7:00 a.m. on Thursday, I know it's Laura, my best friend back in Illinois. It's time for a friendship shot.

After I moved out of state in 1991, Laura and I found that connecting seemed impossible with five kids between us and businesses and homes to run. Our solution was to set a consistent time to talk so we could count on an update each week. Some weeks our conversation lasts three minutes, other weeks it's thirty. Who would you like to stay up to date with? Are you willing to get creative about setting aside a time that works?

Do you have time now? No. Yet, you know there will never be enough time, so make it. Are you nurturing friendships these days? A few months ago, I heard a common theme when I talked to my clients. A surprising number of men and women mentioned they missed the fun, energy, encouragement, and insight they got from friends. Friends remind us of how to laugh and lighten up. Friends remind us how special we are. Friends provide hope and encouragement when we most need it. My cancer diagnosis was an opportunity for me to see this firsthand. The rich and vast network of friends that jumped at the chance to help me (a friend) was humbling and truly awe-inspiring. Each of these friends reminded me of when and where I had been there for them. I believe these friends blessed me ten-fold.

Who was your best friend in grade school? High school? During your twenties and thirties? I'd guess it didn't take you long to think of their names, and I'll bet you smiled when you thought of them. How many of these friends do you still connect with today?

Men are generally conditioned in such a way that they count on their wives to be their friends. Men greatly benefit from the bonding that comes from exploring similar issues with other men. This bonding often comes about when they make time for golf, hunting, or other activities.

While women generally recognize the need for girl time, they often do not make time for female-bonding activities. They struggle with giving themselves permission to step away from their families and careers. It is worth the effort to do so, though. As we get overly busy with work and family, the first thing we do is let go of friendships with other women. We push them right to the back burner. We think, "When I have a bit more time, I'll call." That's really a mistake. Women have a wonderful way of nurturing one another, listening with an antenna that picks up on emotions, as well as the facts. We need time together that is not spoiled by tight time frames and hurried thoughts. This reason is why I believe friendships are important to your health.

One of the best things I did to recuperate the summer following my chemo was to go away with my girlfriend Amy for a week. We went to a log cabin and did nothing but visit, read, sleep, and watch chick flicks. It rejuvenated my soul and my body.

Women Are Wired to Benefit from Friendships

In 2002, UCLA released a report on friendship among women that could be labeled nothing less than a landmark study. The study quickly acknowledged the benefits of friendship among women that included, but was not limited to, helping us through tumultuous times, filling the emotional gaps in our marriages, helping us remember who we really are, and affirming our special place in the world. They also discovered that friendships can also counteract the "kind of stomach-quivering stress most of us experience on a daily basis."[5]

Women respond to stress with a cascade of brain chemicals that causes us to make and maintain friendships with other women. This study turned five decades of stress research—most of it on men—upside down. Until this study was published, scientists generally believed that when people experience stress, they trigger a hormonal cascade that revs the body to either stand and fight or flee as fast as possible. It's an ancient survival mechanism left over from the time we were chased across the planet by saber-toothed tigers.

However, it seems that women have a larger behavioral repertoire than just fight or flights. (Oh surprise, surprise.) Dr. Laura Cousin Klein, Ph.D. described the results this way: "It seems that when the hormone oxytocin is released as part of the stress responses in a woman, it buffers the fight or flight response and encourages her to tend to children and gather with other women instead."[6] In other words, as Dr. Klein and her colleagues point out, women are wired to tend and befriend. Studies suggest that more oxytocin is released, which further counters stress and produces a calming effect. This calming response does not occur in men because testosterone—which men produce in high levels when they're under stress—seems to reduce the effects of oxytocin. Estrogen, Dr. Klein adds, seems to enhance it.

The UCLA research supports the multitude of studies that have found that social ties reduce our risk of disease by lowering blood pressure, heart rate, and cholesterol. Dr. Klein says, "There's no doubt friends are helping us live longer."[7] The famed Nurses' Health Study begun in 1948 has revealed a great deal of health information through the years marking numerous scientific milestones. One of the study outcomes found that the more friends women had, the less likely they were to develop physical impairments as they aged, and the more likely they were to lead a joyful life. In fact, the results were so significant that the researchers came to a startling conclusion: Not having close friends or confidantes was as detrimental to your health as smoking or carrying extra weight.

Friends can rejuvenate you, support you, challenge you, and love you. While friends can also disappoint you, frustrate you, forget you, embarrass you, and anger you, they can share your dreams and lighten your burden. Friends can teach you how to negotiate and express yourself in new ways. Perhaps, most importantly, friends can remind you to laugh.

The bottom line is that when you connect at a deeper level with friends (instant messaging and chat rooms don't count), you get filled at a heart level that fuels your spirit. A person with a filled heart and fueled spirit leads and connects in a more powerful way with others.

Here are four requirements of healthy, worthwhile friendships. These friendship requirements will be followed by three reality checks you can consider for yourself. For each point, I've included some solutions for improving your skill and attention to that area. I've also provided questions to move you to a new level of awareness and action.

Friendship Requirements

1. Friendship Requires Commitment.
Potential Problem

Because we have busy, full lives, we need to make a time commitment to connect with friends, whether they are casual or close friends. It would be impossible (and inappropriate) for me to suggest a specific amount of time because we are each so different in energy and temperament. You need to determine for yourself how much friendship time is enough. Keep in mind that different seasons of life afford varying amounts of time and opportunity to connect.

Solution

Determine what is an optimal, standard, and minimum amount of friendship time you will commit to key friends. Each friend cannot get the same amount of you every week, month or year, but you can set some goals. (Remember: What gets measured, gets done.) My Thursday morning call is my minimum acceptable quantity of time with my friend Laura. Our optimal goal is seeing each other a number of times throughout the year.

I only need to connect with other friends once a month. I have two friends with whom I get together to share a coffee or a smoothie every one to two months. We pick up where we left off the last time. The laughter, camaraderie, and warmth I experience with these friends refreshes me.

I Wonder

Who refreshes you?

When was the last time you were together?

And before that?

How much time would it take to connect just to check in? Would it be worth the time?

2. Friendships Require Honesty and Trust.

Potential Problem

Share your dreams, hopes, fears, challenges, and frustrations with someone. It can be the highest compliment you give. It can act as the glue that melds friends together. Too often we maintain masks that falsely proclaim, "Everything's great, fine, wonderful." Yet, the ramblings in our minds as we drive, try to fall asleep at night, or work during the day are filled with unspoken concerns. Friendships contribute to emotional health when they allow you to express what is turned inward. They enable you to sort thoughts and articulate the confusing situations and issues in life. Real friends provide an environment that allows you to let out the good, the bad, and the ugly. Sometimes solutions to situations emerge by expressing out loud the inner turmoil. Most often, expressing those jumbled, confused, or overwhelming thoughts helps crystallize a healthy perspective.

Solution

Be *honest* with those few friends whom you trust. Tell the truth. When you don't honestly share, even if your friends don't know what your truth is, they sense you are not being authentic. (Caution: Make sure you share honestly with someone who has earned your trust and respect. Someone who doesn't honor the sacredness of your conversations only causes stress and dissension.)

Be trustworthy. Gossip is a real friendship killer. Label gossip anything you like, but talking about others while they are not with you always sets you up for crossing the line. Here's your test. Would you say what you're saying, in the tone of voice you are saying it, if that person were present?

I Wonder

Do you hold back emotions or thoughts that might make you appear weak or powerless?

Do you qualify everything you say? If so, why do you do that?

Do you gossip? If yes, what do you get from it? How does that serve you or your friend?

Do you speak truth with love and kindness? Have you even thought about speaking with love and kindness?

3. Friendships Require Your Physical, Emotional, and Spiritual Presence.

Potential Problem

If you don't feel physically, emotionally, or spiritually grounded, you're going to have a tough time giving your energy, support, and true self to others.

Solution

Take better care of yourself physically (i.e., sleep, exercise, good nutrition), and you'll increase your physical capacity to have energy for friend time.

Take care of your emotional self. Your physical environment (e.g., messy, organized, clean, bright, dreary) impacts your emotional state. Ask for what you need and want. Others won't be able to read your mind or guess correctly.

Spending time with someone who is spiritually grounded is rejuvenating. Be that person for someone else by knowing what you believe, and then live your beliefs in a positive way.

I Wonder

What could you do today that would fuel your body well?

What would give you the energy to connect with a friend, if only for ten minutes?

What are you tolerating from those who drain you?

What do you need from a friend that you haven't asked for? Are you ready to ask?

What spiritual food have you digested today? Who fuels your spiritual self?

What friendship drains you more than energizes you? Are you ready and/or willing to let go of or greatly reduce your time with this person? If not, why not?

4. Friendships Require You to Actively Listen.

Potential Problem

The first step to being truly present is to actively listen and let everything else go. This kind of listening lets friends know they are important and worth your focus. (Few people get that today.) With some friends, you are naturally able to actively listen. The world and its cares vaporize as you connect. With others, you may need to work at it.

Solution

Listen without the need to respond in some brilliant way. Listen to what is being said (the words), and what emotions are being expressed (i.e., fear, joy, anxiety, faith, determination). Trust your gut to listen for what's not being said, yet is probably true or overlooked by your friend. ("She's saying she's angry, but I'll bet she's really hurt.") Ask if your friend would like your observations or thoughts. Share what you think with your friend's permission—she will be more open to your comments if you've asked for her permission to speak your mind. Consider how often you have offered your opinion or insights without checking to see if that is what your friend is looking for. Sometimes, she just may want to talk without your feedback. I used to think I was so brilliant that, of course, she wanted my comments. That was ignorance and arrogance on my part. I sure hope I don't do it as often today. (Note: I say "as often" because I still need to monitor myself.)

While recently doing a seminar, I asked the group to participate in a quick exercise using active listening skills. They were to simply listen to their partner for four minutes. They could neither interrupt, nor question, their partners. Their goal was to connect by listening to hear, see, and feel the person. While this exercise was short and simple, the request to not jump in, speak up, ask questions, or redirect the conversation was surprisingly difficult for people. It was a profound experience for many people. Some said they realized how little they actually listen—even to friends. More frightening was that they realized how *little they felt listened to.* They discovered how quickly they had to bite their tongues because of the tendency to interject their own thoughts and opinions—even when they weren't asked for. During the first year I coached, I think my tongue was perpetually swollen from biting it. My tendency to be the expert almost caused me to go mute from biting my tongue off.

I Wonder

Who has listened closely and fully to you today?

How did it feel to be heard? If you weren't heard, how did that leave you feeling?

Who have you actively listened to today?

If you recognize you listened well, did it take effort on your part to stay focused and present in the conversation? Did you find yourself doing a mental checklist of what you needed to do later in the day? Did you think of that call you need to make? What was for dinner?

I encourage you to take time to thoughtfully answer the "I Wonder" questions above and proactively make something happen. Make a call, write a letter, and set a date. Don't stop with good intentions; *act* on what you discover.

Some Reality Checks on Friendships

While the ideal world exists in our hopes, dreams, and fantasy lives, we exist in the real world. Three important realities impact your friendships. Let's briefly examine each one.

1. You Will Find That Your Friendships Are Not Perfectly Balanced.

It's important to understand the give-and-take of a friendship will shift over time. Like two kids on a teeter-totter, one person will be up and the other down. Sometimes both people will be even. When you evaluate a good diet, you don't want to take too narrow a snapshot of your eating habits to evaluate it. It is wise to look at your eating habits over the course of a week versus twenty-four hours. The same is true with friendships. Be aware of how balanced your friendship is over time. Look at how often you are giving and your friend is taking emotionally, physically, and spiritually and vice versa.

When my clients raise their level of awareness around this issue, many people recognize the reason some friendships feel draining, diminished, or futile is because the friend *has always been allowed to take.*

Solution

You'll probably know in your gut if a friend is capable of participating in an emotionally balanced give-and-take friendship. Some people are so self-absorbed or narrowly focused that they can never be a genuine friend. Friendships need boundaries set, just as work or family relationships need them. It may be that this friend has never realized he or she monopolizes every conversation. It's your responsibility either to make that insight known, give up the friendship, or suffer through it. It's your choice.

I Wonder

Do you feel like the parent or advisor in a particular friendship? Are you always fixing problems and leaving conversations feeling worse than when you started? If so, run, don't walk to a new friend. This person/relationship is a drainer. This friend is someone who most likely uses people to fuel his or her need for attention and drama. While showering and dressing in the locker room after a workout, one woman was commenting to another that she was so amazed. "Kathy is so negative," she said. "She never has anything positive to say. I can't believe I've never noticed that before." I happen to know Kathy. I also know that she has always been someone who finds the one cloud in a bright blue sky on any given day. Kathy hasn't changed. The woman speaking had a new, healthier filter on her vision; her relationship glasses had been cleaned.

2. You Can Outgrow Friends.

While I was recently sitting at the airport, a gentleman struck up a conversation with me. He asked if I was from the area, and I said I was not. He was disappointed because he was looking for advice on housing since he and his wife were moving to the area. The conversation led to a discussion about how he was actually looking forward to the move even though he had lived in his current town most of his life. He said that he and his wife had gone back to school for degrees in their forties. They noticed their friends seemed to resent their new schedules, new interests, and new insights about world issues. Many pastimes that used to amuse them lost their appeal, but their friends still enjoyed them. These differences made the relationships progressively more awkward. The truth was that the couple had outgrown their friends. As difficult as it was for them to think about leaving the friendships, staying in them was proving more painful than fulfilling.

Solution

Two situations occur regarding friendships for busy people. First, friendships continue for years without regard for ones current life. The result is a friendship which exists primarily due to history or convenience. Examples of this could be friendships begun during a past season of life in which you did not have children, yet now do. So, the connection points have changed, yet individuals hang on despite needing to reach out to others for new friendships to develop. Friendships that positively impact your life will likely be based upon having a similar lifestyle, interests, kids that are the same age, professional connections that may flux with time—or not. Your choice of friends is up to you, be intentional.

I Wonder

What friends have you outgrown? Try not to place judgments on friendships that have shifted. The friendship is now different. Consciously choose how much time and energy is appropriate for you to invest.

What friends may you be missing out on spending quality time with because you don't want to hurt someone's feelings?

Do you find yourself avoiding a particular person, yet feeling cornered into spending time together periodically? Who would you prefer to spend time with instead?

What could happen if you intentionally made time for fun friends?

3. You May Shed Season-of-Life Friendships.

Look back over the years. Do you remember with a fond smile some friendships that were terrific at the time, but would not work well today? It's not that these friends are not great people. Life has simply taken you down different paths. Along the way, people step into our lives for a season and move on. I think of a couple my husband and I spent hours, weekends, and vacations with. We had a wonderful friendship. Life choices separated our paths. We went on to have children, and they did not. They took jobs in other parts of the country. Their choices were neither good nor bad. Just different. Yet, our time and energy shifted and so did our friendships. I am a very loyal person. I want close friends to stay close forever. However, that is not how it works. Another familiar and true adage is, "Make new friends but keep the old; one is silver, the other is gold." This wonderful truism certainly relates to season-of-life friendships.

Solution

Give yourself permission to acknowledge that friendships can change and some relationships are better cut loose. Others are not. You can probably think of a few people who you count as close to you who know you and have shared your life. Take stock and consider how you can continue to connect even when life is busy. I send cards, e-mails, and trinkets that remind me of them. Added up over time, small visits, thoughts, and calls make a big difference.

I Wonder

What can you do today or this week to connect with someone and remind this person that he or she is special to you? Let your friend know how you are, what is going on, and find out what is going on in his or her life. It may take days or weeks to actually connect, but this action itself will help you feel proactive.

Make Healthy Friendships A Priority

Pay special attention to your physical health each day. Pay attention to your friendship health. Make the commitment today so you don't pay the cost tomorrow. Charles Caleb Colton put it beautifully, "True friendship is like sound health; the value of it is seldom known until it is lost."

My mom became a working mother when I was in eighth grade. We've talked about the challenges that it presented for all of us. In our conversations, she has shared a nugget I'd like to share with you as it relates to the choices she made about being a full-time working woman. This nugget relates to the years when I had moved out and my younger siblings were teens. She recognizes mistakes she made those twenty years ago. She would have chosen to have done some things differently. However, she keeps two thoughts in mind: She was doing the best she could, and she sees that her ongoing efforts to love, nurture, and support each of her children was enough to heal and make up for the gaps in her judgment. Love, openness, honesty, and a willingness to be vulnerable are blessings for healing any relationship. As we became adults, she intentionally attempted to shift from responding as Mom, to responding as a friend. She also said she prayed for us daily and put our care into God's loving hands. Some days that was all she felt she could do. That proved to be enough.

Thoughts to consider:

When thinking about your relationships, ask yourself this question:

Am I doing the best I can today to honor my values? If yes, then you can ask no more of yourself. If no, then get into gear and begin to take responsibility for the choices you recognize need to be different. Women are wired to tend and befriend. Appreciate and enjoy what that means to you. Act on your instincts and make time for family and friends. Given our culture and the accelerating pace of things, there will never be enough time. You must make it.

Rich With Relationships

Our connection to others is what makes us truly rich. This truth is reflected in the continued desire for most to be married as evidenced by the success of Internet dating services and the growth of speed dating gatherings followed by more weddings. We want to be loved uniquely and specially by someone who has committed himself or herself to us. The same is true of our relationships with children, grandchildren, friends, and co-workers. No one else can have the same relationship with him or her as you can.

Leaving a legacy is about far more than what is written in your obituary. A legacy is built one moment, one exchange, one conversation at a time. At the speed most of us live, it's critical to be intentional about the relationships we want to nourish. Look forward to how you want to be remembered and work backwards. What you do today will determine how you will be remembered tomorrow.

Perfecting your ability to listen deeply and stay in the moment will invigorate your relationships and cause people to love to be with you. Managing your anxiety will nourish you and those around you. There are certain requirements for friendships to work and specific reality checks you can take to guarantee healthy relationships with others. Having deep, honest, and rich relationships with your family and friends is as important—if not more so—than exercising and eating well for great health.

Attitudes to adopt and/or adapt

Adopting the following attitudes can help you experience more joy in your relationships:

- ❏ Enjoy today. Time goes too quickly to spend all of it in the past (in anger, bitterness, or regret) or the future (anxiety, worry, and fear).

- ❏ I can strive to create the kinds of memories that will reflect my heart's desires. Create memories—these are the heart mementos that stay with you as you move onto new and different seasons of life. They are the fertilizer that makes the next season rich and plentiful.

- ❏ Family: acknowledge, accept, forgive.

- ❏ Friends: reevaluate, recommit, release.

TRAINING TIPS

- ■ When you say you're feeling stressed out during a hectic day, you are really saying you have too many demands being placed on you.

- ■ When you handle your responsibilities, other people's expectations, and your schedule in a way that allows you to take care of yourself, you respond more positively to other people.

- ■ Marriage requires energy, patience, time, and flexibility—qualities rarely left over at the end of busy days. You need to *make* the time, *create* the energy, and honestly *pursue* the relationship to keep it alive.

- ■ Friends remind us how special we are. Friends provide hope and encouragement when we most need it.

- While women generally recognize the need for girl time, they often do not make time for female-bonding activities.

- Women respond to stress with a cascade of brain chemicals that causes them to make and maintain friendships with other women.

- Not having close friends or confidantes is as detrimental to your health as smoking or carrying extra weight.

- Too often we maintain masks that falsely proclaim, "Everything's great, fine, wonderful."

- Authentic friends provide an environment that allows you to let out the good, the bad, and the ugly. They help you laugh about life.

- Gossip is a real friendship killer. Label gossip anything you like, but talking about others while they are not with you always sets you up for crossing the line.

- Learn to listen without the need to respond in some brilliant way.

- It's important to understand the give-and-take of a friendship will shift over time.

- Be intentional about making meaningful memories. You don't know the time you have on earth, and you and those in your life will be *this* age only once.

- Submission, service, and sacrifice are positive, relationship-enhancing words. Our culture has made them out to be something to be avoided. Intentional people recognize the power and lasting impact service and sacrifice can make.

WORKINS ➤

Record your answers to the following questions in your journal.

1. What is missing in my relationship with my spouse, children, friends, or co-workers? What can I do to change that?

2. Is there a fear that has been driving my choices and determining where I spend my energy? (Fear of losing other people's approval if I don't maintain a career that is impressive, fear that I will be abandoned and will be unable to support myself and/or my children, fear that I need to prove my worth...)

3. Is the way I'm living today sustainable for the next five years? Twenty years?

4. Are my relationships going to grow and become stronger if I continue to work, live, and communicate the way I have been?

5. What boundaries have I set with those around me that help me maintain my health and role model healthy, smart living to my family and friends?

6. Who do I need to forgive in my life to open up the channels of genuine love and connection?

7. To create the legacy you truly desire requires

forethought followed by action.

Five things I want my family/children/friends to remember about me:

-
-
-
-
-

Five ways I want my clients/peers/associates to remember me:

-
-
-
-
-

What activities, purchases, or conversations have I had today or yesterday that reflect my desire to create the five memories (in each area) I wrote above? If I don't believe my list is convincing and compelling, I can make a new choice today. (Right now, what could you do when you put down this book that would strengthen your intended legacy?)

8. Complete the exercise "It's a Wonderful Life. Your 100th Birthday Celebration" article in appendix I.

9. How are you as a friend? Do I wait for my turn to speak, formulating my response before the person has completed their thought? If I do, I miss much of what they are really saying.

10. Do I have friends who help me be the most that I can be? Who brings me down or gets me caught up in negative behaviors or conversations?

11. List the cost and benefits of these negative friendships. Are there any "shoulds" fueling these relationships? (If your answer is yes, I'd be doubtful it's a *real* friendship. Sounds more like an obligation.)

◀ WORKOUTS

1. Line up a regular babysitter or make arrangements for kid swapping with a friend so that you can have even brief amounts of private time with your husband or wife. It is amazing how rejuvenating an uninterrupted two-hour dinner can be.

2. Answer the statement, "A true friend is _____ _____." Who is/are my true friend(s)?

3. Consider the questions: To how many people am I a true friend? What could I do starting today to be a better friend? Who will I start with? (Do you have a cell phone on you? Hint, hint.)

4. Call that friend you haven't connected with in a long while—TODAY.

Eight

When you think about faith, whether your own or other people's, what comes to mind? What beliefs, feelings, visions, and/or memories come up for you? When I ask that question, most people refer to their religious convictions, rituals, or doctrine.

Let's reflect further to consider on what faith is at its core. For me, it's believing in something or someone more than tangible evidence can prove in the traditional, scientific sense. Which is why the familiar saying, "It's a leap of faith," makes sense. At some point in your life, you reach the end of your energy, resources, creativity, and hope. At *that* point, where do you turn for answers? Who or what do you turn to for insight, wisdom, and confidence for provision and direction? Your beliefs have developed over time through experience, choice, and circumstances. Considering the question of what faith is leads to the next one: Why is faith important?

Why Is Faith Important?

Knowing what you believe in (or whom) is important because you make decisions and choices based upon your beliefs. *Your beliefs impact every choice you make every day of your life.* The conversation of faith can take many directions and have various implications. For instance, we could talk about how you have faith in gravity. Even though you've never seen gravity, you don't jump out of buildings. Why? Because you know, by having faith in gravity, what will happen. The same can be said of having faith in the strength of the chair you are sitting in right now. I doubt you tested its ability to hold you before you sat down.

Spiritual faith is the topic of this chapter. The intriguing questions to ask are: Have you taken the time, as an adult, to evaluate the beliefs you've brought from childhood? Do they fit your experiences as an adult? Most importantly, are you aware of how these beliefs impact the choices you make today?

As an adult, you need to thoughtfully assess your beliefs for their accuracy, authenticity, and congruence with whom you perceive yourself to be. Unless you take the time to reflect upon what you believe in and why, you will unconsciously live life being pulled by an invisible leash. I use the term invisible leash intentionally because if you are not aware of what you deeply believe—especially about your existence here on earth—then you will be unaware of the forces that drive you. That is a dangerous and draining thing.

When my oldest son was in eighth grade, he made a powerful observation. While commenting on his religion class he said, "I think kids grow up and just become whatever [faith] their parents were." "Why do you say that?" I asked. "Well, because when we talk about our differing beliefs and the stuff we do (the rituals of the various faiths), nobody knows *why* they do it. They just do it." His was an insightful and disturbing comment. If you don't own what you believe, your faith may not serve you when you need it most. And, you may not know why you do or don't do what you want to in life.

Having a strong faith foundation is the number one requirement for coping with stress. For many, the crisis of faith is the point at which individuals finally evaluate what they *really* believe and hold in their heart. The crisis of faith for most people comes during challenging and difficult days. Just when you need your faith foundation to mean the most, it may not be strong enough to provide direction and comfort. As with smart financial planning, you don't pay into a retirement fund once or twice or sporadically—you make small, consistent contributions that net a sizable return at your time of need. The same is true of your beliefs and your faith walk.

I believe God acts directly in our lives. The attempt to share faith values and perspectives is often interpreted to mean the judging or condemning of differing values. My goal is not to judge, condemn, or evangelize. My goal is to encourage you to reflect upon what you believe and how it impacts your life on a daily basis. I'm not referring to religion. I'm talking about faith and beliefs, an important distinction. Consider how your faith or belief in a power greater than yourself causes you to think, choose, and live differently.

Faith impacts your health. Faith impacts the degree to which stress and uncertainty will plague you. Beliefs impact your character. Developing your character and becoming a better human being is a benefit of living on purpose and living by faith. Without such reflection, all of the other suggestions I make throughout this chapter (and book) will fall short of making a lasting difference for you. Because, ultimately, what you believe about God, your purpose on earth, and the meaning of your life will determine how confident, proactive, and directed you will be. Antidotal evidence shows that faith is effective in the prevention of disease, the enhancement of recovery from illness, the extension of lifespan, and the sense of well-being.

The vast majority of clients I work with believe in God. They believe in His creative powers and loving presence. Most want to serve and/or honor Him with their lives. I can say that is true for me. That's not to say, though, that if you have different beliefs you need to toss this book or reject the previous contents. It's just to acknowledge that differences between our beliefs will likely become evident as we move along. No problem. I've observed that the clearer I become about what I believe in, the easier my choices become. And isn't making your life simpler a big part of what you want? As you get clearer about what you believe, why you believe it, and how you can and will incorporate your convictions into your life, the easier your choices become.

My hope for you is that you will reflect, evaluate, and reconsider what you believe or don't believe about God, your purpose on earth, and the use of your gifts and talents in and for the world. You need to own your faith. It should act as a springboard for your courage, hope, and joy in the days to come. Your faith can also be a powerful sustainer even for making lifestyle changes. Yes, I believe God cares about how you take care of your body—it's the only one you'll have. Your light shines best when you're in good health. Admittedly, there are those rare souls without their health who shine brightly too. I can only imagine how much more they could do if given good health.

It can be easy to do the deeds of religion without the heart of faith. One of the ways to say it is to develop a faith that comes from an *intrinsic* desire to serve God and others versus an *extrinsic* need to look holy and/or good. Religion can provide a framework of meaning and a network of support, which can serve to anchor you. The discussion of faith in the context of this chapter is truly about you and your individual walk with God.

> *"There comes a time in the spiritual journey when you start making choices from a very different place...And if a choice lines up so that it supports truth, health, happiness, wisdom, and love, it's the right choice."*
> *Angeles Arrien*

It's critical to get spiritually in shape because both historical and contemporary accounts of healing through prayer show that the spiritual dimension of life is important to health in ways we do not fully understand. Despite the fact we don't understand the dynamics of faith and prayer, it does nothing to diminish their impact. What's true of biology is also true of faith; if it isn't growing, it's probably dead or dying.

I have not seen the face of God the way I have looked into the face of my children. I have not touched His hand the way I have held my husband's, yet I believe in God as deeply as I believe in my husband or children. Actually, I believe in Him even more. What I believe about God directly impacts the kinds of choices I make each day. What you believe, understand, and interpret to be about and of God influences your choices each day—whether consciously or not. Faith in someone or something assumes that some things will be left unknown or not understood. And that is acceptable.

Faith and Stress

I mention the Twelve-Step Program here because it became the springboard for my spiritual development. I even attended meetings on Sunday mornings for years. That group and those steps were my church and contributed to my desire to live with intention and purpose. I came to believe (and still do) that the reason the Twelve-Step Program has had ongoing, worldwide success in breaking the bondage of addiction for so many is that the program was divinely inspired—truly divinely inspired. Bill W. and Bob S. were Christian men who I suspect figured that if they brought their Christian values on recovery to the world, their principles would be less accepted and, therefore, less able to help as many people as they hoped. So, instead of having people turn to God, they referred to a Higher Power. That title opened the door for people of all convictions and beliefs to grow in wisdom about themselves and their relationships with others.[1]

Recovery for Life—The Twelve Steps, a Great Prescription

If anxiety plagues you, the Twelve Steps can help. If your relationships are difficult and confusing, the steps can help. If you're a controlling, perfectionist, or fear-based person, the Twelve-Step principles and program can help. There is something different at work in the Twelve-Step recovery program(s). While not a panacea for everyone, the majority of people who apply Twelve-Step principles and approaches to daily living, relationships, and decision-making find them powerful and effective. Why? I doubt I could quantify and prove this answer in a completely scientific way, but I do know all of the steps and principles are Biblically based. Each of the Twelve Steps has a foundation in specific scripture verses.[2] And, I believe that fact lends the program to a different kind of influence and power.

The Twelve-Step Program has a number of slogans that can help you immediately.[3] All you need to do is start applying them moment-to-moment and/or day-to-day. Even as a teen, I believed in God, so the early stages of learning to turn things over as taught in the program was easy to understand. I could turn life and situations over to a loving God. No problem. Or so I thought. I didn't have a hard time letting go; it was taking problems and fears back that plagued me. (As if I would have a better solution or more control than God.) I somehow had developed the mentality that I had to fix people, situations, and circumstances. I discovered I was more controlling and fear-based than I would ever have imagined. I frequently felt like two people—one was wise and confident (as reflected in my relationships with other adults and at work), and the other was insecure and fearful of rejection and failure (with friends, peers, and in situations I was unfamiliar with).

The point is not to recap the entire Twelve-Step Program. However, some of the basic principles taught within it changed my view of faith and life and can do so for you. I learned about myself. I learned compassion and developed insights getting to know people from every walk of life. Members revealed things about themselves few others were ever privileged to learn or see. Watching caterpillars develop into beautiful butterflies was an ongoing experience.

During subsequent years, I've continued to think of myself as a butterfly. At least until recently. Now I think of myself as a preying mantis. Having sons causes me to learn things I never imagined. Kiel came home with a newborn preying mantis one summer. I learned that these insects molt and break out of their shells eight times before they fully develop. And like the butterfly, they have to do the breaking out. If you help them remove their casing, they do not develop the strength they need to survive. The fact is, if a preying mantis survives these moltings, they are guaranteed to be mighty warriors in their own little worlds. It was painful to watch this little creature molt time and time again. Kiel and I both struggled with not taking over the process for him. We both knew it was his job to do to survive. I felt my life was much the same. It sure seemed like it took me a long time and many evolutions (or should I say, moltings) until the steps and slogans became second nature to me. My intuitive response, to this day, remains true to the principles I gleaned from those Twelve-Step [Al-Anon] meetings. So, I guess you could say I'm a *praying* mantis.

The most amazing revelation to me came when I was an inpatient counselor on a drug/alcohol recovery unit in a hospital and came across a resource that showed all twelve steps alongside their twelve accompanying scripture verses. I had not known this stuff was so spirit-filled. Of course, at the time, I couldn't have found any of those verses anyway. I was Biblically illiterate, but that didn't keep me from wanting to learn more about where these great principles for living came from.

One of the most common slogans of AA, Al-Anon, and the other Twelve-Step Programs is to "Live one day at a time." Imagine my surprise when one day I found that referenced in Matthew, a New Testament book of the Bible.[4] Three slogans in particular serve to increase your energy, joy, and peace of mind. Those slogans are live One Day At A Time (ODAT), Let Go and Let God, and K.I.S.S.

Live One Day at a Time. How well do you do that? If you did it really well, I doubt you'd even be reading this book. (And I wouldn't be writing it. I need the constant reminders myself.) Worry and fear come from being outside of the moment and fretting about the what ifs of a future time. Whether that future time is next week, next year, or ten minutes from now, worrying never improves the outcome of something. It merely diminishes your energy and focus in the now.

Anger, guilt, and resentment come from hanging on to things of the past. Past actions, words, deeds, or circumstances ruin the present moment. Think about it. What have you been mad at this week? Today? Yesterday? What have you done to remove that anger, resentment, or guilt? You have a choice. You can simmer in it, rehash comments, replay situations, or be proactive to remove it in the present moment. The reminder to live one day at a time and the resulting shift in emotional, spiritual, and physical energy could save you years of anxiety, negativity, and disappointment. When you are anxious or overwhelmed, tune into your self-talk. I'll bet you find yourself focused on things that are somewhere other than now. If the issue is in the present, act on what you can. Then leave the results up to God, which leads us into the next slogan.

Turn It Over or Let Go and Let God are slogans that really worked wonders in my life. At the time I began wanting to apply these principles, I was working two, sometimes three jobs, had my own apartment, was striving to maintain honors grades at the university I attended, played intramural basketball and racquetball, dated my boyfriend, and maintained my friendships, while attending meetings. (It probably won't come as much of a surprise to hear I was hospitalized for exhaustion at nineteen.)

Through it all, I kept working to turn things over. Teachers and bosses who showed favoritism and partiality caused me to feel frustrated and helpless. Money issues, family challenges, and roommates continued to need to be turned over because there was only so much I could do with limited resources. All my resources were limited—finances, time, energy. The one thing I knew to be true was that God wasn't limited. He had the ability to provide for me. I knew from experience (watching for Him to be at work and hearing about His miraculous ways in other people's lives) that He could and would take care of me. I learned His answers were yes, no, maybe, and not yet.

Not yet was (and is) His toughest answer to me. Let me share one of His most difficult not yet answers I received. My dream had always been to get married and live happily ever after. At twenty-one, I thought I was ready. My boyfriend of three years asked me to marry him, and I said yes. He was a wonderful man, and I knew he would always be a wonderful husband, provider, and friend. Before I said yes, though, I went to one of my favorite places to pray and said, "Dear God, I believe I am ready to be married, and I believe he is the one. If he is not, please help me to see that and do the right thing."

Two months before I was to marry, through a number of unexpected and unexplainable circumstances, I looked to God in pain and disappointment and recognized, that His answer really was, "Not yet. This is not *the* one I have chosen for you." That period of my life was probably among the most painful I have known. I lost not only the dream of being married; I also brought a great deal of disappointment, frustration, and anger to a family I cared deeply about.

But, because I trusted in God and because my faith had been nurtured through prayer, quiet times, and fellowship with others, I could turn it over and trust that all would be well. I can only imagine how difficult it would be to surrender the challenging, draining, mundane things of life (much less the most significant people and situations in life) over if I didn't have a faith relationship that was strong and trustworthy. I find the end of me, my resources, my strength, and my wisdom, comes far more quickly than the solution to problems or difficult circumstances.

What do you need to turn over? What challenges, fears, or situations do you want to take one day at a time? Take small steps to doing so by first being aware, and second, letting go moment to moment.

Finally, K.I.S.S. Keep it Simple, Stupid. Oh, how quickly and easily we complicate our lives. One of the most interesting aspects of martial arts is its foundational belief that all training, all development of the skills goes back to the basics. Masters of any sport or art repeat the basics. You and I need to do that in our faith walk—go back to the basics. Keeping it simple means intentionally reminding ourselves of why we are on earth, asking what difference we want to make today, and how can we best do that given our time, energy, talent, and passion. Titles, status, fame, prestige fade. Striving to impress others or accumulate stuff complicates life unnecessarily. I'm not suggesting you cannot enjoy those things or avoid achieving them. I suggest being intentional about honestly evaluating the cost to you, your family, your health, and community long term of striving for them.

Life is a Powerwalking Marathon

To be in shape to run a race requires diligent training. It requires certain training tools and is greatly enhanced by superb coaching. To be in shape to run the race of life requires spiritual grounding, training, and discipline. To live a life of sustainable success requires a specific focus and attitude about life and how to handle its challenges.

One of the most draining aspects of our culture is the pace at which we run. We are adrenaline junkies, trying to go faster and faster. I once read a quote that went something like this: "Human beings are the only species that, when lost, run faster."

You may be experiencing more stress and energy drain because the pace at which you're asking your body to operate is just too high. Or you're not allowing yourself enough recuperation time between your busy times. Who is setting your pace? If it is you, rethink what you are expecting from yourself. If it seems as if someone else is calling the shots, figure out a way to give yourself permission to slow so you don't get injured—physically, emotionally, spiritually, financially, or interpersonally. While there is more talk these days of pursuing spirituality and faith matters, our lifestyles, in general, allow for little reflection or renewal.

I've referred to my running races and found many helpful analogies to life in them. Here is another important analogy. When I've run races, I've needed to be aware of my wanting to speed up as others pass me—even if speeding up was not going to be to my ultimate advantage. My mental shift was to remember that the race was against myself. It really wasn't about everybody else and their times. And it was unfair of me to continuously badger myself because others ran faster. People will always pass me up; the more important focus is upon whether I'm running the best race I can. If yes, then I strive to let it go. If not, then I pick up the pace. The same opportunity exists for you.

"Take rest; a field that has rested gives a bountiful crop."
Ovid

The desire to accomplish and the need for renewal are competing goals. But they don't have to be. Purposeful planning is required to make time for both productivity and rest. Most people are doing the best they can. I'm sure you have been doing the best you can—up till now. Now, you will have awareness. With awareness comes choice. You set yourself up for fatigue and failure when you ignore the signals your body, heart, and soul give you to slow down and run differently. What mental shifts would feed your soul? Which would nurture your spirit and your walk with God?

Go to that place of asking, "So, why am I here? How do you want me to run the race? What's my best pace? Who do I need to coach me along?"

It's surprising how often people forget to turn to God for support and encouragement when trying to lose weight or get consistent with exercise. The scriptures actually have a lot to say about healthy living. Pray for the support, discipline, and commitment to make better choices.

> "…train yourself to be godly. For physical training is of some value, but godliness has value for all things, holding promise for both the present life and the life to come." 1 Timothy 4:7b-8 (NIV)[5]

One of the important things I've learned as a fitness instructor and with my training as a personal trainer is that your body usually gives off signals if it's in trouble or about to be. It's important to listen for signs of weakness or potential injury. During one thirteen-mile run I noticed my knee beginning to throb. I adjusted my foot strike and speed to protect my knee.

If you do a better job of listening to your body, your heart, and your spirit, you will notice when it is crying out for a break or for nourishment. You may not know what to do about it; however, you will know it's time to stop. Remember, the Titanic got quite a few warnings that it was going to be in trouble unless it stopped and adjusted course.

Warnings do no good unless they are heeded. I will admit that it was my body awareness that sent me in to the doctor when I noticed a painful lump in my breast. I certainly didn't think it was cancer because tumors don't hurt—or so I thought. If I had ignored the lump until my next annual doctor visit—thinking it was just another cyst—I'm afraid to think of how far the cancer would have spread by then. My next appointment would not have been until eight months after my diagnosis. Cancer was already in my lymph nodes—eight more months could have cost me my life. *Listen* and attend to what your spirit and soul need.

Taking Time for Renewal

One principle in fitness training is called reciprocity. This principle describes how you begin to lose the benefit of your last workout anywhere from forty-eight to seventy-two hours afterward. Physically, that's true. Spiritually, I believe the benefits of a great faith boost begins to diminish after twenty-four hours, basically because our news culture is so negative and our lives are stretched so thin. We frequently feel inadequate to achieve everything we want. Most of us need very regular doses of hope and encouragement. Therefore, spiritual renewal and refreshment need to occur on some level *every* day. Our culture is also so negative, sensationalistic, and voyeuristic—you need positive daily input to counteract all the depressing, frightening, and discouraging news of the world. How do you guard your spirit? How do you refresh and renew and maintain your spiritual self?

The goal for growing spiritually is to build and maintain a foundation for life that supports you as you step out into this crazy and often scary world. It's also the world where you find joy, purpose, laughter, renewal, love, miracles, and hope. When you ignore or put off the work on your spiritual foundation you weaken the very supports you need during the difficult times and in times of important decisions. When I want to make a choice that is congruent with my values and vision for life, I go back to my core beliefs about my purpose and calling.

In my early thirties, I wrote this mission statement for my life, "To pursue excellence, and to honor and glorify God through my daily choices and actions. To use my God-given talents and abilities to nurture, challenge, and encourage my family, friends, and community."

That mission statement (which evolved over months of thinking about it and re-writing it) has set the tone and direction for me ever since. I weigh daily choices against the backdrop of this mission. The first part of the sentence, which defines my purpose, has not changed. *How* I live it out has. My children's ages, the evolution of my business, my relationship with Jack and his changing needs all impact how I nurture, encourage, and challenge those around me.

I recognize whether I'm maintaining my spiritual health by my level of contentment and joy. When I'm unsettled, disappointed, frustrated, discouraged, or apathetic, I do two things. First, I do the "H.A.L.T. thing." I ask if I have an unmet need that is draining me. I ask if I am Hungry, Angry, Lonely, or Tired. If I am any of those things, I strive to take care of that need. Second, I do a Connect Check. I quietly review in my heart and mind where my thoughts have been (negative or positive) and whether or not I've been looking to God for my comfort, strength, and direction or to the outside world for affirmation and attention. Am I staying connected to my Source of energy and strength?

Let's examine the beliefs that influence you. The reflection and resulting answers will shed light for you on what you believe, and, therefore, their influence on your choices day-to-day. The hope is that your choices are congruent with what you say you believe.

- ❑ Do you believe you were created with a purpose? Are you living according to that purpose or drawing closer to seeing your purpose fulfilled?

- ❑ Who created you?

- ❑ Does this Creator warrant your attention, allegiance, or gratitude? If yes, how are you to show that in your life?

- ❑ What are your most important beliefs and convictions? What do you believe to be true about life, love, and faith that are undeniable?

- ❑ Do you have a legacy to fulfill? How are you fulfilling it?

- ❑ Where do you get your sense of security? Where would you like to get your sense of security?

- ❑ How are your faith convictions making a difference in your daily living? Are they? If yes, how? If not, why aren't they?

- ❑ Would you be satisfied to have success, power, wealth, and prestige in your community, but not a relationship with God?

- ❑ Does your contentment come from within or from outside circumstances and situations? If both, what percentage would you say is from each?

❑ If you've had a strong faith walk for a while, consider this question: Do you value God's presence in your life more than the greatest achievements you could experience in this world? Do other people recognize that in you? If yes, how?

Look at a clock right now and pause for a mere fifteen minutes before going on. Choose one or all of the above questions to consider before continuing your reading. Your answers will impact how you interpret the rest of this chapter.

Exercises for Developing Faith

One of the most important faith workouts is the one described in the questions above. You need focused discipline to patiently, thoughtfully, and purposefully write out and/or think through those questions.

PRAYER PUSH-UPS

I think of prayer much as I do push-ups—tough to do faithfully, but boy, do they make you stronger. Prayer does the same thing. It makes you stronger and tougher for the day's situations and circumstances. Some days I can whip out push-ups without a lot of anguish, and other days I feel like I can't do any. Some mornings I wake up and can't wait to get down to my prayer table to jump into my quiet time with God. Other mornings, I slack off, postponing it (even though I know it sets the perfect tone for the day), reading through the paper, cleaning the kitchen, filling out kid activity forms—anything but getting myself to sit down quietly. When I do that, I always regret it. Just like when I skip my strength training during any given workout that I planned to do it in. Sometimes I get lazy and do my push-ups on my knees without really putting out the effort to even try doing a couple the challenging way. Likewise, sometimes I sit down without the tools I usually use to pray and wing it. Now, there's nothing wrong with having some winged prayers during the day (I call them arrow prayers shot up throughout the day); I just can't make them my habit. If I were to half-heartedly do push-ups for very long, I would clearly get weaker.

(By the way, if you hate push-ups, can't do them, or wouldn't find any application for them in your life, fill in the term sit-ups for the above analogy.)

Prayer is simply the conversation between you and God. The Twelve-Step Program says it is between you and your Higher Power.

Prayer changes lives far beyond anything I can describe for you. In the book, *The Faith Factor*, Dr. Dale A. Matthews, says "Based on the research data we now have at hand, your doctor could—from a strictly scientific point of view—recommend religious involvement to improve your chances of being able to:

- stay healthy and avoid life-threatening and disabling diseases like cancer and heart disease,
- recover faster and with fewer complications if you do develop a serious illness,
- live longer,
- encounter life-threatening and terminal illnesses with greater peacefulness and less pain,
- avoid mental illnesses like depression and anxiety, and cope more effectively with stress,

- find a greater sense of meaning and purpose in your life.[6]

These benefits of religious involvement have been well documented by scientific studies over the last three decades, with studies published in authoritative, peer-reviewed medical journals like the *American Journal of Public Health, Cancer; American Journal of Psychiatry; American Journal of Medicine;* and *Journal of Heart and Lung.*

Studies have also found spirituality and religion are very important to the quality of life for some people with cancer. (This was certainly true for me.) Although research has not shown that spirituality can cure cancer or any other disease, some studies have found praying for others (intercessory prayer) may be a helpful addition to conventional medical care. The psychological benefits of praying may include reduction of stress and anxiety, promotion of a more positive outlook, and the strengthening of the will to live.[7]

I have witnessed the above results from prayer. And if you've watched for God to be at work in your life, you will too.

A diagnosis of breast cancer was a shock in itself. The distress of surgery was small compared to the trepidation I had about having to receive chemo. However, the first place I went to was my knees—to pray. My prayer was that I would have courage, wisdom, and peace of mind despite the crazy and unfathomable circumstances I found myself in.

Soon after this time of prayer, I was told that I should "get some prayer soakers." Prayer what? Prayer soakers, women who would shower me with love, support, and prayers. That is what I did. I asked five friends if they would be willing to actually come to my house and pray with me and over me each day of the week, one person a day. They all agreed. Kathy came on Mondays, Linda on Tuesdays, Jan on Wednesdays, Joy on Thursdays, and Jean on Fridays. (And Mary Lee backed up Jean when she traveled.) I will never forget the gift that time was. Sometimes, a friend would show up for ten minutes. Other times, it would be an hour. Our time focused upon healing and recovery, but also peace of mind and contentment for me, despite the uncertainty of the situation. Ultimately, I wanted to be able to share the hope I had throughout the journey because of my faith in God's gracious and personal care for me.

Contentment is one of the qualities my clients most want to develop. It is a character quality I highly value. To be content does not mean you don't strive to better yourself, improve your circumstances, or desire to make a contribution to the world. You can pursue excellence without being discontented. However, you cannot try to be perfect or do things perfectly without experiencing frustration and disappointment. Which is why making progress in the direction life takes you is most important; not doing it to perfection. Contentment allows you to do the best you can and leave the results up to God. Contentment frees you to enjoy every good thing God has given you. Contentment demonstrates your belief that God loves you and has your best interest in mind. Strive to be grateful for all that God has given you. Trusting in His timing and provision in all things.

Because I believe God supplies all of my needs, I can be free of envy. Notice, I said, I can be. I have a long way to go

> *"Be content with who you are, and don't put on airs. God's strong hand is on you; He'll promote you at the right time. Live carefree before God, His is most careful with you."*
> *1 Peter 5:6-7 (TLB)*

before I don't ever respond out of envy. That unflattering shade of green colors my heart more often than I like. It does have me go to God in prayer, though. That's a positive.

Have you heard of the Imposter Syndrome? This syndrome describes individuals who question their effectiveness and significance despite external proofs of intelligence, competence, and giftedness. People operate out of fear and limitation because they do not believe that what others say about them is authentic and true. Dr. Valerie Young, a woman who specializes in this subject, put it this way when she recognized herself in the description given in a course in her doctoral training, "It's hard to describe what it was like to discover that these vague feelings of self-doubt, angst, and intellectual fraudulence had a name. This, along with the realization that I was not alone, was utterly liberating."[8]

This syndrome haunts a high percentage of the professionals I work with. These highly qualified men and women fear at some level that "if people really knew what I didn't know, they wouldn't be so impressed with me." If you can relate to these feelings, if you find yourself nodding your head and hear yourself sighing or whispering, "that's me," then listen carefully to this next comment. Your self-worth does not come from your *doing*. It comes from your being, your uniqueness, your special contribution to the world that is given when you be yourself.

STRETCHING REFLECTIONS

The reasons for stretching the body are many. The specific benefits of stretching and the best ways to stretch are debatable. However, one thing remains true—

stretching in one form or another is great for every-body and every body.

Strengthening your faith muscle with sayings, verses, poems, and quotations can revitalize your soul.

As I have tried to describe who God is to me and how I have come to understand and know Him better, I've discovered a wonderful picture of Him through parenthood. I have probably learned more about a strong faith walk with God since having children than ever before. To know how deeply I love my children, that I would die for them, literally, and forgive them (regularly) for breaking the rules, gives me but a glimpse of what God has promised me. I have also developed a better understanding of unanswered prayer. When things don't go the way I want, despite my best efforts, I can trust God is still providing me with the best answer for me. He has a greater perspective than I. I stand above the ants with a broader, more complete perspective about the world around them. The scene at my feet often makes me chuckle. I suspect God might view our scrambling, hectic, cha-otic schedules and smile or shake His divine head in the same way. His perspective is more expansive, more complete, and longer range than mine. I trust in that and experience a comforting peace.

Each year, thousands of little ants scurry all over our front sidewalk carrying tiny crumbs, pieces of leaves, and mysterious objects into their mounds. God, like me looking down on them, must just chuckle at all the hustle and bustle. There is so much more world than those little ants can see; however, I doubt they look up to see me watching and sometimes protecting them from the ravages of boys and bikes.

One of my favorite quotes on prayer is, "Prayer does not change God, it changes me." That's why I pray—to change me. I can get anxious very easily if I don't keep my guard up. When I do the best I can and let the results go to God, I can rest assured. That is true comfort in a world that expects so much out of each of us.

A suggestion for getting and staying in shape spiritually is to be more concerned with what God has to say to you than with what you have to say to God. This is one of those perfect situations to remember that we have one mouth and two ears. God doesn't make mistakes and His designs are perfect.

Meditation: A Different Kind of Prayer

When I first began giving seminars on stress management in the late '80s, I discovered an author whose work I found exciting and helpful. His name was Dr. Herbert Benson. His book, *The Relaxation Response*, explained the effects of stress on human physiology and how these effects can be countered through a simple form of meditation. He said that the effects of this meditation were a decreased heart rate, a lower metabolic rate, a lower rate of breathing, and a slowing of brain waves.

The relaxation response is simple in nature, yet powerful in impact. The meditation follows a series of steps, which include repeating a word, prayer, sound, phrase, or name and passively disregarding the incoming thoughts that float in and out of your mind. Your goal is simply to bring your mind back to the word or phrase without working at it too hard. While it takes practice, the result for many can be seen in physiological and emotional responses, which have been used in the treatment of chronic pain, insomnia, anxiety, depression, infertility, hypertension, cancer (coping with treatment side effects), and irregularities in heart rhythm.[9]

When you take the time to slow down and meditate, you give your body and mind a break from the relentless pace of living. When you slow down to pray or meditate, you have the opportunity to reflectively consider whether you are being the person you want to be. You can evaluate whether you are showing patience or impatience to others, tolerance or self-righteousness, empathy or apathy. I need God's strength and intervention to help me live out these character qualities. If I don't recognize my need for His help and support, I fly through the day and only recognize my need to change too late. Words of apology repeated too often don't matter a whole lot after awhile. Positive action is the gift I give to those I care about, work with, and influence every day.

> *"Health is the ultimate integrity issue."*
> *Dr. Lee Smith and*
> *Dr. Jeannine Sandstrom*

Building Your Character

When someone describes you, what character qualities do they use? When I list my highest values in relation to character qualities, integrity, honesty, creativity, learning, and authenticity rate at the top. When I'm stressed, it's difficult to be patient with others, it's challenging to be creative when my brain can't slow down, and impossible to be compassionate when all I am focused on are the inconveniences and frustrations around me.

Maintaining this attitude will do as much for your health as regular exercise.

Success and Faith

While I'm improving, I still struggle with patience, wanting to see results for my efforts more quickly. I assume because I haven't accomplished more (meaning making more money, booking more business, publishing more books, etc.), I am the one failing and falling short because I am the one not doing something. If I trust God to work things out in His timing, why do I keep telling myself I'm failing? When I'm honest, I realize my life is full and wonderful. I am simply succumbing to the world's definition and benchmarks for success. I am allowing the world to define success for me.

Self-sufficiency is the mantra of our professional world. "Make it happen" is a typical cheer sent our way. As you develop and strengthen your faith walk, you will discover less anxiety haunting you. When you pursue excellence, by doing your best possible work, and give up trying to be perfect, you will discover a freedom in releasing the results of your efforts to God. His wisdom, power, and resources far surpass mine. I can trust in His outcome. So can you.

A Final Thought

What you believe about God and your life purpose influences every thought, every action, and every outcome in your life. If you haven't taken the time as an adult to evaluate, discover, and act intentionally on your beliefs, you will, by default, live according to other people's beliefs. Your stress, your health, and your relationships are dependent upon a positive, active, renewing faith that acts as a compass for everyday living. You can develop and tone your faith muscles the same way you develop your physical muscles—one workout at a time. A strong, empowering faith is developed one small choice at a time.

TRAINING TIPS

- To live a life of sustainable success requires a specific focus and attitude about life and how to handle its challenges.

- You may be experiencing more stress and energy drain because the pace at which you're asking your body to operate is just too high. Or you're not allowing yourself enough recuperation time between your busy times. Do you believe *you* are in control of the results in your life?

- While there is more talk these days of pursuing spirituality and faith matters, our lifestyles, in general, allow for little reflection or renewal.

- It is unfair for you to continuously badger yourself because others ran a faster pace in life. Set your own pace.

- The desire to accomplish and the need for renewal are competing goals for most people. They do not have to be.

- You set yourself up for fatigue and failure when you ignore the signals your body, heart, and soul give you to slow down and run at a different pace.

- The Titanic got quite a few warnings that it was going to be in trouble unless it stopped and adjusted course.

- The goal for growing spiritually is to build and maintain a foundation for life that supports you as you step out into this crazy and often scary world.

- When you ignore or put off the work on your spiritual foundation, you weaken the very supports you need during the difficult times and in times of important decisions.

- Don't run from or avoid the challenges or people you fear. Get support, guidance, and encouragement and then act with faith.

WORKINS ➤

- Faith means/involves _____ _____.

- Have I intentionally sat down and reviewed, reflected upon, and carefully considered what I believe and in whom I believe as an adult? What have I discovered?

- What or whom do I serve with my life?

- Do guidelines exist for me to live by? If yes, what are they?

- How deeply do I believe in these guidelines, laws, or principles?

- Am I willing to follow these laws or principles despite the cost? If not, do I really believe they are valuable and true? If yes, how will I stay strong in my beliefs?

- What do I regularly need to do (or not do) to sustain a strong faith and healthy spiritual perspective in my life?

- What do I want to say is true of me and my faith walk a year from now?

- What is the first step I can take to make that become a reality?

◀ WORKOUTS

- Sit down with someone you respect for their faith walk; that may be someone who you observe manages his or her stress, fears, and anxiety differently or better than you. (Up until now!) Consider where and how God has been a part of your life. If you can't think of any ways in which God has played a part, ask friends where they have seen God at work. (Sometimes their ability to point out how their life has been impacted will enable you to see it in your own life.)

  - Memorize the verse referred to earlier on worry, Matthew 6:34 (TLB). Actually, all of chapter six in the New Testament book of Matthew is called the worry chapter. It's a balm for the anxious soul.

- Memorize, repeat, and reflect upon the Serenity Prayer. "God, grant me the serenity to accept the things I cannot change [other people and circumstances], the courage to change the things I can [that includes proactive attitudes and actions], and the wisdom to know the difference [help get my ego, fear, insecurities, and limiting beliefs out of the way]."

Nine

Financial Fitness

I believe this chapter on finances and the previous chapter on faith may be the most important chapters of this book. These two areas actually influence your daily choices more than any others. Think about it. Most decisions you make are based upon how much something costs, how soon you can get it, how long you have to work each day or week to afford it. And, oftentimes, what you desire (or don't desire and pursue) is based upon your philosophy for why you exist. For many, your faith perspective determines your direction for the way you live and serve. Most of my clients comment on not having time for exercise, friendship time, vacations, or quiet time because they're working or overcommitted to other activities. Yet, they acknowledge that without their health and loved ones, life isn't worth much.

"The thing that differentiates man from animals is money." Gertrude Stein, *1936 American writer*

I am the first person to tell you I am not a financial planner. I strongly encourage you to use one. So, why don't I just refer you to some books or web sites? The reason is that it is important you connect the choices you make regarding money to all of the areas of life we've addressed in *Progress Not Perfection*. The content in this chapter, hopefully, will be a springboard to making conscious decisions regarding your relationship to money and its ripple effect in your life.

So, Where Did Money Come From in the First Place?

Have you ever considered how much of your life is driven and influenced by your need or desire for money? How much of your week (in hours) is spent earning money or traveling to the place you earn your income? Continual thoughts of cost, affordability, debt, and savings are on your mind. You consider the value of services and products, online and in the stores. You read ads, listen to the radio, your kids, peers, and friends. You need to consider the trade-offs of one item or decision over another. If you're married, there's also the tension and frustration of trying to have a united mindset about finances with your spouse. Yes, money is the determining and draining factor for more than we realize.

Ads on TV inform viewers of the challenge of illiteracy in our country and how many organizations are striving to help solve the problem. We have another illiteracy problem in America, which is seriously impacting our country and its people in devastating ways. Adults are having a tough time managing their finances and are conflicted with their attitudes about money. Many adults are financially illiterate. Few adults were ever taught wise money management skills as kids, and few are strategically doing that today with their children. Another challenge perpetuating financial illiteracy is the fact that money is an emotionally charged subject. It takes psychic and emotional energy to deal with the topic—energy many people don't have today.

One of my children's most common complaints is that they have to eat too healthfully. They are only marginally grateful for their resulting health and well-being. I do know, though, that they know *how* to eat wisely. Whether they choose to do so when they're outside the home is up to them. I've done my level best. Kids can learn how to read labels and how to weigh food choices for their benefits (energy). Just as kids develop good eating habits over time, they also develop spending habits over time. The same is true for you and me. You need to know how to save, spend, invest, give, and use money wisely. You cannot do that if you are financially illiterate.

We have endowed money with a great deal of power. Money has been used as a weapon for evil and a tool to do good. It has the ability to change lives—positively and negatively. Money itself has no value. Humans give it value, and it is our response to money that matters.

The History of Money

Money is such an integral part of our lives and psyche. I wonder if you know how it evolved or how it came into existence? Understanding how money (financial management) and consumerism developed is both interesting and important to learn. Knowing how money came to be provides a framework within which we can examine our attitudes about money. A study of money, its origins, and global impact on nations, reveals that *attitudes about money set the core values and focal points of every culture.* These core values and focal points create very different lives. Here's just a glimpse of what I mean.

The Meaning of Money and Trade Around the World

Do you find yourself making decisions throughout your day based upon what you can afford? Is your question, "How can I (we) bring in more?" or "How can I (we) spend less?" If you answer in the affirmative to either question, then you, like most people, have likely made money a determining factor or your focal point for life. Is this the focal point you want to use? Is this your chosen (consciously or unconsciously) point of reference for life and what you organize your life around? If your answer is yes and you're content with your life, you probably don't need this chapter. For the rest of us, including me, spending time analyzing, reviewing, and learning about money and its role in daily life is important because money and our need or desire for it drive the majority of our decisions.

Author and anthropologist Jack Weatherford writes in *The History of Money*, "Only now, after nearly three thousand years, is the full power of money becoming apparent in human affairs, as it supplants or dominates many of the traditional social bonds based on family, tribe, community, and nation."[1]

He is not the first person to make the observation that money, and our quest for it, is taking a toll on our nation. As I studied this topic, I saw that as money swept through history and across societies, its impact seemed surprisingly similar from ancient Greece and Rome to modern day Japan and Germany. Before the creation of money, man bartered and exchanged cowrie shells, beads, copper bells, and other consumable commodities that allowed him to get what he needed.

The Aztecs used chocolate, cacao seeds, for money. With cacao seeds they could buy fruits, vegetables, peanuts, jewelry made of gold or silver, jade, and turquoise. Cacao seeds could also buy manufactured goods such as sandals, clothing, feathered capes, weapons, pottery, baskets, meat, fish, venison, and duck. Chocolate could even be used to buy alcohol and slaves. And I thought our culture had a fixation on chocolate![2]

Whether your money is called dollars, rubes, yen, marks, francs, pounds, pesos, kroners, kwansas, levs, escudos, liras, drachmas, shekels, quetzals, rupees, or shillings, it all operates the same way. The fundamentals of the market differ very little.

Chocolate, like all other types of money, has no inherent value outside of a cultural context. In order for it to have value, people have to want it and know how to use it. Money does not occur in nature, and no version or analog of it exists among any other members of the animal kingdom.

When money was created, it constituted a whole new way of thinking and acting that changed the world immediately.

Have you considered how money, its abundance or scarcity, has affected you? What are your attitudes about money? In all fairness, keep in mind the attitudes of your original family play a huge role in your ongoing perceptions of money as an adult, unless you have purposefully evaluated this subject before. Thinking about these things will play a significant role in getting into and staying in shape for success financially. And your financial health has a huge impact on your overall health. The indirect stress that comes from money concerns negatively affects your body and relationships.

Money and Motivation

Money itself is not bad. Money allows us to structure our lives in incredibly complex ways. Money represents an infinitely expandable way of determining value and social relationships—personal, political, religious, commercial, and economic.

Over time, money has become the medium for the expression of values. The most significant leap in its value may have been when it expanded from defining values of products and commodities (like sheep, sandals, beads, and yams) to defining the abstract—work. Work, or human labor, became a commodity with a value that could be fixed in money according to its importance, the amount of skill or strength it required, and the time it took. Weatherford articulates again for us why this is important today, "As money became the standard value for work, it was also becoming the standard of value for time itself." How often have you heard, "Time is money?"

What is your motivation for working to earn money? For most people, it is to have enough money to do the things that make you (and your family) happy and fulfilled. Rarely is the hope to accumulate wealth for wealth's sake. Unfortunately, due to the level of debt among many, the goal has become to pay back debt.

The intent of this chapter is to encourage you to take control of your finances—one small choice at a time. Money management includes saving, spending, giving, and investing. Money management involves taking purposeful action before, during, and after you have money. Your relationship with money, your perception of it, is more important than the amount you have. When you take control of your finances, you become a wise steward. Being a wise steward enables you to intentionally, thoughtfully, and proactively use the resources you have to accomplish what you desire and provide for those you may be responsible for and to. Proactively using your financial resources wisely is the best way to reduce your stress, fear, and anxiety about money.

Who you really are is most evident by how you react or who you become when life squeezes you. Could you be the person you would want to be if you lost most of your possessions through a medical crisis, economic upheaval, or natural disaster? During the aftermath of natural disasters like Hurricanes Katrina and Rita, the nation had the opportunity to see how people responded to this question. Some responded with grace and poise; many did not.

Excessive accumulation of possessions can be as dangerous to your well-being as having too little. With many physical possessions, it's easy to believe you are invulnerable. Money can give people a false sense of security. Financial well-being can be lost in a moment. A job loss, significant market drop, a health crisis, or divorce can substantially change your financial position in life.

If you are ready to become financially more aware and responsible—congratulations! Keep in mind that while you are ready to address your financial fitness, your spouse may not have the same desire. That difference is one of the greatest challenges I've seen people face when they decide to get financially fit. I have worked with many women who would trade in their salaries, hours, and stress to have more sanity in their schedules, yet they are locked into their current positions because their husbands are content with the status quo—despite the debt, exhaustion, and bondage that goes along with it. (Don't get me wrong; some married men have wives who are not willing to change.) The other reason, mentioned earlier, is that many families cannot afford to have a full salary taken away.

Amanda was tired. Her migraines were becoming more frequent. She felt ineffective and was always feeling behind the eight ball taking care of her clients. When we began working together, her first goal was to "...just plain feel better. I'm tired, frustrated, and anxious all the time." After a few months of working together, Amanda was feeling better and felt more clear-headed. When she felt ready to look at other changes that would be important to her, she said, "I am the breadwinner for our house. I could cut back on expenses, but Jim resists any attempt to reduce our spending. And we can't afford for me to cut back or explore other work options because I have to earn what I do."

She decided she needed to thoughtfully and clearly share her concerns and desire for wanting to make some financial changes so they would both be freer to make other choices about how they spent their time. She was right; Jim did resist making spending adjustments. However, when she sat down and showed him what was going out (in expenses each month) and what she saw them being able to cut down and adjust, he agreed to try the program with her.

Amanda took a couple of steps that helped her cause.

1. She is a financial planner, so she was perfectly comfortable with all the numbered columns. However, she wisely put their financials into a format Jim would understand and grasp clearly. In this case, it was color pie charts that showed the percentages in categories.

2. She was willing to let some of the cutbacks come from her spending. She opted to start bringing lunch more days a week than not. She decided to bring green tea for her afternoon pick-me-up versus coffee from the downstairs coffeehouse.

3. She asked Jim what he was willing to adjust.

4. They agreed to talk again a month later to discuss what was working and what wasn't. Amanda was also going to make copies of the next month's expenses, so Jim would again be reminded of what they were attempting to accomplish.

In most relationships one person tends to be in charge of the money, while the other tends to want to remain oblivious, or at least, not inconvenienced with the details. This manner of dealing with money as a couple will not allow two people to move forward together in life as a team making wise financial decisions. So, the simpler, clearer, and more doable you make the changes, the more likely your success at making changes.

What do the experts have to say? A consistent message from financial experts is that it is critical to set financial goals and objectives, develop a plan to achieve them, and have realistic expectations about your returns. They say to carefully follow your plan, and stay true to the course even in up and down markets.

When humans get scared, they have a compelling drive to act. So, they jump in and out of the market and chase down offers that are too good to be true. Don't question your decisions once they have been thoughtfully made. Thoughtfully put together a plan (with the help of a financial planner, if possible) and trust the plan. Work the plan. Most often, working the plan means creating and living according to a budget.

A good reminder: Every possession requires time, attention, and often additional money to maintain it. Too many or impractical possessions can demand so much time, energy, and money that they harm relationships and negatively impact your health. Recently, a client said, "I don't mean to complain because I've been really blessed with what we can do financially, but the maintenance on a house and cabin and the accompanying toys of the boat, personal watercraft, and motorcycle has become ridiculously exhausting." Having fun gadgets and toys in life isn't bad—unless they are taking more from your energy, finances, and time reserves than you care to really give.

By the way, if you want to get a sense of how much excess you have—start your spring cleaning now. Sort, clean, recycle, or give away what you do not use. You may be very surprised how much you have in your home now that is taking up space.

Defining Financial Security

If you want to develop financial security, you need to familiarize yourself with some basic concepts to competently and confidently make financial changes in your life. You will need to know how you use money in general. How much you save, spend, give away, and invest reflects a great deal about your attitudes about money. Our habits around these issues reflect our *true* values.

I worked with a client Beth who wanted to work differently. She wanted to work, however, she became more and more aware of the drain on her psyche and her body as she carried the financial load for her family. Although married for fifteen years, she and her husband Bill kept separate bank accounts. He had different spending habits and behaviors, and she did not want to baby-sit their accounts to make sure they were managed well. That strategy worked well for a number of years. However, she noticed a growing frustration and increasing resentment toward her husband because he "didn't have a clue about what it cost to live per month." He spent his money (his paycheck) month-to-month the way he wanted. He also overused his checking account and accrued hefty credit card debt. She, on the other hand, paid all of the bills on the house, cars, insurance, summer home, and the needs of their three children.

When I told her that she was actually crippling him financially by keeping him in the dark about their finances and by not holding him accountable for contributing and spending alongside her as a team, she responded, "I know. I think it's a control thing. I don't want to have to depend upon anyone to live. I don't want someone else telling me how to spend, what to spend, or when." She said this with such passion in her voice that it even caught *her* off guard. Bingo! We hit upon something very important.

By controlling the spending and paying of bills for the family, Beth felt in charge. She did not feel like a victim, nor did she have to take the time to teach Bill about finances and fiscal responsibility. What worked in the past was no longer working because she needed his help in two ways. One way was that she could no longer juggle bill paying, software updates, and other maintenance duties for maintaining their expenses. Second, she recognized from our conversation that she and Bill needed to agree to a budget that would give them the freedom to choose the direction of their work and lives. When he was on a different saving, investing, and spending path, he was unknowingly pulling them away from their financial goals.

As I already said, it is very typical to have one spouse handle the financial matters in the home. For the reasons described in Beth's story, it takes coordinated time to work together (even to update the other partner takes concerted effort), and one spouse tends to manage numbers and money better than the other.

However, because you don't like numbers, the stress of money and utilizing it wisely does not excuse you from learning what it takes to manage it well. If you want financial security and financial freedom, you must understand the basics of finance. Many a woman is left financially crippled in her later years because her husband never taught her how to handle money, where to invest, or whom to call on to do so. And she didn't ask.

Financially Unaware: A True Story

Rebecca found herself in difficult financial straits following her divorce. She went back to school and received the degree she needed to start her own business, and got herself on her feet. A short time later she met a wonderful man John who treated her like the special woman she was. In time they became engaged. During their engagement, they talked about all facets of their new life together. She knew, because he paid alimony and child support, they would not be financially flush, but she was confident they would be okay. She did not ask some of the uncomfortable financial questions because she recognized John handled money differently from her ex-husband. At times she recognized that she ignored the urge to go deeper into some financial areas.

When they sat down to budget their income and expenses (unfortunately, *after* the wedding), she was shocked to discover that his ex-wife actually received more than half of his salary. She was devastated to realize they would be financially strapped for years to come. She was also angry with herself for not asking the tough questions: "How much do you make?" and "How will we budget for our new life together?" What brave or uncomfortable questions are *you* avoiding asking today?

Getting Into Financial Shape

Before you start an exercise program, it's important to find out how fit or unfit you are. You don't want to attempt an activity a friend does just because it works for him. What works for another person may cripple you. So, you begin with an assessment of your current level of physical health and well-being. The same plan works for getting into financial shape. You can use the Think, Choose, Act, Win model to financial health.

Consider the following five areas if you want to become financially healthy.

1. Income—identify where you have money coming from and the amounts. The amount is not as important as how you handle it. Aside from paychecks, you can have funds coming in from trusts, retirement funds, interest, and loan repayments to you, etc.

2. Savings—find strategies to insure you are saving a portion of today's income for tomorrow's financial well-being.

3. Debt—teach/know the cost of money and the difficulty of getting out of debt.

4. Giving—believe it or not, giving money away is more than spending it. Of course, that assumes you are budgeting enough to responsibly get by with your current responsibilities.

5. Budgeting—develop a plan for spending—you'll find a three-step process for setting up a budget later in this chapter.

Create a financial plan. Financial planning is nothing more than the proper handling of cash flow and assets to meet your objectives.

One of the best books explaining finances and money management is David Chilton's *The Wealthy Barber*. He gives the wise advice, "...there are many excellent financial planners and when it comes to fine-tuning and implementing your plan, they can be of great help. But when you're originally developing your plan, you must take responsibility for your own future."[3]

Kim is a beautiful example of someone who handled her new money situation wisely. After a very long and drawn-out divorce, Kim was left with the responsibility of handling her finances—for the first time in her adult years. Despite having married at twenty-five, she never got around to investing in anything or learning about things like retirement accounts. Due to the divorce process, she had all of her financial numbers and accounts in order and available to work with. To set herself up with a smart financial plan, she went to a financial planner who helped her co-create the right plan for her. With her finances set up intelligently, she became free to confidently pursue other interests and ambitions. Not having to worry about money management (because she was getting support and advice and was living on a budget) enabled her to reduce her stress and increase her sense of freedom.

Part of the challenge in our culture today is a misperception on the part of many two-income household earners. Many parents believe they have some built-in insurance against layoffs or medical problems because their partner earns a second income or has insurance. Unfortunately, this isn't true. Two-income families are more likely to file for bankruptcy than their one-income counterparts. A generation ago, a non-working (talk about an oxymoron!) mother could offset a layoff or job loss on the part of the husband by going back to work when finances were strapped. That happened in my own family. Today, with most families functioning on two incomes and most often without the benefit of a budget and good self-management skills, they are left floundering and frightened when one partner loses a job.

The mission I have pursued in life has focused on teaching people self-management and leadership skills. However, finances deeply impact your ability to live and choose well because the need or desire to earn and/or acquire impacts most areas of life. Need proof? Consider the fact that most people *know* exercising and eating smart is important, yet few ultimately do it because they are too busy working or making other interests a higher priority. Here is my caution, said loudly and boldly: **You can't afford to wait to take care of yourself!** The small choices you make today could lead to your financial destruction as well as to the destruction of your health and relationships. Families filing for bankruptcy due to medical expenses and bills has been shown to account for 44.2–54.5 percent of the filings.[4]

Creating a Practical Budget

Every exercise CD or video has a warning label to check with your doctor before beginning an exercise program. Here is my warning label: I am not a financial planner, so my recommendations are made on the good faith of the advice and input of professional clients and friends plus my own experience. My goal is simply to get you on the thinking path to what you need, what you believe will work, and the encouragement that today is the best day to begin being financially well-established—one small choice at a time. The foundation for wise spending, saving, and giving is based upon a sound budget.

A budget allows you to pay for what you need and save for what you want. In her book, *Money Doesn't Grow on Trees*, author Neale Godfrey defines a budget as "a plan that lays out what you will do with your money."[5] That's it; the concept is pretty simple. It's the execution, like an exercise program, that's tougher to follow. Self-discipline and self-denial are not among people's favorite personal management skills. They are, however, among the very most important skills to develop. A financial budget provides a framework for practicing self-discipline and self-denial in a positive way.

Steps one and two begin with thinking through your financial attitudes and habits. Reflection and awareness (step three) are key steps to change. Keep in mind, though, that if you're married, your spouse may not be ready to work on finances. Thorough and diligent record keeping may be a longer step than you like. However, it is an important one. Consider this time one of building your case for healthy financial choices.

Step 1: Begin with today. Write down how much you (or your household) earns per year. Record how much you spend each year. If you can break your expenses into categories, you can see specific ways in which to decrease your spending. Like you would with a food log, journal your spending for a month. Remember to write down the amount of interest you pay on each of your credit cards. (We will use that information later when dealing with the concept of debt.)

Step 2: Determine where you want to be financially and personally. Many people work very hard to achieve financial wealth; however, the interest they pay is diminished health and disconnected relationships. Both your health and relationships need ongoing attention.

Step 3: Information is power; learn what you need to learn so you are financially responsible.

Know where your money is going. Information is power when you act on it—especially when it comes to money. One time I went through the check register to find out how much I spent on bagels and was shocked at the number. At approximately six dollars a dozen, the cost adds up quickly. I read in the paper once about a woman who calculated what she spent per year on Starbucks coffee. Most days of the workweek she bought a flavored latte for three dollars and thirty cents, which meant she was spending approximately eight hundred dollars a year on beverages. Instead of small choices make a big difference, it may be better to say, "small change (as in coins) make a big difference."

Debt Is Everywhere

I'm sure, like me, you hear a lot in the news about the rising national debt and the concerns attached to it. Is it the national debt that is running our financial decisions? Is it the national debt that is crushing so many families? No. It's private debt that is killing us. It's private debt that is creating stress and anxiety in marriages and for individuals. While researching this topic, I checked on what the level of American private debt was at: The national debt of our country as of June 5, 2006 was $8,375,141,125,472.30. The estimated population of the US is 298,877,644 citizens, which means each person's share of this debt is $28,021.97.[6] While you may not feel as though you can make a dent in this number, remember a single hair makes a shadow. Small changes, made by one person do make a big difference.

> *"The budget should be balanced; the treasury should be refilled; public debt should be reduced; and the arrogance of public officials should be controlled."*
> *Cicero. 106-43 B.C.*

It said that the debt, like weight gain, is accumulated so slowly over time that you don't notice it until it's an overwhelming problem.

Although it may have been your grandparents (or great grandparents!) who lived during the Great Depression, it's likely you've heard how horribly difficult it was for families to be so broke. Yet, bankruptcy rates for families today exceed the number filed during the Great Depression as a percentage of the population.

Credit card debt has risen from $10 billion in 1968 (inflation adjusted) to more than $600 billion in 2000. That's an increase of more than 6,000 percent.[7]

The Two-Income Trap is a must-read for working professionals. The authors, Elizabeth Warren and

Amelia Warren Tyagi, share their extended expertise and research on why middle-class mothers and fathers are going broke.[8] Regardless of your income, the insights and information they provide in this book are eye opening. Awareness is key to good decision-making. They also offer a different perspective that I hadn't considered until I read it.

The authors offer suggestions for collective action for dealing with the debt level in our country, including recommendations for Congress and state legislatures, political action groups, and faith-based organizations, school districts, and community institutions.[9] However, the focus here is on you and what you can do to improve your financial health and well-being.

The hope is you create an emergency fund, savings outlet, and wise spending habits so you do not cripple yourself with debt.

Many people raise their standard of living through debt, only to discover that the burden of debt controls their lifestyle. When we go into debt, we assume we will earn enough in the future to pay the debt. We plan for our job to continue and our businesses or investments to be profitable. A key way to avoid debt is to shift your attitude about saying no to your impulse to spend. Instead of focusing on what you won't be able to have/get, focus on how freeing it will be to get out of debt or avoid it.

Staying In Financial Shape

When was the last time you said no to yourself when you wanted to buy something? What is something you really wanted, but said, "No, that wouldn't be a wise choice considering …"? I wonder if you, like me, have gotten caught in the I-deserve-it trap. I call it a trap because when I spend money, after I decided not to, I sabotage a higher goal or value. If I am saving for furniture and continually give myself permission to splurge on smaller items, I delay my ability to buy the bigger item (the furniture, a larger college fund, a new car). Eating is much the same way. If I want to lose fifteen pounds, but throughout the week give myself permission to have small (however multiple) treats, I will delay losing weight. As a matter of fact, I may cause myself to go so long without success in little decisions I give up on the big one.

Earlier in this book, I shared that the researchers with the Weight Loss Registry have found that losing weight isn't as difficult as keeping it off. I wonder if the same is true of getting on good financial footing. If the goal is to get out of debt and you achieve that, your greater challenge may be staying out of debt. So, let's talk about handling your money in a manner that will keep you financially healthy.

Guidelines for Handling Money

Answering the following questions will allow you the personal freedom to intentionally and confidently make financial decisions that fit with your budget, values, and goals.

- How much do you need to live on each month given your current financial commitments? Too often we define a want as a need. Itemize what it costs you to work. (Consider gas, monthly parking, clothes, daycare, food expenses, gifts/ contributions you make over the course of the year, and daily coffee or soft drinks in the afternoons.)

- How much do you currently earn (individually or jointly)? By what percentage have your expenses changed over the past five years? What has changed to increase your expenses? If your answer is children, calculate (or situate yourself in a budgeting software program) the cost of education, clothes, sport participation, music lessons, medical and dental expenses, children's hobbies, camps, allowances, etc.

Just as cross training is the smartest way to stay physically healthy long term, a well-thought-out cross mix of investments is the best way to stay financially healthy for the long term. In the financial world, this strategy is called diversification.

A wise financial strategy will incorporate at least these three things:

1. Your personal goals, which will reflect your selected lifestyle.

2. Risk tolerance, which addresses the unknown and various dynamics that will play into your comfort level with your plan, including your spouse's desires and risk tolerance level, the economy, and your own temperament.

3. The time horizon you are looking at for developing and growing your plan. Your strategy will look different at twenty-five, forty-five, and sixty-five years of age.

Keep in mind that the best time to start operating from a strategic financial plan is at the beginning of your career. The next best time is today.

Teaching Children About Finances

Kids watch what we do and feel our energy and emotions more than they listen to us. I came into adulthood completely naïve to the nuances of money management. If you are like the majority of my clients, you have too. Take your awareness of the need to be informed, intentional, and consistent with your financials and give it to your children. These are some of the principles we've used with our kids that have been helpful.

- Teach kids to be wise, discerning spenders. Show them how to comparison shop.
- Help them distinguish needs from wants.
- Teach them how to decipher ads and marketing ploys that sabotage efforts to spend and save wisely.
- Our youngest son had a bank when he was little that offered a wonderful visual expression of the way to manage money. The bank was shaped like three buildings with three slots along the top. There was a store (spending), a bank (savings), and a church (giving). We encouraged him to take 10 percent for savings, 10 percent for giving, and 80 percent for spending. I can't say this will make him a wise

spender into adulthood, but he won't be able to say he was not taught.

- Share with your children when you've resisted the impulse to buy. Show them when and how you delay purchases that reflect discernment and the ability to delay gratification.

- My husband received a promotion and was told he would have a nice car allowance. Our sons got wildly excited going through ads and insisting he get a new car. For days they could not understand why he wouldn't go out and buy a new car. They finally seemed to understand when their dad pointed out, "Employees will be scrutinizing everything I do and every way in which I interact with them. I do not want to give the impression that the first thing I did with a promotion was run out and spend money on a car. They are working very hard themselves and may or may not have the same options. I first want to establish a rapport that reflects well for them and the business. Aside from that, I don't have the need to rush out to get a new car. The one I have works great." They finally seemed to understand the message.

While shopping on vacation with her mom, Kara described to her two teenage daughters how she almost bought a lightweight jacket she loved, but resisted when she thought ahead to the cold winter months and considered how much she would enjoy or value the coat then. (Come on, she lived in Minnesota!) She said, "If I was honest with myself, I knew it wasn't a practical coat. It would never keep me warm during the winter months. So, I'd only get a small window of use out of it each year. The investment in the coat was far bigger than the value it would give me over time. So, I put the coat back. I still love it, but it wouldn't have been a wise purchase." What a great lesson and wonderful message to pass on to her daughters.

Emotions and Behaviors That Sabotage Success

A need is a basic necessity of life—food, clothing, and shelter. A want is anything more than a need. I recognize I have a frighteningly long list of wants. I want to live in a particular neighborhood; I want to have a certain type of car (okay, with three large sons, it's a truck); I enjoy certain clothes that aren't usually bought at discount stores; and I like make-up, shampoo, wines, restaurants, etc. If I'm honest, a car that safely gets me from point A to point B is sufficient to meet my needs. My wants are what drive up the price. The same is true for just about every other purchase I make during the week. The generic brand of allergy medicine should be fine, so why do I need to purchase the name-brand version, which is 40 percent higher? The product is essentially the same. Is it the packaging? Is it the internal message I have about quality? Honestly evaluating the motivation behind my choices helps me choose intentionally. Sometimes I spend more than I need—intentionally.

Watching Too Much Television

Critics of TV give many reasons for not watching it: inactivity, lack of communication that happens when people stare at the tube, increased eating due to commercials and subliminal messages, and the fact that TV offers so much garbage programming. I have another reason to cut out the TV. The commercials are intended to increase my appetite for more stuff. Ads are supposed to cause you to feel left out, inadequate, and dissatisfied with where you fall short, with what you have or don't have, and how you look. Their job is to get you to spend. The best advertisers are those that cause the sale of their clients' products to increase. The less often you subject yourself to the messages the advertisers put before you, the better off you'll be.

Advertising also teaches your children to spend more. During one holiday season the truth of this hit home for one of my girlfriends who had a two-year-old daughter. While we were visiting, Donna said, "Because Abby is my firstborn, I don't know much about dolls and fad toys. We don't watch TV, so I don't pay attention. I've got a ton of friends who are asking me if I'm getting these particular dolls for Abby for Christmas because their daughters are asking for them. Abby has never even mentioned them to me. I realized it was TV ads that were influencing these girls who are only two and three years old!"

Keeping Catalogs—or Not

During my younger years, I often suggested that people keep catalogs to flip through during their short, but important free moments. I suggested looking through them at night when you're too tired to work or maybe even read, because you can enjoy window shopping in the comfort of your own home. However, with a few intentional exceptions, I now recycle—and recommend that clients recycle—90 percent of the catalogs received. Consider this practice a stress reducer. Why? For two very important reasons. Number one, you will tend to spend more because the catalogs stoke your wants and increase impulse purchases. Secondly, while they pile up in a corner screaming to be read, you feel guilty you still haven't gone through them. Let's be honest. When you really want or need something, you carve out the time to get it. My apologies to the catalog companies. I used to be one of their favorite customers. However, I determined I'd rather save the money and recycle the guilt pile. (Keep in mind, however, that during certain seasons of life, catalog shopping may be your most important, stress-relieving avenue for shopping. This is not a black-and-white suggestion.)

Know that what you save today, you can spend tomorrow. That which you forgo today, (e.g., food/alcohol) you don't have to worry about tomorrow.

My hope is that throughout this chapter you have become aware of the holes in your financial management plan—or, especially if you lack one at all—that you now feel compelled to act upon what you have read. Creating a financial road map takes time. Pull out your day planner/calendar or PDA right now, and set deadlines for yourself to gather the information you need to design a financial plan that will work for you long term. Your financial health is absolutely critical to your physical, emotional, and spiritual health. I've also discovered many people make this process of getting financially organized more complicated than it is. One client said she wanted to get her checking and bill paying done online. We set up the plan to make it manageable. In a short period of time she said, "I'm an entrepreneur and professional in every manner of the word except with my finances. I am embarrassed it was so easy to do." The truth is, she was busy enough with the many demands of her life. Avoiding the uncomfortable money topic was not that hard to do. Until it got in the way of her desire to reach new goals that required financial accountability.

Like it or not, money permeates every area of life. The more intentional, deliberate, and purposeful you are about taking control of your finances, the more you reduce your stress and increase your joy. As you know by now, it happens one small choice at a time.

TRAINING TIPS

- Your financial health is absolutely critical to your physical, emotional, and spiritual health.
- Like it or not, money permeates every area of life.
- The more intentional, deliberate, and purposeful you are about taking control of your finances, the more you reduce your stress and increase your joy.
- If you trust God will provide your needs, you can have a different attitude about money, which can and will directly impact your health and well-being.

- When you trust in God (while doing your part), you can relax and be content.
- Have an attitude of discernment about how you spend resources: time, energy, natural, and produced.
- Treat all resources as if they were your own; be respectful and conscientious, i.e., lights and water in hotels, supplies at work, other people's possessions (clothes, camping equipment, power sprayer, bikes, books, tools, etc.)
- Envy is dangerous. Be aware of what gets your envy streak fired up.

WORKINS ➤

- Am I willing to get an accurate picture of my financial health?
- Do I have any fears about what I may discover about my/own financial health? What are they?
- What are my top five, most powerful beliefs about money? How do I think these beliefs impact the way I spend, save, and contribute? What impact do these beliefs have on how I handle my finances?
- Does the long-term benefit of staying out of debt outweigh the short-term benefit of my purchases?
- Envy is dangerous. What gets my envy streak fired up? What people or situations fuel my jealousy bug? What can I

do when I notice I'm envying others and am tempted to go buy new stuff?

- What beliefs do I have about money that get in my way of making and managing my money?

◄ WORKOUTS

- List your assets and liabilities (this is called your balance sheet).

- Look at your credit card statements and record the amount of interest you are paying per month/year. (This is often a shocking dollar amount.) List the interest rate for each of your credit cards.

- Credit card costs vary greatly. List your debts to decide which debts need to be reduced or eliminated first.

- Become more informed. Investigate your workplace plan. Do you have an employee-sponsored retirement savings plan, such as a 401(k) or 403(b)? These can have many advantages including pre-tax contributions, tax-deferred growth, automatic payroll deductions, and, of course, the great deal of the company-matching program.

- Put together a single sheet that lists the location of, individuals to contact, and current phone numbers for all financial accounts, insurance, important papers, and documents you would need in case of an emergency or death.

- If your spouse takes care of your financial investments and strategy overall, you still need to have a basic understanding of what is going on. Meet with your financial advisor, ask the questions you need to so you increase your awareness—think incrementally. If every year you learn just 10 percent more about money management, in just a few years you will feel more capable, confident, and responsible for your financial position. (I gladly give the lead on these things to my husband; that's his area of expertise. I am committed, however, to staying abreast of what our plan is and how it is changing with our seasons of life.)

- Make a date with your spouse to find the answers to the budget, investing, and savings and giving decisions of the last year. With this new information in hand, look to see what you agree to alter for next year.

- Find out what your risk tolerance is. A financial planner or good book on finances can help you. This will be an important aspect of developing your financial plan for the future.

- Do you have a living will? A living will allows either spouse to manage your financials and money decisions in case one of you becomes incapacitated.

- Do you have an updated will? If not, please take care of that. My mother worked in insurance for years and shared the saddest of stories about the loss to families when there was no will. Money to family members was tied up and often lost to the government in taxes. (Many of them were widows who had never handled the finances in their homes, and who had no idea where to begin structuring how they would manage their money.) Also, state laws change, so you need to update your will periodically.

- Did you know you can save money by adjusting your health insurance deductibles if your kids are older? If you have young kids, you probably want the lower deductibles. However, if your kids are grown and you are basically healthy, you can select a higher deductible amount ($2,000-$2,500) and make up for the cost in about eighteen months.

Keep in mind, I did not address the issue of inflation and its impact on your financial plan. Start to pay attention to the newspaper and news commentaries on things like the inflation rate. Just notice. Make a mental note and begin to become familiar with the concepts so you can become conversant on these topics.

Ten

Future Success: Small Choices Made Today Create Your Tomorrow

Your future is altered by the choices you make today. A favorite quote of mine by Nick Murray, a veteran financial planner and author is, "Today is the day you swore was going to be different—yesterday." If you want to change your future, the work begins today. That's great news because you have power over your choices in the moment.

One of the biggest challenges to living positively and healthfully is the fact it takes a daily re-commitment to achieve. Each morning when you put your feet on the floor, you need to intentionally recommit to your desire to make best choices all day—in every area of your life. Each of the small choices makes a big difference. Each choice can seem so innocuous that you overlook it. The world at large will strive to convince you that you are not enough. That what you own is not enough. That what you've accomplished is not enough. That how you look is not good enough.

Hogwash. You are wonderful. You are amazing. You are enough. If you still don't believe me, ask three of your closest friends or family members. Remember that you are the only person who can be who you are to your spouse, kids, siblings, parents, co-workers, and friends. No one else brings the wonderful combination of experiences, skills, hopes, and dreams to the relationship. You are good enough, and you still *get to* grow, change, and improve. Improving does not negate what is.

I have always admired my mother. One of the things I have appreciated most is the graceful way in which she has aged. I find it humorous and stress relieving to moan about my changing middle-aged body. I recognize it's also easy to complain about those changes—and get a lot of commiserating sympathy from peers. However, I've noticed there is a fine line between commiserating and wallowing in self-pity. Commiserating is one of the positive attributes of a great friendship. Wallowing is neither healthy, nor helpful. Mom has continued farther down life's road without a complaint or resistance. She has acted pro-actively on her own behalf taking vitamins, staying connected to friends, taking daily quiet time for prayer and reflection, eating less sugar, keeping to consistent bed and wake-up times, and even walking when she doesn't really want to.

While her skin has changed, her flexibility has diminished a bit, and her speed is slower, she has a feisty, loving spirit that I hope to emulate myself. What a role model for taking charge of your life. Find someone who inspires you and ask what small choices he or she has made to change his or her future.

The Number One Obstacle to a Better Future

A lack of planning is the number one obstacle to creating a life you love and a body that is healthy enough to take you there. One of the requirements of improving your life or health is to look out into the future and determine what you want to play out in your life. I don't believe you or I have ultimate control over the future; however, planning for what you want *is* possible and will make a difference. The mantra I like is, "Act as if it's up to me, pray as if it's up to God." You can trust in that. That sort of motto calls you to be responsible for your choices while not feeling responsible for the outcome. God holds my future in His hands. He does for you too. Do you trust Him with it?

The Greatest Enemy of Your Future

I have rarely worked with someone who didn't list "living with a sense of joy day-to-day regardless of circumstances" as one of his or her top values and aspirations. If that is true for you, let me share what your greatest enemy to joy is—fear.

Living in fear is the antithesis of living in and with joy. When we live in fear, we make ourselves and our world smaller.

F.E.A.R. is False Expectations Appearing Real

Take the time to evaluate the expectations you have for yourself. Many people, possibly you, have created false expectations that feel very real, yet are not. While you need to think and live in the moment, sometimes it's important to step out of the moment and review what is happening. If your "in the moment" is uncomfortable, it's time to take an aerial view of the moment. It may be because you feel lousy or because you've had another argument with your spouse or sibling, or you're angry about your employer's demands. What choices have you made that built up to this moment? Many large and small choices (attitudes, behaviors, responses) created the platform for this moment.

Heidi's work situation provides a valuable lesson in taking the aerial look at the moment. Always aware of how others are reacting and feeling, Heidi very consciously guarded her responses to workplace situations. One day, however, she lost it. After hanging up with another frightened client (she works with money and the markets can scare the most courageous of us), she laid her head on the desk. She ignored the phone as it began to ring again and sighed a sigh that said, "Come take me away." Having learned to coach herself, Heidi sat up a few minutes later and said, "Okay, what is going on here?"

Upon reflection, she realized a pattern that she had begun to ignore. It was a season change, and new sports activities were cropping up on her kids' schedules and, by default, hers as well. They needed new shoes for soccer and baseball. Her husband, who had been helping out more often at home at her request, had slacked off after having a few busy weeks at work himself. She also realized she had initially been cutting down on her exercise times; what had been forty-five minute workout periods were now twenty-five, then zero. Her body was tense from the lack of exercise and the mounting frustration with the sheer volume of requests put before her.

The good news was that she realized she was not going as long ignoring the symptoms of her stress and was realizing she needed to do something different immediately. She also did an attitude or perspective check. She realized she was getting very disappointed, yet frustrated, with her clients. Despite her thorough and consistent work, they were not trusting her judgment and suggestions as readily as she had anticipated. Being on top of the situation was not enough. She recognized that part of the problem was giving too much power to her clients to set the tone for her day. She went back to thought-checking. "How do I want to respond to them? Could I do anything more? How can I let this go?" She immediately began to feel the tension release and her shoulders relax. The headache was probably due to the tight shoulders. "I could go for a twenty-minute walk and just take some deep breaths. I'll take a small pad of sticky notes with me and a pen in case I think of something else I need to consider or remember."

She came back from her walk realizing it was her responsibility to remind the kids and her husband of how they could help her out. Just as family members come to her with needs, she needed to go to them with hers. She needed to remind them of their roles in the family and the importance of pitching in as a team.

Could you hear how Heidi coached herself through the Think, Choose, Act, Win model to feel better and to respond more proactively?

If you find yourself fearful or paralyzed and unable to make permanent lifestyle changes, go back to looking at your beliefs and assumptions. One of the things you may want to consider is how fear is serving you. Yes, serving you. Something about fear keeps you from something else. What is that something else?

Permission to Stay Paralyzed

When you choose to stay stuck, you already know what your future will hold—more of what's not working now. Staying stuck keeps you from mustering up the courage to change, to risk, and potentially fail. People in your life may support your paralyzed state because the status quo is working for them. (Not for you, but for them. Why would they want to rock the boat?)

> *"Those who can command themselves, command others."*
> *William Hazlitt*

Permission to Avoid Self-Discipline

The day I finally sat down to write this chapter, I came home from food shopping, uptight and frustrated. I told my husband I was going nuts trying to carve out the time to write. There are always so many other demands upon my time. It came down to forgoing all things to write. I stopped and said, "I need you to unload the groceries and take over for dinner." I had two friends coming in one hour to work on something that I had committed to, so I had only one hour. Yet, the discipline of making myself focus for one hour was critical. What do you need in order to be able to focus? Ask for it.

Fear will give you the excuse to not exercise self-discipline. Remember the fears regarding exercise? Fear of failure, fear of being confused, fear of looking stupid, not seeing results, not sticking with it, etc. It's easy to spiral out of control when you let fear take over.

So, What Do You Do?

Start with coming back to ground zero. Take a deep breath. Go into your head or heart and ask yourself some important questions. Take six. That means take six seconds to six minutes to answer your self-coaching questions. "Why do I want to commit to this? Why is it worth it to make myself do this? How can I reward myself for having moved forward, even a little bit?" For instance, if I go for a forty-minute walk then I can reward myself with a movie tonight. Or, I'll walk because I'll have peace of mind knowing I followed through on something important. Taking a few seconds or a few minutes to intentionally make the best decision for yourself is so powerful.

To have a more vibrant future, you need to step out in faith or confidence to try new things. When trying something new, ask yourself, "What's the worst that could happen?" A couple of years ago my brother-in-law announced he was taking a sabbatical from his work. The worst that could happen is that he would not come back to find his job and/or his team of people intact. He decided not taking the time off would ultimately cost him more than the possibility of losing his job. After his six-month sabbatical, an amazing thing happened. He quit his job. He searched out another opportunity that was a better personal fit for his interests, skills, and family's season of life, and took a chance. Regardless of how the situation works out, he will *not* have regrets for not having tried, and he has gained more confidence in his ability to be flexible in a difficult market.

The Ability to Act

We need to overcome fear in our heads before we overcome it in our hearts. Then behaviors will change. Every day that you make good decisions, intentional choices that influence yourself or others—the deeper and stronger you build your foundation, the more you improve the possibility of getting the future you desire.

Our lives go by so quickly. The people I have talked with and worked with have all said they want to live wisely; they want to connect deeply with others and have the energy and capacity to live independently until the end of their lives.

To accomplish these things you will need to pay attention to all that I've shared throughout this book. The truth is: Relationships count more than anything else in the lives of people. Without your health, you cannot *do* the things you want, *be* the person you long to be, and *serve* those you love.

Stop Comparing Yourself to Others

As I sit here writing at the library, I have found myself taking breaks by wandering to bookshelves peeking inside various books that look interesting to me. Of course, I am primarily drawn to those I would like to one day write or contribute to the world. I noticed something. I was beginning to lose my writing energy. I was starting to feel overwhelmed. I had an insight that caused me to put down the book I was looking at and go back to writing again. The realization I had was that the more I looked at other people's works, the less capable and inspired I felt. I was doing too many unconscious comparisons, which were keeping me from writing. What in your life do you compare to others that is keeping you from action? Is it your pants size, pocketbook, career, marital status, or health that you evaluate against someone else that's keeping you stuck?

Become aware of the sneaking comparison bug. Small comparisons are like mosquito bites. They seem innocuous but keep in mind this saying from my kitchen window calendar, "Beware of little sins. Mosquitoes drink more blood than lions." E.P. Brown

Stepping Out of the Lie

On Mother's Day, my then forty-one-year-old brother said to my mom, "Thank you for stepping out of the lie. Thank you for giving us permission to tell the truth about what was real and what wasn't. You gave us the chance to choose differently." As Mom reflected upon his comment, she came to realize how profound it truly was. She had somehow, someway achieved what she aspired to most in life. She had created a legacy that will live on for generations. We have all, I believe, chosen different spouses, careers, and lifestyle approaches based upon her single act of telling the truth—life wasn't working the way we were living it. She then, one small choice at a time, changed the course of our lives.

You have the same power and the same opportunity to change your life. *Up until now*, certain choices have been challenging. That's fine. However, now you are aware, and you *get to* choose to live, making healthy choices that enhance your life, your relationships, and your work. Life is about the journey. As Ursula K. LeGuin said, "It's good to have an end to journey toward, but it's the journey that matters in the end." Live purposefully, intentionally, healthfully, and lovingly and the progress you make on your life journey will matter in the end.

Appendix A

I Choose To...

Designing clear agreements is important to avoid or minimize miscommunication, disappointment, and/or frustration with others. Just as important is creating clear agreements with yourself about how you will live your life.

First you need to determine *what* you want to accomplish with your life so you know *why* you are making the choices that you are and *how* you will accomplish the goals you want in the manner that fits with your values. I have found that the finishing the statement which starts with "I choose to," and ends with the implied or stated answer to "so that," establishes clear boundaries and directions for the way I will or will not live my life.

Your statements will need to incorporate *your* values. Revisit the Values Clarification exercises for a list of possible values that you have determined are important to you and complete these statements including these values.

1. I choose to _____
   so that _____

2. I choose to _____
   so that _____

3. I choose to _____
   so that _____

4. I choose to _____
   so that _____

5. I choose to _____
   so that _____

6. I choose to _____
   so that _____

7. I choose to _____
   so that _____

8. I choose to _____
   so that _____

Use these statements as guiding principles or boundaries for making decisions.
Make sure your life vision or wellness vision supports these statements and vice versa.

Appendix B

VALUES CLARIFICATION
Identifying and defining the values you desire to live by

	1 Highest value– essential	2 Highly valued– but not essential	3 Don't feel strongly either way	4 Little value for me	5 Absolute no value for me
Name:					
Date:					
1. Achievement—a sense of accomplishment, realization of a goal, a sense of competition					
2. Admiration—receiving respect, positive feedback or credit for contributions, recognition					
3. Advancement—recognized growth, progress toward a higher professional level, promotion					
4. Adventure—unusual, exciting, dangerous or risky activities or pursuits					
5. Aesthetics—appreciation of beauty and/or refinement in art, nature, ideas and one's surroundings					
6. Affluence—prosperity, financial well-being, wealth, financial freedom					
7. Authority—permission through position or title to influence or control events and other people					
8. Autonomy—the ability to act independent of others, self-reliant, self-sufficient, high level of control over work, choices and direction					
9. Balance—lifestyle that allows for healthy proportions of time for one's various roles; self, family, peers, work, community					
10. Challenge—opportunity to solve problems, find resolutions, overcome odds					
11. Competency—demonstrating high proficiency and knowledge, a level of mastery, efficiency and positive impact					
12. Cleanliness—neatness, order, organized, without messiness or dirt					
13. Contentment—appreciative acceptance of one's personal traits, temperament, and/or circumstances, peace of mind, lack of anxiety, happiness					
14. Contribution—ability to donate, add to, give away, support; the ability to make a difference to individuals or organizations that can provide nothing in return, fulfillment comes in the giving					
15. Connection—the feeling of being tied to and affiliated with others, having camaraderie, interpersonal relationships that are meaningful					
16. Courage—the ability to move beyond fear and act, a willingness to act on one's beliefs					
17. Creativity—the desire to use one's imagination, be innovative and nonconforming					
18. Duty—respect for rules, regulations, following standard expectations, honoring authority					
19. Emotional Intelligence & health—the ability to understand oneself and others' emotions and know what to do with them (emotions), emotional stability					
20. Environmentally responsible—lifestyle choices and behaviors that directly support and preserve the natural world					
21. Exercise—the physical pursuit of activity through sports, formal fitness routines or competitions					
22. Fame—public affirmation of one's achievements, impact, contribution, being well known					
23. Family—immediate/extended					
24. Friendships—close personal relationships that enrich one's life					
25. Geography—the ability to live in a specific location of choice					

	1 Highest value– essential	2 Highly valued– but not essential	3 Don't feel strongly either way	4 Little value for me	5 Absolutely no value for me
26. Health—physical energy, vitality, strength, lack of illness or disease, positive/effective management of illness/disease					
27. Humility—meekness, modesty, lack of ego					
28. Humor—the ability to laugh at oneself or life					
29. Integrity/honesty—wholeness, presenting oneself without illusion, doing what one says one will do, trustworthiness, ethical					
30. Inspire—to nurture, encourage or help others achieve their goals, help them feel important and capable					
31. Justice—fairness, equitable treatment, impartiality					
32. Learning—desire to continually learn, grow, develop, accumulate knowledge, improve skills and expertise					
33. Love—intimacy, close personal, affectionate relationships of transparent interdependence and nurturing					
34. Loyalty—true, faithful, steadfast commitment to a person, cause, tradition or organization, allegiance					
35. Margin—the ability to balance the needs of one's various roles and needs in life, personal breathing space, perspective					
36. Order—systems, clear processes for organization, clarity of purpose and direction, routine, stability					
37. Personal Development—dedication and effort toward developing one's potential					
38. Pleasure—fun, enjoyment, laughter, joy					
39. Quality Time—time spent with intimate or extended family, or friends in a manner that is fulfilling and meaningful					
40. Self-Discipline—mental, moral or physical training, control or order exercised over self					
41. Servant's Heart—perspective that one's mission is to serve and think of others more often than the norm, a willingness to do what is needed to help others succeed					
42. Spirituality—strong spiritual or religious beliefs, convictions, pursuit of moral fulfillment					
43. Variety—change, lack of routine					
TOTAL					

List your top ten values starting with your number ones, then adding number twos if you do not have ten number one values:

1. _____
2. _____
3. _____
4. _____
5. _____
6. _____
7. _____
8. _____
9. _____
10. _____

Take these top ten values and write out:

1. Your definition of that value if it differs from the one provided.

_____

2. In what ways your life and choices show evidence of this being an active value for you today.

_____

3. Take your list and whittle it down to your top five values.

_____

4. Do any of these top five values conflict with one another?

_____

5. Select the top three values you want to make sure you live by.

_____

6. What actions or attitudes do you recognize that need to be added or taken out in your life to better live by your top three values?

_____

Appendix C

Creating Your Life or Wellness Vision

Paint a picture of what you would like to have to be true about you and your life. If you write the elements down, include how you will feel, how you will carry yourself, how others with describe you (physically) and experience you (emotionally, intellectually, interpersonally, and spiritually.) What would be true about your character and the congruence in the way you live your life.

Write for thirty minutes without stopping. Let your thoughts, ideas, hopes, and dreams flow. You may actually write on a number of occasions over a week or two. Keep all your writing in one place.

Once your ideas seem thoroughly written, pull out the key adjectives that define the person you've described. For instance, you may hear vitality, energy, health, strength, contentment, focus, joy, creativity pour forth from your writing. Write a statement that captures the essence of these descriptors which, if experienced in your life, would thrill you. Make it a statement that you can *own* and get inspired by. If you were to read it to someone (or memorize it and say it), would others feel your conviction and energy captured within it?

EXAMPLE

"I am a woman who lives each day with energy, conviction, vitality, and joy. I express my creativity in a way that focuses on those most important to me: my family, friends, and community. While content with my choices, I continue to grow and learn, enjoying each day with health to drive me and purpose to keep me to the course." (It does not need to be poetic or perfectly written. It's yours!)

If your statement causes you to sit up straight or challenges you to be feisty about achieving your goals, you've nailed your vision statement. It can be focused on your health or your life. A life vision statement can also incorporate your wellness. The focus is up to you. The goal of your statement is to direct your choices and make them easier.

Life is full of many great choices. Making the best choices is your goal.

If you express yourself better artistically, paint, collage, or draw your vision. Or write music that says in lyrical ways what you would say verbally. Take your art or music and write the adjectives that you see or hear in your creation to capture your vision.

After you have created your life or wellness vision, you can create the individual goals that will enable you to achieve your vision. Your wellness vision statement should capture your dream in a statement that does not list goals, it describes an outcome. You will set goals and objectives to make the dream/vision come to life.

Appendix D

Goal Setting Exercise

Write your life/wellness vision statement here to act as a reminder and guide as to why you are selecting the goals you are.

Before drilling down to specific goals, consider the answers to the following questions. Seriously consider your answers honestly and reflectively.

The *outcomes* I want for my health (or life) are _____,

_____,

and _____.

Write out in succinct, clear language a goal you have:

What is motivating you to achieve this goal?

Have you attempted this goal before?

If no, skip the next question.

If yes, what is different now about you or your circumstances that makes you believe you are ready to diligently and persistently pursue this goal?

If nothing has changed, think deeply about what would motivate you to achieve this goal now. What is that reason or motivator?

How will you, your life, or your work be different when you achieve this goal?

How does this goal support or enhance your life or wellness vision? If you haven't written yours yet, you can come back later and make sure your goals fit with your vision.

How will you know you are making progress toward your goal?

At what point along the way will you reward yourself for your effort?

How will you reward or acknowledge yourself?

How will you know the goal has been achieved?

Will people see you or experience you differently when you achieve this goal? If yes, in what way?

Who will support you in achieving this goal?

Who may get in your way?

How will you deal with their resistance?

What specific support do you need? What exactly will you request of others?

What other obstacles could/will make achieving this goal a challenge?

List your obstacles:

For each obstacle, determine steps you can take to overcome these roadblocks.

EXAMPLE

Overall Goal: I will exercise three times a week. This supports my vision because I see myself as a healthy, active, vital woman, and exercise is a key component to that outcome.

The outcome I want is: the confidence I gain about myself when I exercise regularly. I also want to be at a healthy weight. I want to be more toned, strong and flexible.

This goal for fitness has three components that I will need help in achieving. I want to be more toned (requiring some strength training). I want to be strong. (Muscularly that will mean strength training. Aerobically, that will mean running, walking, swimming or some other activity that gets my heart rate up.) If I want to be more flexible, I will need to do stretching activities.

Sub-goal of overall fitness goal: (I will describe only one.)

I will walk three days a week for thirty minutes. I will strive to get my heart rate up to a challenging level by using my heart rate monitor to guide me.

My motivator is that I am getting older and can feel my capacity changing. I do not want to be limited and have a diminished life quality because I wasn't active when I could have been. I am also motivated by the fact I have more time because my children are in school or grown now. I am inspired by my older sister who has reduced her blood pressure through consistent exercise.

As I achieve this goal, I expect to be less fatigued and have more energy and lose weight. I also expect to see my health statistics (heart rate, blood pressure) improve. I will have a better quality of life and feel proud of my efforts.

One of the obstacles I will experience is my habit of putting everything else ahead of my exercise/activity time. I will need to schedule my exercise and not let any other activities take precedence.

My strategy will be to review my week on Sunday to schedule my exercise into my weekly appointments. I will keep my walking shoes and heart rate monitor in the same place each day so I can quickly and easily get out the door. In the winter months, I will walk at our nearby indoor mall. I will repeat my vision statement to myself everyday until it becomes a part of me.

I will ask my neighbor and girlfriend Carol to do two things: #1 I will ask her if she would like to walk with me, and #2 I will stay accountable to her even if she doesn't walk, reporting on how I am doing and what I am feeling.

I will ask that she remind me of my promise to myself if I start to slack or become distracted from my new routine.

Appendix E

Real vs. Ideal
My Evolution and Growth

Look at each of the qualities or descriptions of energy, style and temperament. Without over-thinking, mark an X on the line along the range that best describes you and this strength or shortcoming at this point in your life.
See sample: Patient...◄─┼─┼─┼─┼─**X**─┼─┼─► Impatient *(which would indicate you are more impatient)*

QUALITIES		SHORTCOMINGS
Awareness of Others	◄─┼─┼─┼─┼─┼─┼─►	Self-centered
Helpful to others	◄─┼─┼─┼─┼─┼─┼─►	Self-indulgent
Generous	◄─┼─┼─┼─┼─┼─┼─►	Selfish
Thoughtful	◄─┼─┼─┼─┼─┼─┼─►	Self-pitying
Open-minded, gracious	◄─┼─┼─┼─┼─┼─┼─►	Smug, stubborn
Constructively critical	◄─┼─┼─┼─┼─┼─┼─►	Judgmental
Respectful	◄─┼─┼─┼─┼─┼─┼─►	Disrespectful
Patient	◄─┼─┼─┼─┼─┼─┼─►	Impatient
Tolerant	◄─┼─┼─┼─┼─┼─┼─►	Intolerant
Realistic	◄─┼─┼─┼─┼─┼─┼─►	Unrealistic
Reasonable	◄─┼─┼─┼─┼─┼─┼─►	Unreasonable
Assertive	◄─┼─┼─┼─┼─┼─┼─►	Submissive
Cooperative	◄─┼─┼─┼─┼─┼─┼─►	Domineering
Outgoing	◄─┼─┼─┼─┼─┼─┼─►	Withdrawn
Forgiving	◄─┼─┼─┼─┼─┼─┼─►	Resentful
Trusting	◄─┼─┼─┼─┼─┼─┼─►	Suspicious
Trustworthy	◄─┼─┼─┼─┼─┼─┼─►	Prone to gossip
Content	◄─┼─┼─┼─┼─┼─┼─►	Envious
Agreeable	◄─┼─┼─┼─┼─┼─┼─►	Disagreeable
Cheerful	◄─┼─┼─┼─┼─┼─┼─►	Depressed
Courteous	◄─┼─┼─┼─┼─┼─┼─►	Discourteous
Kind	◄─┼─┼─┼─┼─┼─┼─►	Unkind
Loving, caring	◄─┼─┼─┼─┼─┼─┼─►	Indifferent
Discreet	◄─┼─┼─┼─┼─┼─┼─►	Lacking discretion
Stable	◄─┼─┼─┼─┼─┼─┼─►	Panicky, violent
Consistent	◄─┼─┼─┼─┼─┼─┼─►	Inconsistent
Sincere	◄─┼─┼─┼─┼─┼─┼─►	Insincere
Honest	◄─┼─┼─┼─┼─┼─┼─►	Dishonest
Willing to admit faults	◄─┼─┼─┼─┼─┼─┼─►	Self-righteous
Humble	◄─┼─┼─┼─┼─┼─┼─►	Arrogant
Calm	◄─┼─┼─┼─┼─┼─┼─►	Worrisome
Relaxed	◄─┼─┼─┼─┼─┼─┼─►	Tense
Confident, having faith	◄─┼─┼─┼─┼─┼─┼─►	Fearful, apprehensive
Hopeful	◄─┼─┼─┼─┼─┼─┼─►	Despondent
Optimistic	◄─┼─┼─┼─┼─┼─┼─►	Pessimistic
Living for today	◄─┼─┼─┼─┼─┼─┼─►	Living in the past or future
Industrious	◄─┼─┼─┼─┼─┼─┼─►	Lazy
Prompt	◄─┼─┼─┼─┼─┼─┼─►	Procrastinating
Purposeful	◄─┼─┼─┼─┼─┼─┼─►	Aimless
Responsible	◄─┼─┼─┼─┼─┼─┼─►	Irresponsible
Using talents and abilities	◄─┼─┼─┼─┼─┼─┼─►	Disinterested in self
Thankful	◄─┼─┼─┼─┼─┼─┼─►	Ungrateful
Willing to continue to seek	◄─┼─┼─┼─┼─┼─┼─►	Smug, complacent
Emotional and spiritual balance	◄─┼─┼─┼─┼─┼─┼─►	Numb to own needs

© 2003 Winning LifeStyles, Inc. • (952) 943-1430 • 1-888-Lif-Walk • www.katelarsen.com

Appendix F

What I Really Need in My Life Right Now is More...

Physical	Mental/Career	Emotional and Relationships	Spiritual/Self
❑ vitality	❑ self-esteem	❑ tenderness	❑ composure
❑ security	❑ recognition	❑ generosity	❑ centering
❑ activity	❑ confidence	❑ caring	❑ awareness
❑ health	❑ motivation	❑ sharing	❑ solitude
❑ strength	❑ knowledge/skill	❑ music	❑ devotion
❑ energy	❑ opportunities	❑ laughter	❑ contemplation
❑ fitness	❑ challenges	❑ support	❑ serenity
❑ relaxation	❑ variety	❑ self-expression	❑ trust
❑ comfort	❑ structure	❑ companionship	❑ insight
❑ nutrition	❑ accomplishments	❑ harmony	❑ joy
❑ touching	❑ control	❑ romance	❑ commitment
❑ sex	❑ imagination	❑ intimacy	❑ communion
❑ sleep	❑ money	❑ patience	❑ integration
❑ coordination	❑ responsibilities	❑ beauty	❑ forgiveness
❑ flexibility	❑ education/training	❑ sensitivity	❑ surrender
❑ exercise	❑ experience	❑ receptivity	❑ faith
❑ self-control	❑ freedom	❑ self-awareness	❑ purpose

Appendix G

The Life Inventory Wheel

Directions: The eight sections in the Wheel of Life represent overall life balance. Seeing the center of the wheel as 0 and the outer edge as 7, rank your level of satisfaction with each life area by drawing a straight or curved line to create a new outer edge (see example). The new perimeter of the circle represents the Wheel of Life. How bumpy would the ride be if this were a real wheel?

Example

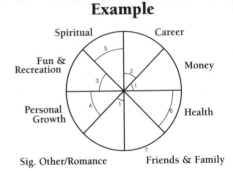

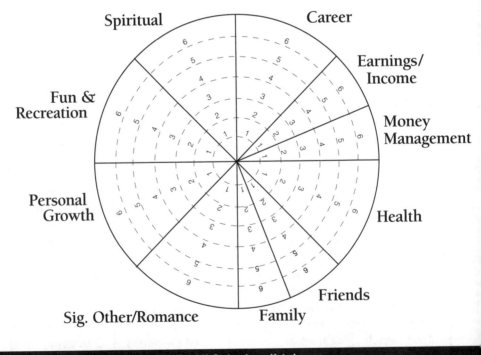

Spiritual

Career

Fun & Recreation

Earnings/ Income

Money Management

Personal Growth

Health

Sig. Other/Romance

Family

Friends

Winning LifeStyles, Inc. • Kate Larsen
P.O. Box 385522 • Minneapolis, MN 55438 • (952) 943-1430 • 1-888-Lif-Walk • Fax: (952) 941-3521
E-mail: thinkchoosewin.com • Web site: www.katelarsen.com

Appendix H

PROGRESS REPORT FOR
STRESS BUSTING AND ENERGY BUILDING

HAVEN'T STARTED (WOULD LIKE TO) PLANNING	HAVE STARTED (APPLYING) IN ACTION	HAVE INCORPORATED (REGULAR BASIS) MAINTENANCE

Consider behaviors and attitudes you want to change.
© 2003 Winning LifeStyles, Inc. • (952) 943-1430 • 1-888-Lif-Walk • www.katelarsen.com

Appendix I

Winning LifeStyle™ News

| Volume 1, Number 1 | *Centennial Edition* |

It's a Wonderful Life...

_____ Celebrates 100 Years
(Your name)

Notes

Introduction

1. Swenson, R., *The Overload Syndrome: Learning to Live Within Your Limits* (Colorado Springs, CO: Navpress, 1998), 15.

Chapter 2 Build On Your New Foundation

1. Colditz, G.A., "Economic costs of obesity." *American Journal of Clinical Nutrition.* (1992): 55:503-507s. (This figure represents consumer dollars spent in the early 1990s on all efforts at weight loss or weight maintenance including low-calorie foods, artificially sweetened products such as diet sodas and memberships to commercial weight-loss centers.)

2. Creagan. E., *Mayo Clinic on Healthy Aging: Answers to Help You Make the Most of the Rest of Your Life* (First Edition) (London, UK Kensington Publishing Corp., 2001), 25.

3. Locke, Edwin A. and Latham, Gary P., "Building a practical use theory of goal setting and task motivation: A 35-year odyssey" *American Psychologist.* (Sep. 2002) Vol. 57(9): 705-717

4. Prochaska, J.O., Norcross, J., and Diclemente, C., *Changing for Good: A Revolutionary Six-Stage Program for Overcoming Bad Habits and Moving Your Life Positively Forward* (New York, NY: Avon Books, 1994), 38-46.

Chapter 3 Keys to Living an Intentional, Joy-filled Life

1. Covey, S., *Seven Habits of Highly Effective People* (New York, NY: Free Press Publishers, 1990), 188.

Chapter 4 Mantras, Attitudes, and Perspectives—M.A.P.s That Will Change Your Life

1. Muoio, Anna. "Balancing Acts." *Fast Company* (Issue 22, February, 1999), 83.

Chapter 5 Food: Friend or Foe

1. National Heart, Lung, and Blood Institute, "Calculate Your Body Mass Index." http://nhlbisupport. com/bmi/bmicalc.htm (accessed June 4, 2006).

2 University of Arkansas for Medical Sciences, "Dangers of Obesity" (10/3/05) http://www. kthv.com/news/health/ask-the-doctor/story. aspx?storyid=20041 (accessed June 4, 2006).

3. Klem, M.L., Wing, R.R., McGuire, M.T., Seagle, H.M., and Hill, J.O., "The National Weight Control Registry Research Findings: A descriptive study of individuals successful at long-term maintenance of substantial weight loss." American Journal of Clinical Nutrition (1997): 66, 239-246.

4. Nelson, M., Ph.D., Wenick, S., Raichlen, S., *Strong Women Stay Slim* (New York, NY: Bantam Books, 1999), 20.

5. Shapiro, H.M., *Picture Perfect Weight Loss Diet* (New York, NY: Rodale Publishers, 2000).

6. "Are Growing Portion Sizes Leading to Expanding Waistlines?" Study *in Journal of the American Dietetic Association* Sizes Up Trends (accessed June 6, 2006). http://www.eatright.org/cps/rde/xchg/ada/ hs.xsl/media_3073_ENU_HTML.htm.

Chapter 6 Fitness: Privilege or Pain

1. U.S. Department of Health and Human Services, "A Report of the Surgeon General: Physical Activity and Health" (1996) http://www.cdc.gov/ nccdphp/sgr/ataglan.htm (accessed June 6, 2006).

2. Franklin, Barry A., Senior Editor, *ACSM's Guidelines for Exercise Testing and Prescription*, Sixth

Edition, American College of Sports Medicine (Philadelphia, PA: Lippincott Williams & Wilkins, 2000), Medicine & Science in Sports & Exercise. 33(2): 4.

3. United States Department of Health & Human Services, News Release, "The Surgeon General Issues First-Ever Report On Nation's Bone Health" (HHS Press Office, October 14, 2004). http://www.hhs.gov/news/press/2004pres/20041014.html (accessed June 6, 2006).

4. Ibid.

5. Franklin, Barry A., Senior Editor, *ACSM's Guidelines for Exercise Testing and Prescription*, Sixth Edition, American College of Sports Medicine (Philadelphia, PA: Lippincott Williams & Wilkins, 2000), Medicine & Science in Sports & Exercise. 33 (2): 189-190.

6. Ibid, 145-162.

7. Department of Health and Human Services, Centers for Disease Control and Prevention, "Physical Activity for Everyone Activity Terms" (March 22, 2006). http://www.cdc.gov/nccdphp/dnpa/physical/terms/index.htm (accessed June 11, 2006).

8. LookSmart, "Natural Health: How much exercise do you really need?" (Welder Publications, 2003) http://findarticles.com/p/articles/mi_m0NAH/is_3_33/ai_10483 (accessed June 11, 2006).

9. Cotton, Richard T., editor, *Personal Trainer Manual: The Resource for Fitness Professionals* (San Diego, CA: 1996) American Council on Exercise, 214-217.

Chapter 7 The Care and Feeding of Family and Friends.

1. Putnam, R. D., *Bowling Alone: The Collapse and Revival of American Community* (New York, NY: Simon & Schuster, 2000), 367.

2. Deveny, Kathleen, "No Sex, Please, We're Married: Are Stress, Kids and Work Killing Romance?" *Newsweek*, (CLXI 26, June 30, 2003), 41.

3. Gerzon, G., *Finding Serenity in the Age of Anxiety* (New York, NY: Macmillan, 1997), 22-27.

4. Ibid.

5. Taylor, S.E., et al. "Biobehavioral Responses to Stress in Females: Tend-and-Befriend, Not Fight or Flight." *Psychological Review* (2000), 107 (3), 411-429.

6. Ibid.

7. Ibid.

Chapter 8 Faith in Action

1. Alcoholics Anonymous, *Alcoholics Anonymous: The Story of How Many Thousands of Men and Women Have Recovered from Alcoholism* (Center City, MN: Hazelden, 1986), 1-16.

2. Anonymous, *The Twelve Steps: A Spiritual Journal* (San Diego, CA.: RPI Publishing, Inc., 1988), 256-257.

3. Alcoholics Anonymous, *Twelve Steps & Twelve Traditions* (Center City, MN: Hazelden, 2002), 5-6.

4. Matthew 6:34 (TLB).

5. 1 Timothy 4:7b-8 (NIV).

6. Matthews, D.A., with Clark, C., *The Faith Factor: Proof of the Healing Power of Prayer* (New York, NY: Penguin Putnam Inc., 1998) 35-36

7. American Cancer Society, "Spirituality and Prayer," June 1, 2005. http://www.cancer.org/docroot/ETO/content/ETO_5_3X_Spirituality_and_Prayer.asp?sitearea=ETO (accessed June 5, 2006).

8. Young, V., "The Imposter Syndrome: Finding a Name for the Feelings" (2005) www.impostorsyndrome.com (accessed June 9, 2006).

9. Benson, H., with Klipper, M.Z., *The Relaxation Response* (New York, NY: Harper Collins, 1975), 98, 106.

Chapter 9 Financial Fitness

1. Weatherford, J., *The History of Money* (New York, NY: Three Rivers Press, 1998), 27.

2. Ibid, 17.

3. Chilton, D., *The Wealthy Barber* (Roseville, CA: Prima Publishing, 1998), 29.

4. Marshall, J.M., *Talking Points Memo*, March 19, 2005, http://www.talkingpointsmemo.com/bankruptcy/archives/2005/03/index.php (accessed June 5, 2006).

5. Godfrey, N.S., & Edwards, C., *Money Doesn't Grow on Trees* (New York, NY: Fireside, A Simon & Schuster Imprint, 1994), 39.

6. U.S. National Debt Clock, http://www.brillig.com/debt_clock (accessed June 9, 2006).

7. Durkin, T.A., "Credit Cards: Use and Consumer Attitudes." 1970-2000. *Federal Reserve Bulletin 76* (September, 2000), 623.

8. Warren, E., & Warren Tagi, A., *The Two Income Trap: Why Middle-Class Mothers and Fathers are Going Broke* (New York, NY: Basic Book Publishers, 2003), 83-84.

9. Ibid, 163.

Index

A

accidental eating, 127
accountability partner, 51
action
    beliefs influence, 50
    commitment to relationships as, 65
    knowing when not to take, 22–23
    lifestyle change requires, 12–14, 40
    making a choice is not, 131
    money management as, 269
    overcoming fear for, 302
    spiritual faith in, 258–59
    in steps to change, 33, 35–36
    TCAW model for, 38–42, 54
addiction recovery, 33
    . *see also* 12-step programs
additives, food, 142
advertising, 288
aerobic exercise, 161–63
aging
    commiserating over, 296
    finances and, 284
    fitness and, 151, 160
    lifestyle choices and, 177–80
    values and choices when, 192
    wellness vision for, 28, 152
Al-Anon, xx, 240–41
Alcoholics Anonymous (AA), 241
    . *see also* 12-step programs
alcoholism
    family history and, xviii–xx, 2, 178
    impact on life's perspectives, 2

    lifestyle choices and, 50
    12-step programs and, 239–41
American College of Sports Medicine (ACSM), 118, 165
American Dietetic Association, 144
American Journal of Medicine, 252
American Journal of Psychiatry, 252
American Journal of Public Health, 252
American Psychologist, 29
anger
    eating habits and, 116, 121–22
    learning to let go of, 41, 241
    M.A.P.s for, 97–98
    recognizing and dealing with, xxvi–xxviii, 198
anxiety
    eating habits and, 116
    journaling for dealing with, 108
    lifestyle change to reduce, 19
    recognizing and dealing with, xxvi–xxviii, 206–09
    . *see also* stress
assessment
    in achieving goals, 30
    by comparing self to others, 182–83, 302–03
    of eating habits, 135–38
    F.E.A.R., 297–99
    of financial health, 275–78
    of lifestyle choices, xiii–xiv, xxiv
    of personal beliefs, 234–38
    as step toward change, 22–24
    visualizing success, 172–73

E

F

SMART achievement in, 29–33

goal statements, 32–33

goals

change requires practice, xxxi

creating a foundation of, 1–3

in earning money, 268

importance of vision in, 27

in the journey of life, 57

M.A.P.s for, 95–96

patterns for unachieved, 31–32

risking to reach for, xxvi

willpower vs. wantpower, 134–35

God/faith in God, 7, 235–36

. see also spiritual faith

Godfrey, Neale, 279

Goethe, Wolfgang Von, 4, 191

gossip, 99, 217, 228

guilt

exercise as relief from, 169–70

learning to let go of, 41

as motivation, 68–69, 181

negative motives and, 102

self-care and, 7

"workins" for defining, 81

H

habit

change requires action, 12–14, 156

change requires practice, xxxi

change requires reflection, 20

eating wisely as, 115–17, 127–28, 135–42

emotional eating as, 121–23

food history as origin of, 123–25

negative communications as, 208

recognizing and dealing with, xxvii

self-care is a, 63–64

thinking better = choosing better as, 21–22, 35

vision for a healthy, 26–27

willpower vs. wantpower, 134–35

H.A.L.T.. see "Hungry, Angry, Lonely, or Tired" (H.A.L.T.)

Hazlitt, William, 300

health

authenticity and, xxviii

burned up vs. burned out, 11–12

creating a foundation for, 2–3

creating a wellness vision for, 25–27, 308–09

eating habits and, 135

exercise and, 28–29

fast-food and, 143–45

female bonding for, 213–14

lifestyle choices and, xiii–xvi, 20–22, 139–43

obesity and, 117–21

OSO concept of disease prevention, 177

physical and mental flexibility for, xxx–xxxi

physical conditioning and, 159–60

prevention vs. treatment for, 3–6

productivity and, 74–75

self-sabotage of, 63–64

spiritual faith and, 235–36, 251–52

. see also physical fitness

heart disease

aerobic exercise and, 161–63

M

maintenance
  of changed relationships, 222–24
  in loving relationships, 224–25
  as stage of change, 36–37
  weight loss, 120
mantras, defined, 86
M.A.P.s (mantras, attitudes, and perspectives)
  Build Reserves, 106–07
  Choices Make a Difference, 88–91
  Learning Never Stops, 93–94
  Life is a Journey, 91–93
  Make Gratitude Your Attitude, 96–98
  Making Choices That Won't Lead to Regret, 94–95
  Motives Are the Key, 98–99
  Reflective Writing, 107–10
  Scale Your Choice, 95–96
  Time Warps Work, 95
marriage
  expectations in, 202–06
  faith in God in, 242–43
  finances and, 270–71, 275, 281–82
  love and commitment through, 226
  money management in, 264–65
  nourishing the relationship in, 200–201, 208
  recognizing changes in, 34, 105–06
  . see also children; family
masks, hiding behind, xviii, xxviii, 121
Matthews, Dale A., 251

Mayo Clinic on Healthy Aging (Creagan), 28
McCarthy, Bill, 67
media. *see* culture
meditation, 174, 256–57
memories, creating, 191–94, 227–30
menopause, exercise and, 155, 157
mental fitness, 169–77
mental illness, 2
money
  guidelines for handling, 283–84
  history and origins of, 265–68
  as motivation, 268–72
  as sense of security, 269
  . see also debt, managing; finances
Money Doesn't Grow on Trees (Godfrey), 279
mothers. see family; woman/women
motivation
  for achieving goals, 29–30
  comparing self to others as, 182–83, 302–03
  creating a foundation of, 1–3
  exercise, 154–55
  family and relationships as, 191–93
  guilt as, 68–69, 181
  identifying values in, xxiv, 126, 287
  money as, 268–72
  and Six Stages of Change, 33–38
  stuck from lack of, 9
  visualization for, 172–76
  weight loss, 120–21
  wellness vision as, 25–27, 308–09

T

tactical nutrition, 119
target heart rate, calculating, 161–63
television, 288
termination, as stage of change, 37–38
Think, Choose, Act, Win Model (TCAW)
    components of, 38–42
    eating habits and, 116
    eating wisely with the, 130–32
    examples for applying the, 42–54
    self-talk and the, 179–80
think first, then act, 22–23
thinking better = choosing better, 39–40, 43–50
toxic anxiety, 206–07
Training Heart Rate (THR), 162
training tips
    creating a foundation, 14–15
    financial management, 290–91
    food and eating habits, 145–46
    for healthy relationships, 227–29
    M.A.P.s, 110–11
    physical fitness, 183–84
    for recognizing success, 79–80
    for spiritual faith, 259–60
    TCAW model, 54–55
Tubesing, Donald A., 62
12-step programs
    for dealing with addiction, 238
    decision-making and, xx
    "Keep It Simple, Stupid", 243–44
    "Let Go and Let God," 242–43
    "One Day At A Time", 241–42
    as prescription for life, 238–41

Serenity Prayer, 262
The Two-Income Trap (Warren & Tyagi), 281–82
Tyagi, Amelia Warren, 282

U

U. S. Surgeon General, 165
undivided attention in relationships, 65, 68, 75–76
University of Arkansas for Medical Sciences, 118

V

value statements, 4–5
values
    balance and alignment in, xiii
    of "being" vs. "doing," 65–66
    creating a foundation of, 1–3
    eating habits and health, 135
    exercise as, 179–80
    identifying and living one's own, xxiv–xxv, 6–8, 257
    a life message of, 193–97
    living successfully through, 3–6
    money and, 264–66, 268–72
Values Clarification exercises, 7, 15–16, 306–07
victimization, xx–xxi, xxviii
vision
    communicating a life message, 193–97
    goal setting for a long-term, 24–25
    SMART goal setting and, 29–33
    statement of your own life's, 103, 248
    . *see also* life vision; wellness vision
visualization, 172–76

W

walking, 139, 164

"The Wall". *see* "hitting the wall"

Warhol, Andy, 85

Warren, Elizabeth, 281

water, importance of drinking, 140–42

wealth, 71, 268, 279–80

The Wealthy Barber (Chilton), 276

Weatherford, Jack, 266, 268

weight gain, 128–29

weight loss

  eating habits and, 115–17

  exercise motivation and, 155

  food additives and, 142

  getting out of debt is like, 283

  looking better vs. living better, 20–22

  maintenance of, 120

  self-discipline and, 104

  . *see also* nutrition

weight training, 163–64

wellness vision

  creating a, 25–29, 308–09

  fitness and your, 152–53

  in your life statement, 103

"What I Really Need in My Life Right Now is More...," 56

The Will to Believe (James), 109

willpower, 134–35

winning, 127, 131–32, 318

  . *see also* Think, Choose, Act, Win Model (TCAW)

woman/women

  balancing career and family, 192–93, 224–25

  career options and, 76–77

  cultural expectations of, 202–06

  finances and, 227, 271–74, 281–82

  friendship bonding by, 212–14

  making choices as, xxiii–xxiv

  as role model, 296, 303

  support networks for, 209–10

  wellness vision for, 25–27

working mothers. see woman/women

"Workins"

  changing self-talk with, 13

  for defining success, 80–82

  financial management, 292–92

  food and eating habits, 146–48

  M.A.P.s, 111–12

  physical fitness, 185–87

  relationship, 229–31

  spiritual faith, 260–61

  TCAW model, 55–56

  values clarification, 15–16

"Workouts"

  as action exercises, 13

  congruence test of values, 16–18

  financial management, 292–94

  food and eating habits, 149–50

  God/faith in God, 261–62

  journaling and, 37

  M.A.P.s, 112–13

  physical fitness, 188–89

  for recognizing success, 82–83

  relationship, 231

  TCAW model, 56–57

worry. *see* anger; anxiety; stress

Y

Young, Valerie, 31, 254

About the Author

Kate Larsen is a seasoned business and life coach, experienced professional speaker, and faculty member teaching coaching skills to leaders. She excels at challenging others to realistically live up to their potential.

Kate helps busy professionals assess their leadership skills while examining their health and fitness lifestyle choices. Kate works with those who want to achieve great results and function with a positive, powerful, and proactive energy and style at work and at home. She has a gift for helping others develop their decision-making skills. Through her coaching, Kate enables others to take charge of their lives in a powerful way.

Kate provides workshops and keynotes, which emphasize simple, achievable behavior change and provide tangible tools that allows individuals to reclaim their enthusiasm and health. Her ability to effectively teach, speak, and coach on these topics comes from her experience as an addictions counselor, professional speaker, professionally certified business and life coach, certified personal trainer, and group fitness instructor.

Kate is a corporate leadership coach and coaching skills workshop leader for the Ken Blanchard Companies. Since 2002, Kate has served as an advisor, faculty member and mentor coach for the Wellcoaches Inc. organization, training health and wellness professionals the skills required to help people make healthy lifestyle changes that last. She has been an active member of the National Speakers Association since 1989. Kate has coached individuals since 1992 and has been a Professionally Certified Coach (PCC) through the International Coach Foundation since 1999, completing training through the Coaches Training Institute, CoachU and Corporate CoachU.

Kate has appeared in and written for more than forty magazines (i.e., *Fitness, SHAPE, Experience Life, Self, Club Industry, Training Magazine, Cosmopolitan, Weight Watchers, Prevention,* and more) and newspapers. She has also appeared on television and radio programs as a lifestyle expert.

Kate is also a breast cancer survivor who truly knows the importance of living intentionally and proactively. She and her husband live in Minnesota with their three teenage sons.

To contact Kate Larsen or request information
on Kate's speaking, coaching, writing,
or consulting services
call 1-888-Lif-Walk
or e-mail kate@katelarsen.com.

Visit www.katelarsen.com
for updated information, resources, and
web links related to this book,
Progress Not Perfection: Your Journey Matters.